Diversity in Health Care Research

Strategies *for Multisite, Multidisciplinary, and Multicultural Projects*

Joellen W. Hawkins, RNC, PhD, FAAN, is a professor in the William F. Connell School of Nursing, Boston College. For over 30 years, she has been engaged in multisite, multidisciplinary research projects and served as principal investigator for a project investigating abuse during pregnancy.

Lois A. Haggerty, RNC, PhD, is an associate professor and coordinator of the master's entry into nursing program at the William F. Connell School of Nursing, Boston College. She has been a coinvestigator on a multisite research project investigating abuse during pregnancy.

Photos by Chad Minnich, Media Specialist, William F. Connell School of Nursing and doctoral student, Lynch School of Education, Boston College.

Diversity in Health Care Research

Strategies for Multisite, Multidisciplinary, and Multicultural Projects

Joellen W. Hawkins, RNC, PhD, FAAN
Lois A. Haggerty, RNC, PhD,
Editors

 Springer Publishing Company

Springer Publishing Company, Inc.
536 Broadway
New York, NY 10012-3955

Acquisitions Editor: Ruth Chasek
Production Editor: Sara Yoo
Cover design by Joanne Honigman

03 04 05 06 07 / 5 4 3 2 1

Library of Congress Cataloging-in-Publication Data

Diversity in health care research : strategies for multisite, multidisciplinary, and multicultural projects / Joellen W. Hawkins, Lois A. Haggerty, editors.
    p.   cm.
    Includes bibliographical references and index.
    ISBN 0-8261-1814-3
    1. Medical care—Research—Methodology. 2. Public health—Research—Methodology. 3. Health surveys—Methodology. 4. Medical care surveys—Methodology. 5. Interdisciplinary research. I. Hawkins, Joellen Watson. II. Haggerty, Lois A.
R850.D585 2003
362.1'07'2—dc21
                                                           2003041617

Printed in the United States of America by Maple-Vail Book Manufacturing Group.

Contents

Part II   Lessons Learned From Specific Research Projects

Contributors

Cynthia S. Aber, RN, EdD, is an associate professor, College of Nursing, University of Massachusetts, Boston. Her research includes multisite and multidisciplinary work, the latter as part of a team investigating abuse during pregnancy.

Dyanne D. Affonso, PhD, RN, FAAN, is professor and dean at the University of Toronto, Toronto, Canada. Dr. Affonso was principal investigator on a multisite, multicultural, international research project focused on comparison of depression symptoms among postpartum mothers.

Susan Anderson is the Project Manager with the Women's Health Initiative Clinical Coordinating Center, Fred Hutchinson Cancer Research Center, Seattle, Washington. She has provided administrative and management support to multicenter, multidisciplinary, and multicultural research teams in cancer prevention for over ten years.

Doris Williams Campbell, PhD, ARNP, FAAN, is Director of Diversity Initiatives for the University of South Florida Health Sciences Center, Tampa, and professor in the Colleges of Nursing and Public Health. Her multisite, multidisciplinary, multicultural research focuses on violence and abuse in the lives of African-American women.

Jacquelyn C. Campbell, PhD, RN, FAAN, is the Anna D. Wolf Endowed Professor and Director of the Doctoral Programs at Johns Hopkins University School of Nursing, with a joint appointment in the School of Hygiene and Public Health. She has been engaged in multisite, multicultural, and multidisciplinary research exploring intimate partner violence and femicide.

Barbara Cochrane, PhD, RN is a senior staff scientist at Fred Hutchinson Cancer Research Center and affiliate assistant professor in Family and

Child Nursing, University of Washington, Seattle. She is a coinvestigator with the Women's Health Initiative Clinical Coordinating Center. She is also a member of the Family Functioning Research Program team at the University of Washington, which has been engaged for nearly two decades in multicenter, multisite, and multidisciplinary research to help families that are experiencing chronic illness.

Anindya K. De, PhD, is a Senior Research Fellow at the Centers for Disease Control and Prevention, Atlanta, Georgia. He also works as a statistical consultant and was a team member on a multisite, multicultural, international study on comparison of depression symptoms among postpartum mothers.

Mary E. Duffy, RN, PhD, FAAN, is professor and director of nursing research at the William F. Connell School of Nursing, Boston College. She currently serves as a coinvestigator and methodologist on several nationally funded, multidisciplinary, multicultural, and multisite clinical trials.

Joyce M. Dwyer, RN, MS, MPH, is an associate professor at the William F. Connell School of Nursing, Boston College, and a member of a multisite, multicultural research team investigating abuse during pregnancy.

Barbara A. Given, PhD, RN, FAAN, is a Senior Scientist, Institute for Health Care Studies, and University Distinguished Professor, College of Nursing at Michigan State University, as well as a Senior Scientist at the Walther Cancer Institute. She has been engaged in multisite, multidisciplinary research for several decades.

Charles W. Given, PhD, is a Professor in the Department of Family Practice, College of Human Medicine, Michigan State University and Senior Scientist, Walther Cancer Institute. He has been part of a multisite, multidisciplinary research team investigating family caregivers.

Loretta P. Higgins, RN, EdD, is an associate professor and associate dean at the William F. Connell School of Nursing, Boston College. Her research includes multisite, multicultural projects, and membership on a team studying abuse during pregnancy.

Ursula A. Kelly, RN, PhD candidate, APRN, is a clinical assistant professor at the Massachusetts General Institute of Health Professions and a doctoral candidate at the William F. Connell School of Nursing, Boston College.

Her dissertation research is multicultural and multidisciplinary and she has also been part of a research team on a multisite, multicultural project investigating abuse during pregnancy.

Christine King, EdD, RN, is associate professor, University of Massachusetts, Amherst. She is codirector of a primary health care project for abused women and engaged on a team of researchers studying intimate partner violence.

Sharon L. Kozachik, MSN, RN, was a research assistant at Michigan State University, Family Care Studies, Walther Cancer Institute, on a multisite, multidisciplinary project on family caregivers. She is currently a doctoral student at Johns Hopkins University School of Nursing.

Patricia Price Lea, RN, PhD, is currently serving as the Dean of Nursing at North Carolina A&T State University. She has been part of a multicultural, multisite research project on intimate partner violence.

Bernedine Lund, MS, is the Technical Coordinator with the Women's Health Initiative Clinical Coordinating Center, Fred Hutchinson Cancer Research Center, Seattle, Washington. She has served as a project manager on multicenter and multidisciplinary research teams in cancer prevention for two decades.

Linda J. Mayberry, RN, PhD, FAAN, is a professor at New York University, School of Education, Division of Nursing and Director of the Muriel and Virginia Pless Center for Nursing Research. She has developed and directed several multisite international projects addressing pregnancy health issues.

Carole W. Pearce, RNC, PhD, is a professor in the Department of Nursing, College of Health Professions at the University of Massachusetts, Lowell. She has been part of several interdisciplinary research teams, including one studying abuse during pregnancy, and a coalition to address violence in a community.

Ross Prentice, PhD, is a Member in the Public Health Sciences Division, Fred Hutchinson Cancer Research Center, Seattle, Washington and is Professor of Biostatistics at the University of Washington. He is the principal investigator of the Women's Health Initiative Clinical Coordinating Center and has been engaged in multicenter, multidisciplinary, and multicultural research in cancer prevention for over two decades.

Josephine Ryan, DNSc, RN, is associate professor at the University of Massachusetts, Amherst, and part of a study team on intimate partner violence and femicide. She is also studying teen dating violence.

Rachel F. Schiffman, PhD, RN, FAAN, is a professor and associate dean for research, University of Wisconsin-Milwaukee. She served as a member of the Early Head Start Research and Evaluation Consortium which coordinated the national evaluation of the Early Head Start program and as principal investigator for the Michigan State University site.

Eleanor Lowndes Stevenson, RN, MS, is a research fellow and is currently participating on a multidisciplinary research team in conjunction with her doctoral studies at New York University, Division of Nursing.

Sara Torres, PhD, RN, FAAN, is Dean at the University of Medicine and Dentistry of New Jersey School of Nursing, Newark, New Jersey. She has been part of a research team studying intimate partner violence and femicide. Her particular interest is the Hispanic community: family violence, cross-cultural health care, mental health of Hispanic women, and substance abuse.

Nancy W. Veeder, MBA, PhD, a professor in the Graduate School of Social Work, Boston College, has been engaged in health and mental health services, planning, marketing, and research for over 30 years in the United States, Jamaica, the West Indies, and Mauritius, Indian Ocean.

Foreword

The human genome has been completed. We now know that, from a biological perspective, we are almost identical. The genetic variation within ethnic and racial groups is greater than the variation between groups. Schwartz (2001) tells us that race is a social construct, not a scientific classification (p. 1392).

Yet, incredible disparities in health status continue to exist. The Surgeon General of the United States (2000) has set a goal of eliminating health disparities among segments of the population, including differences that occur due to gender, race, ethnicity, education, income, disability, geographic location, or sexual orientation.

Lewis (2001) asserts that, since these disparities are not due to scientific classification, they may well be due to social classification and issues such as prejudice, discrimination, and lack of access to services.

In order to eliminate disparities and improve health status for all, it is important to understand the complex relationships that lead to these differences. It is, however, critically important to conduct this research in an atmosphere that is respectful of differences, and using research designs that are sensitive to cultural and economic issues among populations. The very nature of this type of work demands that it be conducted by investigators with a variety of disciplinary perspectives, in a variety of settings, and among participants with a variety of backgrounds. Since each individual has a unique ethnic background and a specific disciplinary lens with which she or he views the world, the ability to be successful requires a special set of learned knowledge, skills, and abilities.

Hawkins and Haggerty have produced a masterful work that will assist researchers to develop the skills and sensitivities necessary for this success. They and their contributors have provided us with a broad theoretical perspective that is both enlightening and pragmatic. This book will help researchers anticipate and plan for the challenges of conducting research in several sites, from gaining entry to working with clinicians who have competing job responsibilities.

The several exemplars of multicultural, multisite studies conducted by multidisciplinary teams provide the reader with a wide range of projects that have successful outcomes. The authors of these chapters provide the pragmatics that demonstrate how the theoretical components come together in actual situations. Each chapter provides a unique perspective and, when taken together, weave a tapestry that both enlightens and instructs.

This book is a valuable addition to the literature and will inform researchers at every stage of their careers. It will certainly help us as we work together to understand and appreciate differences, celebrate our unique diversity, yet work to eliminate health care disparities and improve the health of all members of society.

JUDITH A. LEWIS
Professor
School of Nursing
Virginia Commonwealth University

REFERENCES

Lewis, J. A. (2001). The social construction of diversity. *Issues in Interdisciplinary Care, 3*, 175.

Schwartz, R. S. (2001). Racial profiling in medical research. *New England Journal of Medicine, 344*, 1392–1393.

U.S. Department of Health and Human Services. (2000). *Healthy people 2010: Understanding and improving health* (2nd ed.). Washington, DC: Government Printing Office.

Prologue

Joellen W. Hawkins and Lois A. Haggerty

We seem to be awash in a palette of "multis" in our current research agendas for the health care professions. For the past two decades, research policy statements, requests for proposals, and program announcements have touted interdisciplinary, cross-disciplinary, transdisciplinary, and multidisciplinary research teams (O'Connell, 2001). Multisite research is heralded as producing richer data and more generalizable findings than single-site research. Then there is the third multi: multiethnic or multicultural. While in theory all of these sound like great concepts, in practice we haven't always produced well-thought out projects or well-executed plans for their implementation.

Sometimes we resemble disparate schools in our research more than we do a multifaceted and coherent portrait of investigation. Each addition of a multi makes a project exponentially more complex. For example, as O'Connell (2001) pointed out, each discipline has its own language, and we sometimes erroneously believe that everyone on a research team speaks that same language. This is without even suggesting multiple sites in different countries. When members of a team come together early in a collaborative effort, some engage in posturing, displays of credentials, and just plain bad manners. The latter is best exemplified in the name-dropping of important works and researchers in their individual fields. The behavior of the individual members of a discipline reflects the culture of that profession and its historical positioning in relation to the others.

Each discipline has its own culture, complete with rituals, rites of passage, and patterns of leadership. Each health care agency or institution has its own culture as well. Proposing that the sample for a study be multicultural or multiethnic imposes more languages, traditions, and meanings of participation in research with all the inherent fears, biases, prejudices, and possibilities of exploitation. Soon the whole project can take on the complexity of a cultural smorgasbord. Adding to these difficulties are enhanced concerns about the selection and protection of participants in research.

This increased vigilance for the protection of human subjects hangs over many critical decisions facing a multifaceted research team. Each member of that team brings from her or his own discipline an ethical framework that underlies both the research and the clinical practice of that discipline. One compelling necessity for a multidisciplinary team is the skill set needed to implement a multisite and especially a multicultural investigation. As Roberts and Reich (2002) pointed out, health professionals need skills in ethical analysis and applied philosophy. In the context of HIV/AIDS research, but more broadly applicable, Lansang and Crawley (2000) urged that particularly for international research, all participants need a voice in the discussion of the ethical issues. Adding to the burden for researchers, Benatar and Singer (2000) and Benatar (2002) pointed out that no standard of care for research subjects has even been set for international studies, particularly in developing countries. Thus engaging in international, multidisciplinary, and multicultural studies is happening simultaneously with engaging in the ethical debate (Wang & Huch, 2000).

This book represents some of the best examples of multisite, multidisciplinary, and multicultural research, both national and international. The authors of each chapter provide unique perspectives on their projects and address the many bonuses and barriers facing researchers undertaking studies incorporating one, two, or all three of the multis. We are particularly excited about the authors' excellent abilities not only to tell the stories of their own research, but to examine the larger issues embedded in those stories. Of course, we anticipated that the authors would present compelling tales of their adventures in undertaking research involving many sites, working with researchers from a variety of disciplines, and encountering samples rich with diversity. Never did we imagine that the chapters would be so highly illustrative of the diversity in research from such exciting and interesting perspectives.

In chapter 1, Veeder lays out the critical role management plays in the success of any study. As she points out, "Without good management, the most elegantly designed single or multisite research project will fail." Of course, without funding, every project is doomed to failure as well. Duffy, in chapter 2, skillfully presents resources useful for novice as well as expert investigators, providing practical information such as the use of websites. All but the most experienced investigators can benefit from suggestions and information in chapter 3 on how to navigate the Institutional Review Board (IRB) maze as painlessly as possible.

Few researchers can afford to launch multisite projects without research assistants. Lessons learned from one multisite, multiethnic study and shared in chapter 4 may be useful to those considering such projects. A companion to this chapter is number 5, which examines the clinical support at study sites. The theme continues in chapter 6 with examples of managing multidisciplinary projects.

Lending an international perspective, Mayberry and colleagues, in chapter 7, have prepared a detailed portrait of the relationship-building process and other essential components of a multisite, multicountry study. Their experiences illustrate the creation of a community partnership.

Campbell and colleagues' contribution fills out the multicultural aspects of the study. Their description in chapter 8 is of the cultural competence essential to a multisite, multicultural investigation.

When a study design demands more than one site, researchers are faced with many tasks and problems. When the sites are in disparate locations, the problems multiply. Creative solutions are posed in the second part of the book. Kozachik and colleagues provide the unique perspective of a study of family caregivers in the community. Many of us are far more familiar with conducting research on comfortable turf—clinical sites. This team added several new dimensions to the study, those of investigators as telephone intruders in persons' homes, of caregivers rather than patients, as research subjects, and as those who add to the burdens of family caregivers. The most complex study, the Women's Health Initiative, required 40 clinical centers to meet its objective. The authors of chapter 10 have clearly delineated the management and coordination challenges necessitated by so large a study. What they have learned and shared will benefit researchers immensely.

Schiffman, in chapter 11, focuses on the development of relationships necessary for a project to succeed. This theme of relationships is interwoven through all the chapters. The national perspective introduced here, with its emphasis on building key relationships, should be required reading for any investigator proposing a project.

"The complex nature of systems, diseases, and human response patterns demands both a broad brush and many pigments for designing studies to answer questions of primary importance to changing and guiding practice" (Hawkins, Veeder, & Pearce, 1998, p. 166). The contributing authors to this book have painted a vivid mural, indeed, of what is possible when researchers dare to dream in many dimensions.

REFERENCES

Benatar, S. R. (2002). Reflections and recommendations on research ethics in developing countries. *Social Science & Medicine, 54,* 1131–1141.

Benatar, S. R., & Singer, P. A. (2000). A new look at international research ethics. *British Medical Journal, 321,* 824–826.

Hawkins, J. W., Veeder, N. W., & Pearce, C. W. (1998). *Nurse social worker collaboration in managed care: A model of community case management.* New York: Springer.

Lansang, M. A., & Crawley, E. P. (2000). The ethics of international biomedical research. *British Medical Journal, 321,* 777–778.

O'Connell, K. A. (2001). Barriers to interdisciplinary research. *Journal of Professional Nursing, 17,* 153–154.

Roberts, M. J., & Reich, M. R. (2002). Ethical analysis in public health. *The Lancet, 358,* 1055–1059.

Wang, C. H., & Huch, M. H. (2000). Protecting human research subjects: An international perspective. *Nursing Science Quarterly, 13,* 293–298.

I

Strategies for Implementation

.

1

Managing Multisite, Multidisciplinary, and Multiethnic Research Projects

Nancy W. Veeder

OVERVIEW OF MAJOR ISSUES

Multisite, multidisciplinary, and multiethnic research projects have a good deal to recommend them. Multisite studies enable increased sample sizes and consequent wider generalizability of findings. They also afford opportunities for increased power and sophistication of statistical analyses based on large and diverse sample sizes. Further, findings derived from collaborations among many disciplines and diverse ethnic and cultural populations augment the ability to answer increasingly complex socioeconomic, political, health, behavioral health, and socioeconomic policy questions.

The defining goal of multisite research is to gather and analyze *original data from many sites*. Multisite evaluations fall into two categories: retrospective and prospective. The retrospective multisite study takes different past evaluations and reanalyzes them in relation to a topic of current concern. The difference between a retrospective multisite evaluation approach and a meta-analysis is that the meta-analysis describes past studies, whereas the retrospective multisite evaluation reanalyzes past findings using the usual summary statistical methods (Sinacore & Turpin, 1991).

Methodological problems in describing or reanalyzing retrospective findings abound. This book focuses on prospective, rather than retrospective, multisite research. While retrospective analyses pose problems of recall and interpretation, prospective multisite research projects suffer from many planning, interorganizational, research methodological, political, and process issues. Add to these the ongoing human interactional and communication factors, and the challenges increase exponentially for the researchers.

Conducting prospective multisite, multidisciplinary, and multiethnic research projects is even more complicated and fraught with potential obstacles than it would seem at first glance. Multisite research projects entail simultaneously dealing with all of the following aspects, each one a complicated system within itself: multisites, multiprofessionals, multigoals, multiagendas, multiethnicities, multivalues, multistakeholders, and multihidden agendas. Multisite research may range from needs assessments across communities, states, and nations; to qualitative studies of the course of single and multiple interventions; to qualitative and quantitative outcome evaluations of a variety of human services interventions in widely differing communities.

Many complex human interactional issues must simultaneously be addressed: span of control; leadership power and initiatives; decision-making authority; researcher vs. practitioner issues; researcher vs. clients; differing views of responsibility for completing projects; different funding "masters" to serve; different agendas and investments, both hidden and overt; methodological disagreements about sampling, data collection, and measurement across different disciplines and organizational sites; and procedures with human subjects that differ among sites.

Four major concepts crucial to implementing multisite research are discussed in this chapter: interorganizational planning and implementation issues, research methodological issues, political issues, and the principles of management that underlie successful negotiation of the complex maze of organizations, methodologies, people, and investments that characterize multisite, multidisciplinary, and multiethnic research projects.

INTERORGANIZATIONAL PLANNING AND IMPLEMENTATION ISSUES

Complications of the New Collaborative Research Model

The task of planning, organizing, and coordinating numerous collaborating sites and people begins at the initial fund-raising and design phase of the research project. Obtaining funding is discussed in another chapter in this book. However, it must be noted that it is in the fund-raising phase that initial and ongoing collaborative roles are hammered out between and among the various sites.

One important issue in multisite study collaboration across several sites and participating disciplines is that of centralization versus decentralization. The essence of interdisciplinary professional collaboration on any task is lateral, collegial, equal interaction (Rice, 2000). This flies in the face of the old research model, which was anything but collaborative and collegial.

The old, classical research model was hierarchical, linear, causal, and controlled. The classic model mandated that one or a few skilled researchers were in charge; a research project leader had clearly designated power and authority to see that the job got done. It was with this leader or director that the complete responsibility for project completion lay.

There is no question that in this older model of project design and implementation, the ultimate judgment of success or failure was not based on team performance. Quite the contrary: final judgment stopped at the doorstep of the project director. The director was ultimately responsible for the success or failure of the project.

The new multisite research model relies on lateral, collaborative research efforts, usually carried out by a number of inter- and intraprofessional teams. Although there must be a project director, responsibility for project implementation lies across sites with any number of actors with different disciplines, agendas, statuses in the collaborating organization, political and power interests, and a variety of investments in successful completion of the research project. Somehow all of these must be planned, organized, and coordinated *centrally,* while simultaneously sharing implementation decisions and power laterally in teams across decentralized organizations.

Thus, even in the new collaboration era, part of the old research model is of utmost importance in multisite research. There must be a centralized *project director* or *principal investigator* who holds all researchers to mutually agreed-upon standardized protocols for research design, implementation, and training, and provides oversight to the on-site *project coordinators,* who provide local management and adherence to all research protocols.

The entire multisite research enterprise is facilitated by collaboration, which is the cornerstone of the new research model. Collaboration means shared leadership and team membership, especially in relation to maintaining team motivation and advocacy for the project. The crucial issue is to establish clear and ubiquitous communication patterns from the inception of the project and to carry these throughout the life of the research.

Planning, Organizing, Coordinating, Implementing, and Collaborating in Multisite Research

Plans, Protocols, and Communications

Project planning must be conjoint among all research team members in all sites. From the outset of the research project, there must be written conceptual, research methodological, and specific implementation agreements among all project personnel. It cannot be overemphasized that *all* conceptual, design, sampling, data collection, and analysis issues, as well as joint and individual study implementation responsibilities (including time frames for completion of each phase and the overall project), must be written out in contractual fashion at the outset of the project. All collaborating sites must literally sign on to the written agreement.

These conjointly designed research protocols that are read and agreed to by all participants must contain time lines, milestones, delegated tasks with responsible personnel, and dollar resources needed for completion. The protocols must also contain joint team evaluation times and responsibilities. In short, every aspect of the research design and implementation plan must be cast into standardized protocols across sites and agreed to by every site management and project coordinator.

Specifically, the protocols must assign clear responsibility for task completion and an evaluative "as evidenced by" (AEB) statement for each major task. The AEB statements delineate those collaborating team members who are responsible for all tasks, clear task descriptions, expected outcomes, and strict time lines indicating when products are to be delivered and evaluated. Such protocols must be jointly designed for all aspects of the research project and for all sites. The AEB protocols must also be reviewed and evaluated regularly, perhaps monthly, in order for time lines to be met and participants' roles regularly reevaluated and clarified. The design of the implementation plan and protocols must be jointly hammered out collaboratively among participating sites.

Plans for timely meetings among all collaborators must be made in order to clarify potential misunderstandings, deal with both general and site-specific problems, and reinforce the need to meet products and time frames. Conference telephone calls are essential, with sufficient frequency (at least monthly) and length (1–2 hours, depending on the number of project issues to be ironed out). Telephone conference-call agendas should be generated by the project director, sent to all participants in timely fashion by e-mail, and in sufficient time for participants to add to or modify the agenda. Frequent and timely e-mail contacts with those on the project are also essential. Interactive websites should be utilized extensively and updated constantly as well. Fortunately, technology has made the centralized-decentralized issue much more manageable.

In short, well before the research project is launched, great care must be taken to ensure instant communication among collaborating sites and between collaborating sites and the project director and on-site coordinators. Wherever possible, potential surprises should be anticipated and articulated to the research team from the project's inception. It is normal in all research projects to have numerous unanticipated occurrences, even in single, centralized research sites. Obviously, the greater the number of sites, the greater the number of project-obstructing surprises is possible.

Implementing the Research Project: Who on the Research Team Does What, with Whom, and When?

Organizationally, there must be one project director with clear authority for ultimate decision-making. Collaboration among team and site equals the desired model. However, in research projects (as well as almost all other projects), one person must ultimately be "more equal" than cocollaborators. That person is the project director, who is usually off-site. Clearly, the project director must be the ultimate authority for substantive, methodological, and administrative decisions, along with any specialized consultants on the central team.

In each separate site there should be a project coordinator. The project coordinators, who receive funding that is written into the overall research budget for the duration of the project, should be responsible for all on-site research project information dissemination, staffing, and all training relating to the research project in the individual site.

In addition to site coordinators, the various collaborating sites should have small (3–7) on-site teams specifically charged with implementing that site's part of the research project. The project coordinator communicates directly with other site coordinators and with the central project director. Communication among the coordinators is helpful in suggesting strategies for mutual problem resolution.

A good deal has been written about the development of teams. Functional teams have structure, definition, direction, and focused, purposeful action. Teams are based on communication and mutual trust. Teams may be derailed by role and goal conflicts and conflicts in professional identity, interpersonal strife, and vying for preeminence in decision-making (Rice,

2000). The site coordinators have a major role in assuring that study goals are reached through positive team efforts.

Staffing and standardized training are important tasks for the on-site project coordinators. Staffing patterns in sites will depend on many factors, not the least of which are funding and personnel resources on-site. Ideally, the overall budget for the multisite project will have monies built in so that on-site data collectors and others conducting research-specific activities receive appropriate remuneration.

It is far preferable to have line project staff (such as data collectors and data entry personnel) at the various sites rather than centrally located, especially when distances between sites are great. Having on-site project staff also increases local investment in obtaining study results and motivation to take the time from busy schedules to carefully collect and/or input data. However, standardized training of data collectors and data input personnel should be done in larger centralized conference formats or at the sites. Again, technology has enabled us to utilize the web to put up and make available to participants the entire training module and requisite manuals. This is a highly cost-efficient, reliable, and effective way to train study staff.

In terms of overall management and standardization throughout all sites, an *oversight audit committee* for the entire life of the multisite project must be established. This should be composed of the project director, all project coordinators in the sites, and all CEOs of the collaborating sites. This group oversees that all of the research protocols, staffing, and training are standardized throughout the length of the project. This group should be in regular, scheduled communication, with its own special e-mail communication list.

Inter- and Intradisciplinary Collaboration on the Research Team

One of the most important areas in multisite research is interdisciplinary and intradisciplinary collaboration. Both types of collaboration are crucial. *Interdisciplinary* means between different disciplines. Rice (2000) defined interdisciplinary practice as "an integrated approach to care and services across disciplines, where members collaborate and come to consensus regarding decisions" (p. 60). Elements of successful interdisciplinary collaboration include: "consistent two-way communication and sharing, interdependence between roles, mutual trust and respect, mutual goal setting and the ability to compromise, and shared responsibility and decision making" (Rice, p. 62). Health and behavioral health care research offers extensive examples of interdisciplinary collaboration on practice, education, and research projects among nurses, social workers, physicians, psychologists, psychiatrists, physical and rehabilitation therapists, veterinarians, dentists, podiatrists, teachers, lawyers, statisticians, and epidemiologists.

Intradisciplinary collaboration can be clearly seen in the profession of social work which has many "wings" within the profession. For example, in social work one has clinical line practitioners with a wide variety of specialties and fields of practice. In addition, social work has administrators, researchers, policy makers, community organizers, private clinical practitioners, and group workers. Nursing has the same specialization divisions, as do medicine, law, and teaching. These within-discipline divisions may impact collaborative efforts in multisite research projects.

Rice (2000) extensively discussed interdisciplinary collaboration in education and practice. Veeder, Williams, Pearce, and Hawkins (2001) explored interdisciplinary nurse–social worker issues in case management practice, research, and model building. Those problems seen in education, practice, and interdisciplinary research collaborations would, one surmises, be compounded in multisite research. These collaboration problems may include the dominance of one or another member or profession, turf and territory issues, sense of autonomy fostered in professional education, lack of understanding of other members' skills and roles, ambiguous or lack of common goals and values, and communication barriers (Rice, 2000).

Collaboration between and among agencies has also been discussed, although not collaboration in relation to research efforts (Breznay, 2001). Although interagency collaboration is seen as a positive, there is no research to date to confirm this.

Several recent observers have supported interdisciplinary collaboration in research (Browne et al., 1997; Henneman, Lee, & Cohen, 1995; Lorentzon, 1995; Watson et al., 2000). Although much less has been written about interdisciplinary research per se, in the past decade researchers have begun to note positive outcomes specifically for client care when complex health and behavioral health care issues are addressed by multidisciplinary research teams (DiBiaggio, 1992; Lorentzon, 1995; Martin, 1994; Rabkin, 1998; Watson et al., 2000).

RESEARCH METHODOLOGICAL ISSUES

Project Design Issues

Designing and implementing research in multiple, complex settings is difficult at best, as has been described in the previous section. Further difficulties arise in trying to apply experimental research designs that satisfy the basic tenets of scientific inquiry. However, a number of things can be built into the design phase in order to approach good scientific method and to ensure reliability and predictability of the findings. One of the major issues to be kept in mind during the design phase is that, although it is important to build consensus at every phase of the project, there is one ultimate decision-maker: the project director.

For example, it might be desirable to sample interventions across different sites. It might be possible to give standard interventions to a group of welfare mothers who refuse to utilize prenatal care and well-baby clinics, offer a structured and highly focused telephone call to urge utilization to the intervention group, and provide no contact to a third, similar group of underutilizing mothers.

If a research site is wary of taking a large, randomly selected sample from its caseload at the outset, the researchers could do a delayed intervention, or mini-experiment. In the example above of the three groups of welfare mothers, the researcher could field a small randomized study into these three groups and see how the experiment is going in a relatively short period of time. If the experiment does not seem to warrant the trouble of randomized sample assignment, it could be discontinued without further undue burden on the site.

Another approach that has been utilized when randomly assigned experimental and control groups are neither available nor feasible in most or all of the research sites is to use the waiting list as a control group. The basic idea here is that the waiting list group is like the intervention group in all important ways, such as demographic characteristics, presenting problems, socioeconomic variables. They were deemed appropriate to receive services at intake, with the exception that they sought help at a time when there were not sufficient staff or material resources to offer immediate help. The waiting list group, therefore, serves as the "no intervention" control group during the time that they are on the waiting list. When these control group individuals receive interventions, they are added to the experimental groups.

Many of the questions asked in the human services are not amenable to an experimental design approach. These questions range from what the complex family correlates of domestic violence are; to why those most in need of health, mental health, and social services don't utilize such services, even when they are freely made available; to what the qualitative factors in race and ethnicity are that need to be addressed before interventions can be successfully applied.

A comparison group should always be built into the research design when a control group is not desired or feasible. This is one of the biggest strengths of multisite research: it provides countless opportunities to get different and similar groups in one large study in terms of demographics, ethnicities, problems, and interventions.

Another important need in multisite research is for overall coordination of the study design, sampling, data collection and analysis, and report-writing aspects of the research project. This coordination needs to be controlled centrally by the project director and the previously suggested audit committee for the research project. This is not to say that collaboration in overall study design, sampling, and data collection planning isn't desirable, both initially and along the way. However, it is to say that too many cooks do spoil the broth, especially in research design and implementation.

Sampling

The requirement for equivalence, representativeness, and reliability of sampling across study sites poses numerous potential problems. Sample selection needs to be closely monitored across sites. The exact criteria for sample selection need to be clearly written in protocols. Those charged with selecting the sample need to be trained on-site according to standardized protocols (as previously noted, all on-site training is the responsibility of the on-site project coordinators). The sample selection needs to be closely monitored not only by the on-site project coordinators, but by the project director as well.

Sinacore and Turpin (1991) suggested that selecting a random sample is sometimes neither feasible nor desired by stakeholders. To get around this, it is desirable to get a deliberately heterogeneous sample by selecting individuals who represent the widest range of demographic characteristics such as gender, age, race, education, ethnicity, cultural background, and socioeconomic status. As noted in the previous section on research design, there are many ways to simulate a random sample.

The inability to obtain a simple random or stratified random sample can also be offset by taking both a purposive and quota non-probability sample, making sure that the proportions of those desired demographic characteristics are present in the populations in each research site. To sample with these issues in mind does not enable prediction in meaningful ways to the larger population. However, sampling focused on ensuring heterogeneity does help to increase the reliability, generalizability, and validity of study results.

Data Collection

Multiple sites offer particular challenges to preserving the integrity of data collected. If data are collected on-site, those responsible must also be trained. Data collection must be standardized, with clear protocols, across all sites.

This is not to prohibit the collection of idiosyncratic, largely qualitative data (in addition to standardized protocols for the larger study) in substudies in selected sites where specific insights are available. The management and line site personnel can be extremely helpful in designing these special substudies. Staff investment in generating data for these substudies will also be enhanced, as will their investment and motivation to cooperate in the larger study. Finally, management in these sites will appreciate obtaining site-specific data that will answer specific, idiosyncratic, programmatic questions for them.

Data collection must be appropriate to ethnic and cultural groups and to different educational levels, ages, and genders. There may be great disagreement across sites about idiosyncratic needs or taboos in data collection. Considerable skill is needed among the project team members to juggle two important aspects of meaningful data collection (and subsequent analysis) that may be at variance across complex settings: relevance to the groups from whom data are being collected and relevance to the central study issues. The bottom line is that standardized data collection protocols must be strictly adhered to, whatever the site-specific needs.

Measurement Issues

Reliability and validity are especially crucial in measurement. The operational definitions of concepts need to be clear. The protocols for data collection also need to be written in clear terms. However, across sites, if language is an issue and translation from one language to another is desired in order to collect data from the different ethnic, cultural, and racial groups in which the study may be interested, multiple opportunities for unreliability and invalidity are possible. Again, on-site, in-depth training is essential to offset multiple possibilities for misunderstanding.

Data Analysis and Final Report Writing

Data analysis must be centrally located, under the direction of the project director and a variety of statistical experts. Trained coder and data entry persons must do data input at a centralized site such as a university. The project director should be responsible for developing all codebooks and for designing the data analysis plan. The project director must also be primarily responsible for data analysis interpretation and writing all final reports.

The reason for the centralization of the data analysis, interpretation, and report writing functions in multisite research is that it is highly unlikely that such specialized expertise is present in the various sites. This is not to say that drafts of the findings should not be circulated among participating sites. They should, and there should be several drafts generated until all sites agree on the basic findings and how they are articulated in the final report.

Ethical Considerations

Multiple systems of different, sometimes conflicting, human subjects research review (IRB) mechanisms and procedures in each individual research site may pose potential conflicts. These must be understood and negotiated on a one-by-one basis by the project director. There need to be overall project human subject protocols generated for the project as a whole. These then need to be flexibly adapted to conform to the mechanisms and procedures in every participating research site. All project participants must review the human subjects part of the research design (as part of the entire design) and sign off on it.

Another pitfall across sites alluded to in the sampling section above is the ethical difficulty inherent in sample selection procedures, especially randomization. Many direct service practitioners fear that clients will be harmed when, in fact, this is not the case. Such fears must be addressed initially in each site, and throughout the life of the multisite research project.

Randomization into experimental and control groups sometimes disturbs practitioners. Of concern might be giving no services to an abused child and her or his family in the short run so that the tenets of "scientific" inquiry for a true control group with no intervention can be met. However, as has been discussed in both the design and sampling sections of this chapter, rarely, if ever, is the absolute withholding of treatment a research option. In keeping with ethical standards of research conduct, experimental treatments can be offered as long as the comparison groups receive standard treatments.

The most useful delineation of worldwide research ethical considerations has been published in the World Medical Association Declaration of Helsinki, "Ethical Principles for Medical Research Involving Human Subjects" and "Perspectives on the Fifth Revision of the Declaration of Helsinki" (2000). Two of the most important points for multisite research in these broad-ranging documents, which are not limited strictly to medical research, are that "the research protocol should always contain a statement of the ethical considerations involved," and that "the design and performance of each experimental procedure involving human subjects should be clearly formulated in an experimental protocol" (pp. 3043–3044). For further ethics review by multicenter research ethics committees in the United Kingdom, see Tully, Ninis, Booy, and Viner (2000).

POLITICAL ISSUES

Those of us who have engaged in multisite research are all too aware that the best designed and planned research project can fail miserably due to lack of understanding of the so-called political climate in all of the sites in which the research project is launched. The political climate of an organization, frequently cited among "contextual factors" in the research literature, includes social and communication issues as well as idiosyncratic organizational cultures. The project coordinators in each research site can be very helpful in clarifying idiosyncratic and ever-changing political climates in each of their study sites.

The classic political situation in community-based research arose during the 1960s when university-based researchers came out into the community, which was usually ethnically and culturally different, to study the effects of community-based, frequently idiosyncratic, interventions. The researchers wanted data about what did or didn't work. They usually had a middle-class orientation to the design and implementation of the research. In other words, the researchers had their own agenda, which they did not bother to share with the community within which they wanted to gather data.

Needless to say, the grass roots community activists did not take kindly to these outsiders barging into a situation which, by definition, they could not or would not understand, or, more precisely, understand in a way that went with the grain of these communities of color and a variety of other ethnic and cultural compositions.

Data quality depends in large measure on understanding and working within widely varying organizational, political, and cultural environments.

Failure to attend to these environments may result in outright sabotage, passive-aggressive foot dragging, disregard of tight time schedules, and wish for independence and autonomy from the centralized authority represented by the multisite research project director and on-site project coordinators. Exquisite research methodology can be easily torpedoed by such factors if they are not understood a priori and dealt with as they are observed.

Factors such as role confusion and deteriorating staff morale on site can also jeopardize study findings. If the project is too time consuming or too jeopardizing to client care, or the direct practitioners are not kept informed of the study, serious problems may also arise. The crucial role of the on-site project coordinator in relation to staff problems is obvious.

PRINCIPLES OF MANAGEMENT FOR SUCCESSFUL MULTISITE RESEARCH PROJECTS

The span of control and decentralization issues in multisite research projects provide the potential for fragmentation and poor research outcomes. The overriding need in multisite research, therefore, is for the overall project director and project coordinators at the various research sites to consciously and systematically exercise traditional corporate management skills such as planning, organizing, coordinating, motivating, advocating, and monitoring and evaluating in all aspects of the research process.

The important management functions and skills that must underlie all successful multisite research projects are:

- *Planning*—planning underlies all other management functions. It entails laying out what is to be accomplished, who is responsible for each aspect and task, what specific actions are to be taken within a given time frame, why such actions are necessary, and specifying the means and timing to assess and evaluate the success of the plans. In Skidmore's (1990) parsimonious view, planning is a process of anticipating goals and objectives and preparing a plan to reach them, a process that involves knowing where you are, where you want to go, and deciding the best means to get there.
- *Organizing*—organizing is creating a formal series of role structures and responsible relationships that enable the organization to attain its stated goals and objectives.
- *Coordinating*—coordination has been widely described as the glue that holds organizations together. Operations coordination, like

planning, is one of the most ubiquitous management functions. Coordination not only pertains to coordinating the various units and teams within the organization but outside the organization as well, which is of primary importance in implementing multisite research.

- *Motivating*—motivating entails creating reward systems that meet human needs within an organization. Motivating activities can be carried out with individuals, groups, teams, and units within the organization and organizations outside the primary organization.
- *Advocating*—advocating activities consist of convincing other individuals or systems to produce something that is needed by an individual, family, group, organization, or community for whom one is advocating. Key personal attributes in advocacy are communication, persuasion, exchange, and organizational and political savvy.
- *Monitoring and Evaluating*—the monitoring function has to do with creating processes, tools, and motivations for monitoring, measuring, evaluating, and correcting outcomes of the project's stated goals and objectives (Veeder & Dalgin, 2002). Clearly, this area is the one in which the research project audit committee must be most active and vigilant in maintaining standardized procedures and processes.

Table 1.1 outlines management skills needed to successfully implement multisite research in three major areas: interorganizational, research, and political. The table indicates that these aspects of the multisite research process rely heavily on the management functions of planning, organizing, coordinating, motivating, advocating, and monitoring.

Other personal management skills required for successful multisite research implementation are insightful interpersonal skills, leadership abilities, decision-making prowess, team-building and sustaining skills, and high capacity for multidisciplinary collaboration. In other words, it is necessary but not sufficient to the successful outcome of multisite research to be a competent researcher. Of crucial importance for successful multisite research project outcomes is skilled management.

CONCLUSIONS: THE CRITICAL ROLE OF MANAGEMENT IN A SUCCESSFUL RESEARCH PROJECT

From the very beginning of any project, the primary concern must be with planning, organizing, coordinating, motivating, advocating, and monitor-

TABLE 1.1 Management Skills Needed in Interorganizational, Research, and Political Aspects of Multisite Research Implementation

Implementation Areas	Management Skills					
	Planning	Organizing	Coordinating	Motivating	Advocating	Monitoring
1. Interorganizational	Fundraising Agreement Protocols Tasks Time lines Milestones Persons Responsible Meetings Communication	On-site Teams Coordinators Training Staffing	Interdisc. Collab.	All involved Intradisc. Collab.	For Research Team & Design	All aspects of Process Audit Committee
2. Research	Design Sampling Process Data Collection Measurement Data Analysis Report Writing	All aspects	All aspects of Process	All aspects of Process	All aspects of Process	All aspects of Process Audit Committee
3. Political	Potential Sabotage	Clear lines of authority	Communication	Communication	Turf Sensitivity	All aspects of process Audit Committee

ing. An equally important concern is to fashion, nurture, and constantly support task-oriented teams in each of the research sites. Strictly research concerns are important, but are clearly secondary to organizational and political issues attendant to implementing multisite research projects.

In order to maximize the considerable strengths of multisite research projects, such as obtaining larger and more diverse samples and the richness of multidisciplinary approaches to data gathering and analysis, the project director and project coordinators must systematically fashion a management team at the top. Built into this top management team must be instant, clear and timely communication vehicles; clear operational protocols for the entire project to include tasks, responsibilities, time frames, and monitoring and evaluation criteria; and the overall and site-specific goals for the project. On-site teams must also be similarly designed and implemented as management entities.

Managing professionals, especially those engaged in highly technological research and development, can pose added complications. Miller (1986) pointed out that professionals, by definition, seek a high level of autonomy that is seemingly at odds with the control issues inherent in the close management necessary in multisite research. Ensuring the free flow of information and decision making across sites and professional collaborators will nonetheless maximize cooperation in the accomplishment of research tasks.

Without good management, the most elegantly designed single- or multisite research project will fail. The difference between a single site and a multisite research situation is that by virtue of having numerous research sites, lack of centralization, more personnel involved, and a more complicated span of research control, good management is both more complex and difficult and more essential to success.

REFERENCES

Breznay, S. (2001). Liaison teams: A strategy for building interagency collaboration in caring for children with serious emotional disturbances and their families. *Issues in Interdisciplinary Care, 3*(2), 101–106.

Browne, G. B., Watt, S., Roberts, J., Gafni, A., Byrne, C., & Partners in Affiliated Health and Social Service Agencies. (1997). Within our reach: Evidence-based practice resulting from alliances in health and social services. *Clinical Excellence for Nurse Practitioners, 1*(2), 127–140.

DiBiaggio, J. (1992). Allied health in a contemporary university: Strategies for survival. *Journal of Allied Health, 24*, 117–123.

Henneman, E. A., Lee, J. L., & Cohen, J. I. (1995). Collaboration: A concept analysis. *Journal of Advanced Nursing, 21,* 103–109.

Lorentzon, M. (1995). Multidisciplinary collaboration: Lifeline or drowning pool for nurse researchers? *Journal of Advanced Nursing, 22,* 825–826.

Martin, K. (1994). Coordinating multidisciplinary collaborative research: A formula for success. *Clinical Nurse Specialist, 8*(1), 18–22.

Miller, D. B. (1986). *Managing professionals in research and development: A guide for improving productivity and organizational effectiveness.* San Francisco: Jossey-Bass.

Perspectives on the fifth revision of the Declaration of Helsinki. (2000). *Journal of the American Medical Association, 284*(23), 3045–3046.

Rabkin, M. (1998). A paradigm shift in academic medicine. *Academic Medicine, 73*(2), 127–131.

Rice, A. H. (2000). Interdisciplinary collaboration in health care: Education, practice, and research. *National Academies of Practice Forum, 2*(1), 59–73.

Sinacore, J. M., & Turpin, R. S. (1991). Multiple sites in evaluation research: A survey of organizational and methodological issues. In J. M. Sinacore & R. S. Turpin (Eds.), *Multisite evaluations* (pp. 5–18). San Francisco: Jossey-Bass.

Skidmore, R. A. (1990). *Social work administration: Dynamic management and human relationships.* Englewood Cliffs, NJ: Prentice Hall.

Tully, J., Ninis, N., Booy, R., & Viner, R. (2000). The new system of review by multicentre research ethics committees: Prospective study. *British Medical Journal, 320*(7243), 1179–1182.

Turpin, R. S., & Sinacore, J. M. (Eds.). (1991). *Multisite evaluations.* San Francisco: Jossey-Bass.

Veeder, N. W., & Dalgin, R. E. (in press). Social work as management: A retrospective study of 245 care management practice outcomes. *Journal of Social Service Research.*

Veeder, N. W., Williams, S. L., Pearce, C. W., & Hawkins, J. W. (2001). Building an interdisciplinary practice model through interdisciplinary research. *Issues in Interdisciplinary Care, 3*(1), 51–58.

Watson, B., Proctor, S., van Zwanenberg, T., Byrne, C., Browne, G., Roberts, J., & Gafni, A. (2000). Interdisciplinary, intersectoral, and international collaboration in research. *National Academies of Practice Forum, 2*(3), 217–222.

World Medical Association Declaration of Helsinki. Ethical principles for medical research involving human subjects. (2000). *Journal of the American Medical Association, 284*(23), 3043–3044.

2

Obtaining Funding

Mary E. Duffy

A ll health-related disciplines are responsible to society for providing quality, cost-effective care and for finding ways to improve that care. Conducting research is the primary way members of a discipline develop knowledge to underpin their practice. Although the focus of research may vary from one health-related discipline to another, researchers in all disciplines need to seek funding, and they usually follow the same routes to secure it for their individual projects and programs of research.

The purpose of this chapter is to provide an overview of the most common ways to find and secure funds to carry out research projects. It includes information on:

- How to become a funded researcher
- Public funding mechanisms with a focus on the National Institutes of Health (NIH) extramural research and peer-review process and tips for seeking federal funding
- Private funding mechanisms and grant-writing tips for seeking private funding
- The most common reasons grants are not funded
- Grant-writing resources available on the Internet and in print

BECOMING A FUNDED RESEARCHER

Targeting funds for health and human services research is all about raising money to carry out a research project in an efficient, cost-effective, and competent way. All that is needed is a good research idea (project); a good match between the proposed project and the mission of the funding agency; a carefully thought-out approach to the project, including what it would cost in time and money; and a well-written, focused proposal including a proposed budget submitted to, and reviewed by, a specific funding agency or foundation (Burns & Grove, 2001; Reif-Lehrer, 1995a).

The old adage "success begets success" is also true in research. Experienced researchers who have already garnered significant amounts of research funding are more likely to receive subsequent funding from public and private grant-making groups. They became funded researchers because they have mastered grant writing, the art of acquiring peer-reviewed research funding (Kraicer, 1997).

WHY SEEK RESEARCH FUNDING

It is important to researchers and to their respective disciplines to seek research funding. Scientific credibility and research funding go hand-in-hand (Burns & Grove, 2001). An investigator who seeks and secures research funding from federal agencies such as the National Institutes of Health (NIH), National Science Foundation (NSF), the Centers for Disease Control and Prevention (CDC), and the National Endowment for the Arts (NEA), through their competitive, peer-review process can be assured the funded study has scientific and social merit. In fact, each funding award enhances the status of the researcher, increases the researcher's chances of securing greater funding for subsequent studies, and contributes to the scientific credibility of the researcher's discipline (Burns & Grove, 2001).

Over the past five decades, grant writing has become the business of scientific disciplines in general and professional disciplines in particular. Substantive scientific research in health-related disciplines is labor intensive and requires uninterrupted time and effort by teams of personnel to complete one or more research projects. Research scientists are made, not born to the role. Their programs usually begin with an idea of how to answer a particular problem germane to improving one or more segments of that portion of society they serve. Once the idea is developed, the scientist designs a systematic way or method to find the answer to the identified problem; writes up the method in a proposal, commonly called a grant; and submits it to a federal or private group that funds this type of research. By way of illustration, in fiscal year (FY) 2001, the NIH budget for funding health-related research grants was $22.43 billion (NIH, April 9, 2001) and the President's budget for FY 2002 was $23.04 billion, an increase of 13.5% over 2001 (NIH, May 23, 2001). Had it not been for this research sponsorship in past decades, there would have been 80 fewer Nobel prizes for scientific advances, including breaking the genetic code governing all life processes and discovering new ways to prevent, treat, and cope with diseases and related disabilities (NIH, April, 2001).

TYPES OF FEDERAL RESEARCH GRANTS

The largest source of grant monies for health and human services research comes from the federal government, usually through the NIH extramural grants program. There are two main approaches for pursuing NIH funding: researcher-initiated proposals and federal agency requests for proposals (RFP) or requests for applications (RFA). The researcher-initiated proposal, the most common type, begins when the researcher identifies a significant research problem, develops a method to study it, and submits a research proposal to the appropriate NIH Institute, which will review and, it is hoped, fund the project. An RFP is a written invitation by a funding agency to submit a research proposal on a particular topic by a stated deadline. An RFA is the term used for an RFP within the NIH Institutes. It is a formal announcement that describes an NIH Institute(s) or other federal agency initiative in a well-defined focal area inviting anyone in the field to submit a grant application for a one-time competition for a specific amount of funds set aside to be used for a specific number of awards (Reif-Lehrer, 1995a). Basically, an RFA is a contract for which researchers submit a bid (Burns & Grove, 2001).

RFPs and RFAs are published in the *Federal Register*, a daily publication of all federal grant opportunities and program deadlines. Since the advent of the Internet, finding RFAs has become very easy. Potential applicants need only go to the *NIH Guide for Grants and Contracts* found on the Office of Extramural Research (OER) web page at *http://grants.nih.gov/grants/guide* and click on Requests for Applications. This website will then take visitors to the latest RFAs sorted by year, beginning with the most recent. Using the Search mechanism eliminates the need to plow through all of the RFAs to date. Just type in a key word or phrase, separated by commas. The site also provides a process for subscribing to the free weekly content notification service via e-mail.

Types of NIH Grants

The NIH has several different grant mechanisms, each with its own objectives and review criteria. The grant mechanisms most often used by health researchers are the traditional Research Project Grant (RO1), the Academic Research Enhancement Award (AREA, R15), the Small Grants Program (RO3), and the Mentored Clinical Scientist Development Award (K08). Each of these grants is discussed below. Information about other NIH grant mechanisms is available at *http://grants.nih.gov/grants/funding/funding.htm*.

Research Project Grant (RO1)

The most common funding mechanism at NIH is the RO1, so-called because the alphanumeric "RO1" precedes the assigned NIH proposal number to designate this program (Ogden, 1991). RO1s are generally researcher initiated and used to support scientific research or training. An RO1 usually provides a commitment of support for an average of four years of funding. After the initial year of RO1 funding, the grantee receives noncompeting continuations each year for the specified length of the grant. The bulk of NIH funds allocated to RO1 grants in any given year supports noncompeting continuations that permit important research to continue. In FY 2001, 58% of NIH's total budget of $2,442 billion was spent on RO1 grants, with 75% of those funds going to noncompeting continuations. Only about 25% of total funds allocated for research projects are available to fund new projects or initiatives (NIH, April, 2001).

NIH RO1 reviewers' guidelines. Peer review is the cornerstone of the NIH extramural research funding program. Scientific consultants, chosen for their expertise in research methods, serve as members of each Institute's study section where they evaluate the scientific merit of RO1 grant applications. As of July, 2001, the stated criteria used by NIH study section reviewers are: (National Institutes of Health, July 12, 2001):

1. Significance. Does this study address an important problem? If the aims of the application are achieved, how will scientific knowledge be advanced? What will be the effect of these studies on the concepts or methods that drive this field?
2. Approach. Are the conceptual framework, design (including composition of study population), methods, and analyses adequately developed, well-integrated, and appropriate to the aims of the project? Does the applicant acknowledge potential problem areas and consider alternative tactics?
3. Innovation. Does the project employ novel concepts, approaches or methods? Are the aims original and innovative? Does the project challenge existing paradigms or develop new methodologies or technologies?
4. Investigator. Is the investigator appropriately trained and well suited to carry out this work? Is the work proposed appropriate to the experience level of the principal investigator and other researchers (if any)?

5. Environment. Does the scientific environment in which the work will
be done contribute to the probability of success? Do the proposed
experiments take advantage of unique features of the scientific environment or employ useful collaborative arrangements? Is there evidence
of institutional support?

6. Additional Considerations.

a. Are the minority and gender characteristics of the sample scientifically acceptable and consistent with the aims of the project?

b. If Human Subjects' Exemptions are claimed, are there any concerns
about the appropriateness of the Exemption(s) claimed? [Note:
Claiming an Exemption status means the investigator states on
the grant application that the proposed research does not require
Institutional Review Board (IRB) approval because the research
does not involve human subjects as defined in Subpart A of the
*Common Rule of the Code of Federal Regulations (45CFR46) Protec-
tion of Human Subjects*; or the only involvement of human subjects
is in one of the six "exempt" categories listed in the Code (Code
of Federal Regulations, 2001). See this reference's website for
more detailed information about the six exempt categories.] If No
Exemptions are claimed, are there concerns about the applicant's
responses to the six required points? Are the risks to the subjects
reasonable in relation to the anticipated benefits to the subjects
and/or in relation to the importance of the knowledge that may
reasonably be expected to result from the research?

c. Is the Total Budget appropriate for the proposed project? Are
modifications in amount or duration of support needed?

The RO1 Grant and New Investigators

Since 1998, new investigators are encouraged to use the RO1 grant mechanism for researcher-initiated proposals. The NIH (2000, August 21) defines
a new investigator as one who has not previously served as a principal
investigator (PI) on any NIH-supported research project other than a small
grant (RO3), an Academic Research Enhancement Award (R15), an explor-
atory/developmental grant (R21), or certain other career awards directed
to investigators at the beginning of their research careers (KO1, KO8, K22,
and K23).

NIH believes that new investigators are critical to the future of health
research. Since they are typically less proficient in preparing grant applications expressing their research plans than experienced PIs, NIH revised
its PHS398 application form to let new investigators indicate this status.
In so doing, NIH ensured that new investigators would be evaluated in a
manner appropriate for the present stage of their research careers (NIH,
August 21, 2000). In addition, RO1 reviewers are instructed to keep in

mind the experience of, and the resources available to, the new investigator. When considering a new investigator's RO1 grant application, the RO1 study section reviewer should evaluate the RO1 criteria in a manner appropriate to the expectations for and problems likely to be faced by a new investigator (NIH, August 21, 2000). The following statements have been added to the NIH study section review criteria:

1. Approach. More emphasis should be placed on demonstrating that the techniques/approaches are feasible than on preliminary results.
2. Investigator. More emphasis should be placed on their training and their research potential than on their track record and number of publications.
3. Environment. There should be some evidence of institutional commitment in terms of space and time to perform the research.

Academic Research Enhancement Award (AREA, R15)

NIH began the AREA (R15) program in 1985 as a special effort to stimulate research in educational institutions that provide the baccalaureate training for a significant number of U.S. research scientists but that have not been major recipients of NIH support (NIH, July 18, 2001a). In 1999, the AREA program was expanded from its annual RFA to a standing, ongoing program announcement (PA) with current submission dates of January 25, May 25, and September 25 (NIH, February 11, 1999).

The purpose of the AREA grant is to support small-scale research projects conducted by faculty in institutions that are not research intensive. In contrast to most RO1s that use actual budget line items, an AREA application must be submitted with a budget of one to four modules of $25,000 for up to 36 months (three years). For example, an investigator determined that she needed $75,000 to complete a clinical study in two years (24 months), and the major portion of the funds would be needed in Year 1. Using the Modular approach, the researcher's budget would ask for two $25,000 modules for Year 1 and one $25,000 module for Year 2, for a total of three modules ($75,000). For detailed information about all aspects of the NIH Modular Research Grant Applications, go to the NIH OER web pages at http://grants.nih.gov/grants/funding/modular/modular/modular.htm.

Typically, AREA grant applications are reviewed by NIH study sections that handle a significant number of these at any one time. Frequently, at least one study section reviewer is from an AREA-eligible school. In addition to evaluating the AREA application using the RO1 Reviewer Guidelines discussed earlier, reviewers must evaluate the following additional elements (NIH, July 18, 2001a):

4. Investigator. Is the principal investigator's experience appropriate for supervising students in research?
5. Environment.

- How suitable is the applicant's school/component for an award in terms of strengthening the research environment and exposing students to research?
- Does the applicant document the likely availability of well-qualified students?
- Does the applicant provide evidence that students have in the past, or are likely to pursue, careers in biomedical and behavioral science?

The Small Grants Program (RO3)

The RO3 grant mechanism provides research support, specifically limited in time and amount, for activities that are not yet ready for RO1 support. These research activities include pilot projects, testing of new techniques, or feasibility studies of innovative, high-risk research, which would provide a basis for more extended research (NIH, December 11, 2000). Applicants may request nonrenewable funds of either $25,000 or $50,000 direct costs for projects of one year or, in some cases, two years duration. Not all NIH Institutes employ the RO3 grant mechanism, so it is wise to check the OER Small Grant Program (RO3) website at *http://grants.nih.gov/grants/funding/r03.htm* for which NIH Institutes currently use it. It is important to contact the NIH Institute most likely to fund the proposed research project to verify that the RO3 mechanism is in effect prior to submitting an application.

The National Institute of Nursing Research (NINR) is one NIH Institute that does not use the RO3 mechanism. In contrast, the National Institute of Aging (NIA) has issued two recent Program Announcements (PAs) seeking small grant (RO3) applications for specific types of research: *NIA Pilot Research Grant Program* (NIH, December 20, 2000); and *Data Analysis and Archiving in Demography, Economics, and Behavioral Research on Aging* (NIH, April 12, 2001). Even though the PHS398 form is used for RO3 applications, each Institute sets its own page limits. This information can be found only in the PA issued by the specific Institute or at the Institute's website.

Mentored Patient-Oriented Research Career Development Award (K23)

The K-series funding mechanisms are called Research Career Awards, offered by various NIH Institutes. There are several types of career awards to research and academic institutions for scientists with evident research potential. Each K award is part of an integrated program designed to develop a cadre of outstanding scientists and help them to expand their potential for making important scientific contributions (NIH, December 11, 2000).

The *Mentored Patient-Oriented Research Career Development Award* (K23) is particularly relevant to beginning health researchers. Its purpose is to support the career development of investigators who have made a commitment to focus their research endeavors on patient-oriented research. Patient-oriented research is defined as research conducted with human beings (or on material of human origin such as tissue, specimen, and cognitive phenomena) for which a researcher directly interacts with human subjects. It includes (1) mechanisms of human disease, (2) therapeutic interventions, (3) clinical trials, and (4) new technology development (NIH, October 8, 1999).

The K23 mechanism provides funding for three to five years of supervised study and research to clinically trained professionals who possess a doctorate or its equivalent. Candidates must identify a mentor with extensive research experience who agrees to serve in this capacity. The candidate must agree to spend a minimum of 75% of full-time professional effort conducting research career development and clinical research. Allowable costs under the K23 mechanism are candidate salary and fringe benefits based on a 12-month staff appointment; research development support up to $25,000 per year for tuition, fees, and books; research expenses; travel to research meetings or training; and statistical services, including personnel and time. There is no salary for mentors, secretaries, and administrative assistants (NIH, October 8, 1999). If you are interested in this award, you should contact the specific Institute's program staff during the planning phase of your K23 application.

Federal Funding For Minority Research and Researchers

Since 1985, the NIH has dedicated specific funds to increase the number of underrepresented minority scientists participating in biomedical research and the health-related sciences (NIH, April 9, 2001b). The U.S. Department of Health and Human Services (DHHS) Office of Minority Health (OMH) was created then to improve the health of racial and ethnic populations by developing effective health policies and programs to eradicate disparities in health (USDHHS, 2001, June). The OMH Resource Center maintains a database of funding resources that can provide support for minority health projects and other health-related programs (USDHHS, 2001, January). This searchable database provides information on private and public foundations; federal funding and community resources; pharmaceutical and insurance organizations; journal articles, directories, and books; and fellowships, scholarships, and internships for members of minority groups.

There are several NIH-wide Minority Researchers' Training and Enhancement Programs: the Minority Biomedical Research Support Program, Minority Access to Research Careers Program, Research Supplements for Underrepresented Minorities Programs, and Research Centers in Minority Institutions (National Institute of Allergy and Infectious Diseases, 2001). For more specific information about these programs, see the website listed in the cited reference.

The NIH Review Process

This section briefly describes what happens to NIH-submitted grant applications. Review can occur either in the NIH's Center for Scientific Review (CSR) or in a specific Institute. Most investigator-initiated grants such as the RO1 and AREA (R15) grant applications are reviewed by a scientific review group (SRG) Study Section in the CSR. Institute-specific grants such as the research career (K) grants, program (P) projects, cooperative agreements (U), training (T) grants, and specific PAs and RFPs are reviewed by Institute SRGs.

Submitting the NIH Application

After you send your grant application to NIH, it arrives at a mailroom along with about 10,000 other grants received during each review cycle (NIH, August 24, 2001). Once an application is received, it is first checked for compliance with NIH Policies. If mistakes are found such as incorrect numbers of pages, missing pages, wrong information, or lack of signatures on the face page, this may delay the processing of the application for the current review cycle. The project is then assigned to an Institute for funding consideration. This determination is based on the focus and mission of each of the NIH Institutes and centers. An application may receive primary and dual assignments to two Institutes (NIH, July 11, 2001). If this happens, each Institute receives copies of the application and the application undergoes two reviews. Finally, the grant application is assigned for review to the appropriate CSR Study Section(s).

In a cover letter accompanying the grant application, an investigator can ask which Institute or Institutes might be most appropriate for the review of the proposed grant. This request will be taken into account by the CSR Division of Receipt and Referral (DRR) personnel when assigning the NIH application. Within six weeks of this assignment, the DRR sends a notice to the investigator and to the business office of the applicant institution. This notice contains information on the timetable for review and funding consideration; the assignment number of the project; whether there is a dual assignment; the review assignment, including the name of the Study Section or panel; information about the primary Institute to which the application is assigned; and the address of the investigator. If information is incorrect in this notice, the investigator should immediately contact the DRR staff to inform them about the situation.

Study Section Review

The NIH has a dual peer review system. The SRG constitutes the first level of review and is called the Initial Review Group (IRG), which is composed of a subcommittee called a Study Section. Each CSR Study Section is composed of about 18–20 individuals nominated for multiyear terms by Scientific Review Administrators (SRA) from among the active and productive researchers in the respective scientific disciplines germane to the Institutes. The goal of the SRA is to make sure that each Study Section has sufficient and varied expertise so as to be knowledgeable about the diversity of subject matter to be encountered when reviewing grant applications in the particular Institute (NIH Center for Scientific Review, August 24, 2001).

One week before the particular Study Section convenes, the SRA solicits from all members a list of research applications believed not to rank in the top half for scientific merit. Called streamlining, the SRA combines the individual lists from Study Section members and establishes a final list of those applications deemed to be in the lower half for scientific merit. Although these applications are not scored or discussed at the Study Section meeting, investigators will receive reviewers' written comments and may subsequently revise and resubmit their applications at a later date. The streamlining process does not indicate that a grant application has been disapproved per se; rather, it represents the Study Section's decision that the application does not rank in the top half of applications generally reviewed by the Section (NIH, August 24, 2001).

Determining Priority Scores and Percentile Rankings

Using the appropriate Review Criteria discussed in the previous section, at least two or more Study Section members serve as primary and secondary reviewers for each grant application. Their task is to determine the strengths and weaknesses of applications assigned to them for this review cycle. The reviewers present each application to the entire Study Section and indicate their level of enthusiasm by suggesting a priority score, where 1.0 = the best and 5.0 = the worst (NIH, August 24, 2001). If streamlining takes place, then the score will range from 1.0 to 3.0; those higher than 3.0 will be in the bottom half of the ranking.

After full discussion of the merits of the application, each Study Section member assigns a priority score. The Summary Statement that the investigator receives within six to eight weeks after the Study Section meeting contains the overall priority score for the application. This score was computed by taking each Study Section member's priority rating, adding these scores together and dividing by the number of Study Section members at the review to form an average priority rating, then multiplying that average priority rating by 100. Reviewed research grant applications are then assigned a percentile rank, based on the priority scores assigned to them during the current plus past two review rounds. In other words, applications that have been revised by a standing Study Section are percentiled against all applications reviewed by that same Study Section for the three consecutive rounds (NIH, July 18, 2001b).

Summary Statements

Following the Study Section meeting, the SRA prepares a Summary Statement, formerly called pink sheets because of the color of the typing paper used, and sends it to the investigator within eight weeks. The Summary Statement contains the reviewers' critiques; a summary of the Study Section deliberations; an average priority score; recommended changes in the budget; administrative comments, if any; and a roster listing the reviewers in the Study Section with no identifiers as to which reviewers were assigned to the investigator's application. The Summary Statement also contains the name of the Institute program staff responsible for the application (NIH, August 24, 2001).

Investigators should usually wait until after they receive their Summary Statements before contacting the specific program officer to learn if their applications are likely to be funded. The priority score is a good indication of the likelihood of success. The closer a priority score is to 100 (the highest possible score), the greater the likelihood of being funded. A good question to ask the program officer is: What is the payline, that is, the funding cutoff point, for this funding cycle? If the program officer can provide an answer to this question, investigators will be better able to ascertain whether their projects will be funded this cycle, deferred until the next one or two cycles, or not be funded at all. Percentiles better than the payline are likely to be funded; those worse than the payline (except for some high-priority applications around the payline margin) are likely to be deferred until later in the fiscal year or not funded at all. Keep in mind that the payline is not a fixed number, but a budget management tool that can change as the fiscal year progresses and changes occur in available funds for the particular Institute. Paylines also vary among Institutes so that the same percentile that is funded in one Institute may not be funded in another (National Institutes of Allergy and Infectious Diseases, August 30, 2001).

Institute Advisory Council

The second step in the NIH peer review process is the National Advisory Council of each Institute, consisting of 12 to 16 members from the scientific and nonscientific communities. About 25% of the membership are lay persons and 75% are scientists. Each Institute Advisory Council considers the Summary Statements from each Study Section and adds its own review based on judgments both of scientific merit of the application and its relevance to the specific Institute's program goals. In some cases, relevance of the application supersedes its percentile ranking. The Council can concur with, or modify, Study Section action on grant applications or defer an application for further review (Reif-Lehrer, 1995a). Funding of a particular application is based on two considerations: scientific merit and program considerations. However, keep in mind that neither the Study Section nor the Advisory Council has the power to make funding decisions. These are advisory bodies only with the final decision about funding awards made by the Director of the relevant Institute or funding component (NIAID, August 30, 2001; Reif-Lehrer, 1995a).

Appeal

An investigator can appeal a review if (s)he thinks the review process had serious flaws such as errors due to conflict of interest or bias on the part of reviewers. However, differences of opinion between the investigator and the reviewers cannot be appealed. An investigator who believes an appealable error(s) has occurred, can contact the Institute program officer for the project and discuss the best course of action. An excellent discussion of the NIH appeals process can be found in the NIH Guide: Appeals of Initial Scientific Peer Review (November 21, 1997), found at *http://grants1.nih.gov/grants/guide/notice-files/not97-232.html.*

GRANT-WRITING TIPS FOR SEEKING FEDERAL FUNDING

A basic principle of writing grants is that no amount of good writing can fool grant reviewers into funding a research proposal that springs from a poorly formulated idea. Success in obtaining grant funding for research depends on a good research idea (project), a good match between the proposed project and the mission of the funding group, a carefully thought-out approach to the project, and a well-written, focused research proposal. In addition to capturing the reviewers' interest in the project, a good proposal must be feasible, defined as doable by the principal investigator and research team, and relevant to the mission of the funding agency (Rief-Lehrer, 1995a).

As Reif-Lehrer (1995b) noted, getting funding takes more than just a good idea. In today's very tight funding market, more and more grant seekers are looking for extramural funding to move their research programs forward. Consequently, it is important to develop the needed skills and use the resources available to carefully think through the proposed project. Here are several tips that can help you when preparing a federal grant application.

1. Start with a good research idea that is significant, timely, and carefully focused so as to be doable in a specified period of time for a certain amount of money.
2. Dream big, but start small (Grey, 2000). A researcher needs to envision a program of research and then carefully delineate the best research project for which to seek funding. Most projects in the early phase of a research program will not be suitable for significant amounts of competitive, extramural funding. Rather,

      small intramural or extramural funds should be sought first to undertake pilot work to gather evidence that can be used as the base for larger, extramurally sought, competitive federal research grants (Burns & Grove, 2001; Grey, 2000).

3.   Once you have decided on what NIH Institutes might be appropriate for the proposed project, contact program officers at the Institute(s) to discuss your research idea with them. This is particularly important if the proposed project is methodologically innovative or outside the current mainstream of research (Lorian, 1995).

4.   Develop a 3–5 page prospectus, or concept paper, delineating your proposed research questions and a brief methods description prior to meeting with NIH program officers. This will greatly help them in advising you on what steps to take next. It is also a good idea to consult research colleagues, particularly those who have received federal research grant funding. The more help you get at the outset, the better the proposal should be.

5.   Carefully listen to the advice NIH program staff and experienced research colleagues give you about the proposal. These individuals know what is currently being funded, what is likely to be funded, and how your project may fit within the Institute's current grant portfolio (Grey, 2000; Lorian, 1995).

6.   Make sure that your proposal is not overly ambitious for the amount of money you seek and for the proposed time frame. Beginning researchers very often bite off more than they can chew in one proposal. Experienced researchers and NIH project personnel can often help you to revise your project to fit the time and the funds available.

7.   Make sure that the proposal you submit is clearly focused. It should not have too many general-sounding aims that convey great ambition but little specificity (Lorian, 1995). The research problem should be important and significant to society. Federal reviewers want to be assured that the proposed work for which you seek funding "will contribute to more than improving the investigator's health" (Grey, 2000, p. 91).

8.   Carefully read the published NIH instructions provided by the Institute, PHS398 form, the PA or RFA, and follow them to the letter. This includes formatting, spacing, font size, and page limits. Make sure you follow the format in the instructions. NIH reviewers expect the research plan to be organized exactly as described in the instructions (NIAID, August 30, 2001).

9. Start the grant-writing process early so that the first proposal draft is written at least six weeks before the Institute submission deadline. This will give you enough time to have your proposal critically appraised by colleagues who can provide guidance in making revisions.

10. When writing your research grant application, make sure that you convey a sense of the current state of the science in your focal area. You need to show links between what has already been done, what is currently needed, and how these will contribute to new knowledge in the field (Lorian, 1995).

11. You also need to convey in the application that you will be able to cope with potential problems that could arise when implementing the study. This is particularly important if you are a novice grant seeker.

12. Assess areas where outside expertise is needed to help you conduct the research. Choose and name a consultant who can provide the needed assistance. If the consultant is critical to the conduct of the study, provide a curriculum vitae.

13. Request only enough funds to carry out the proposed research. Make sure the budget is realistic and appropriate for the aims and methods of the project, eliminating any extravagant requests or resources that would already be available to you. Provide a rationale for all requested expenses, especially for any expensive equipment. Reviewers will evaluate the budget for whether it is realistic and justified by the aims and methods of the project (NIAID, August 30, 2001).

14. Remember that everything takes longer than you think. In developing your project time line, provide sufficient time to carry out the project to its successful completion. Reviewers are concerned that the time frame is a realistic picture for the research involved. They do not want a blow-by-blow description of everything you need to do; rather, they want assurance that you have really thought through the various project steps and know what needs to be done when (Reif-Lehrer, 1995a).

15. Carefully read the application instructions for specific requirements for the protection of human/animal subjects and for the responsible conduct of research. Follow instructions to the letter. Failure to include this necessary information can result in a grant application not being reviewed (NIAID, August 30, 2001).

16. Make sure that your research plan includes diverse populations unless it requires specific groups. State how you will ensure ade-

quate numbers of minorities, children, and both genders. Carefully justify all exclusions (US DHHS Public Health Service, August 8, 2001).

PRIVATE FOUNDATION GRANTS

Other excellent funding sources for health-related research are private foundations, entities established as nonprofit corporations or charitable trusts with a fundamental aim of funding grants for unrelated organizations, institutions, or individuals for scientific, educational, cultural, religious, or other charitable purposes (The Foundation Center, 2001a). In the United States alone, there are over 60,000 foundations offering grants to individuals, organizations, institutions, and other nonprofit groups (The Foundation Center, 2001b). A foundation can be classified as private or public. A private foundation receives most of its funds from one major source: an individual, a family, a corporation. In contrast, a public foundation normally receives the bulk of its assets from multiple sources, including private foundations, individuals, government agencies, and fees for service. Such a foundation must continue to seek funds from multiple sources in order to keep its public status (The Foundation Center, 2001b).

The first, and often the most difficult, problem for health researchers who wish to seek private foundation funding is to identify the right foundation(s) to approach. In contrast to federal funding, foundations are less bound by regulations about the types of projects they can fund and the way they make decisions about funding. Their funding priorities can, and may, change annually (Burns & Grove, 2001; Gitlin & Lyons, 1996). Thus, it is really important for grant seekers to find out as much information as possible about the foundation(s) before writing and submitting a grant proposal.

An excellent first step is to visit The Foundation Center website at *http:// www.fdncenter.org*, where you will find a wealth of information on private philanthropy and available grants. Founded in 1956, The Foundation Center's mission is to support and improve institutional philanthropy by promoting public understanding of the field and helping grant seekers succeed. To achieve their mission, The Foundation Center collects, organizes, and communicates U.S. philanthropic information; conducts and facilitates research on trends in the field; provides education and training on the grant-seeking process; and ensures public access to information and services through its website, print and electronic publications, five library/learning

centers throughout the U.S., and a national network of Cooperating Collections (The Foundation Center, 2001c). Some of the free services available
at the website are Online Librarian reference assistance, database searches,
an online Foundation Finder tool, and online bibliographic citations of
the nonprofit sector literature. For example, you can submit reference
questions to the Center's Online Librarian and/or search its online database
containing information on almost 61,000 U.S. private, community, and
corporate philanthropic giving programs. You can also look up basic facts
on U.S. private and community foundations simply by typing in the name
using the Center's free, online look-up tool. In addition, you can search
its nonprofit sector database containing about 19,000 full bibliographic
citations for books, periodicals, and Internet resources on philanthropic
topics (The Foundation Center, 2001c). The Foundation Center also has
a well-written *Short Proposal Writing Course* available at *http://fdncenter.org/
learn/shortcourse/prop1.html*.

Another valuable online resource for grant seekers is GrantsNet, a
searchable, continuously updated database of funding opportunities in
biomedical research and science education (GrantsNet, 2001). Although
this website requires you to register before using it, membership is free
and well worth the few minutes it takes to provide basic information and
get a user name and password. Once registered, you have full access to
special tools and resources as well as programs that offer training and
research funding. The programs are subdivided into those for graduate
and medical students, postdoctoral fellows, junior faculty, undergraduate
faculty, and students in science, math, engineering, and technology. Currently, the website is unavailable every Thursday from 8:00 am to 8:30
am Eastern Time for routine maintenance (GrantsNet, 2001).

GRANT-WRITING TIPS FOR SEEKING PRIVATE FUNDING

In addition to the tips mentioned for writing federal grants, there are
several tips for writing a successful private grant. Determine which founda-
tion(s) have awarded grants in your geographic region similar to the proposed project. In other words, carefully match your research project with
an appropriate funding source. It is better to send appropriate requests to
fewer foundations than to send many requests in the hope that one might
pay off. The key to success is homework done well and thoroughly.

1.   Carefully read the written guidelines for those foundations that you
     deem appropriate. Make sure you know their deadlines, funding

priorities, proposal formats, required content, desired attachments, page length restrictions, and the maximum funding amount. If the directions state that a cover form must be completed, an audited financial statement is required from nonprofit organizations, and/ or a protection of human/animal subjects approval is/are required, follow these directions scrupulously.

2. Collect a sample successful grant(s) to use as a boilerplate model. Many foundations, if requested, will send you proposals from past funded projects and/or provide you with names and addresses of past grant recipients so that you can contact them directly for copies of their proposals.

3. Use the same terminology in your proposal that the foundation uses to describe what it wants to fund. If a foundation tells you what it wants to underwrite, listen and be very clear and specific as to how your project dovetails with the posted guidelines. Successful grant seekers tailor each proposal to meet the desired format, priorities, funding type, and grant amount of a carefully selected foundation (Grantproposal.com, 2001).

4. Talk with persons who know the foundation to which you are applying. Program officers, particularly those with long histories at foundations, have become experts in what their foundations wish to fund and they interact regularly with funded and potential grant-ees. It is important to note and carefully review their suggestions after interacting with them in person, by telephone, or by other electronic means. Their ideas will provide you with suggestions and hints that can help you focus your proposal. Foundations appreciate grant seekers who take the time to gather all the facts. So make yourself personally known to foundation personnel and pay careful attention to what they say about what to emphasize and what to tone down in your proposal (Lone-Eagles.com, 2001).

5. The proposal should be written clearly and succinctly. Less is more when writing a proposal. With each written draft, tighten the language and let details, rather than empty, descriptive jargon, convey the project's worthiness. Grant reviewers quickly learn how to scan proposal text, particularly proposal abstracts, so as to get a quick overview of exactly what you plan to do, with whom, when, how, and toward what measurable outcome. A comprehensible and fundable proposal should be short, to the point, well organized, and understandable.

6. Consider the abstract as the single most important paragraph in your research proposal. You should convey that you know what to

do with the foundation's money, and express it in elegant simplicity. Providing the grant reviewer with a well-written abstract will lead to an important first impression that you know what you want to achieve, with whom, at what cost, and exactly how to go about it (Lone-Eagles.com, 2001).

7. Make sure you use the latest research literature. It should be written by respected experts, and come from reputable journals and periodicals, governmental sources, up-to-date census, and other such data. In other words, the grant seeker needs to convey a command of the most current and best research literature.

8. The proposed project should not be too ambitious because it will be a red flag to reviewers that you plan to accomplish more than your budget makes realistically attainable. It is better to keep your proposal within limits so that the objectives can be realistically achieved, given the budget and time frame specified in the proposal. It is best to be realistic and conservative.

9. Project personnel listed in the proposal should have the educational and professional credentials needed to achieve project aims. Make sure that the curricula vitae (cv) of key personnel are current and that any job descriptions are tailored to meet project goals. Reviewers carefully examine each curriculum vitae or biosketch included in the proposal, so pick your research team carefully. The more experienced the team, the more confident reviewers will be that project aims will be achieved if funding is awarded.

A FINAL NOTE ON PRIVATE FUNDING

Because it takes a long time to secure funding for a research project, the best advice is to start planning early. Think carefully about your topic well in advance of writing the proposal. Write the first draft about three months prior to the submission deadline; ask at least two colleagues to review and critique it; write a second draft based on their revisions; give it back to colleagues for more revision; then rewrite as needed. Review each draft for substance, appropriate language, style, form, and correct spelling and grammar. Nothing hurts a researcher's chances of getting funded more than a sloppy-looking grant proposal. It may give the reviewers the idea that this is a reflection of how the grant seeker carries out scientific work (Reif-Lehrer, 1989). The most successful grant proposals are clearly and concisely written and targeted to foundations or other donors funding that area of research. The winning proposal reflects planning, research, and vision.

COMMON REASONS GRANTS ARE NOT FUNDED

Most grant applications do not get funded the first time around, particularly when competing for NIH funds (NIAID, August 30, 2001; Pequegnat & Stover, 1995). Competition for research funding has become increasingly tough in recent years. Researchers should be prepared to revise and resubmit applications more than once. Many grant applications succeed on the second or third submission, provided the applicants have made revisions cited in the Summary Statement (NIAID, August 30, 2001).

There are a number of reasons grants do not get funded. The following list has been adapted from Wiggins (2001) and Bowman and Branchaw (1992):

1. The grant writer failed to demonstrate a clear understanding of the problem.
2. The proposal did not arrive by the submission deadline.
3. The grant writer did not provide information requested by the funding agency in the grant application guidelines. Essential data were not included in the proposal.
4. Study objectives/aims were not well defined.
5. The wrong audience was addressed.
6. Hypotheses were ill defined, superficial, lacking, unfocused, or unsupported by preliminary data.
7. The methods and procedures were not specific, were unsuitable or defective, and were unlikely to produce desired results.
8. Data collection methods were confusing; design and/or instrumentation was not appropriate.
9. There was limited access to the specific population needed for the proposed study.
10. Data management and analysis plan was vague, unsophisticated, or inaccurate.
11. Curriculum vitae or biosketches of key personnel were inadequate. The principal investigator had inadequate expertise or knowledge of the field or had too little time to devote to the proposed project.
12. Resources or facilities available for the proposed project were inadequate. The proposal failed to show that essential equipment and facilities were available.

13. The proposal was poorly written or not well organized according to the specifications in the proposal guidelines. The completed proposal was unattractive.
14. The proposal did not provide adequate assurance that completion deadlines could be met. The proposed time line was unrealistic.
15. The proposal failed to include the qualifications and/or resources of the submitting organization.

KNOWING WHEN TO REVISE

The major mantra of grant writers is to revise and resubmit as soon as feasible. In the federal grant process, the Summary Statement provides the grant writer with excellent reviews of what is good and what needs fixing in the proposed research project. If the grant writer uses the reviewer critiques, reworks the proposed project, and resubmits a revised proposal, there is a good chance that this proposal may be funded. A rejection by a private funding organization may not provide such feedback to a grant writer. However, a call to the organization staff usually proves very helpful and informative.

There are several common fixable problems in a grant proposal. These are poor writing, insufficient information about experimental details or preliminary data, an unconvincing statement of the rationale for funding the proposed study, concerns about the ability of the proposed project personnel to complete the project, and insufficient discussion of the obstacles the researcher may encounter and alternative approaches that may be needed (NIAID, August 30, 2001).

There are also problems that may not be fixable. These include philosophical issues based on reviewers' beliefs that the proposed work is not significant; hypotheses that are not sound or not supported by the data presented; work that has already been done, making the proposed project unnecessary; proposed methods that are deemed unsuitable for answering the research questions; reviewers without the expertise needed to appropriately evaluate the proposal; and biases operating when the review took place. If you think the latter two reasons are the basis for not funding your proposal, you should revise the application as needed and resubmit. In a cover letter accompanying the revised application, request that the review be submitted to another scientific review panel. Provide reasons for the request and suggest an alternative scientific panel if possible (NIAID, August 30, 2001).

GRANT PROPOSAL WRITING RESOURCES

In addition to the citations provided in the references, there are many grant writing resources available on the Internet and in print. An easy, efficient, and effective way to find resources is to use a specialty search engine such as Google (*http://www.google.com*) or AltaVista (*http://www. altavista.com*). Just type the words, grantwriting resources, in the search line and, within seconds, you will have a host of very useful website addresses. If you have access to a major university or health science center library, ask the librarian where the grants references are located, and then use these print resources to identify funding sources. Regardless of what method you use to find resources, the important thing is to use them to help you find the right funding agency, write an effective proposal, and submit it prior to the funding deadline.

CONCLUDING THOUGHTS

Even if you are able to incorporate all or most of the ideas about grant writing contained in this chapter, there is no guarantee that you will secure funding. Most grant writers revise their research proposals two or three times before securing extramural funding. Grant writing is a craft that takes practice. The trick to getting funded is to carefully use the comments of colleagues, reviewers, and organization staff to rewrite your proposal prior to resubmission. It is essential that you address every reviewer criticism, no matter how small it is. If you can't incorporate the suggested revision, give a plausible reason why not. This is a far better strategy than ignoring the criticism, which gives the reviewer the impression that you did not even think it worth considering.

Don't let frustration stop you from writing and/or revising a grant application. Remember, if you don't submit a grant, you have no possibility of getting funded. It is far better to submit a project, get rejected the first time, revise, and resubmit. This will give you an even better chance of winning the award. My final advice to a potential grantwriter is:

When in doubt, submit.
When rejected, revise and resubmit.
When rejected again, cry, then revise and resubmit.
When awarded, rejoice and roll up your sleeves for
    now the work begins!

REFERENCES

Bowman, J. P., & Branchaw, B. P. (1992). *How to write proposals that produce.* Westport, CT: Oryx.

Burns, N., & Grove, S. K. (2001). *The practice of nursing research: Conduct, critique & utilization* (4th ed., Rev.). Philadelphia: W. B. Saunders.

Department of Health and Human Services. (December 13, 2001). *Code of federal regulations Title 45 Public Welfare Part 46 Protection of Human Subjects.* Retrieved March 23, 2002, from DHHS National Institutes of Health Office for Protection from Research Risks Web Site: *http://ohrp.osophs.dhhs.gov/humansubjects/guidance/45cfr46.htm*

Gitlin, L. N., & Lyons, K. J. (1996). *Successful grant writing: Strategies for health and human service professionals.* New York: Springer.

Grantproposal.com. (2001). *Six guidelines for successful proposals.* Retrieved August 19, 2001, from *http://www.grantproposal.com/proposal_inner.htm*

GrantsNet. (2001). *About GrantsNet.* Retrieved September 20, 2001, from *http://www.grantsnet.org*

Grey, M. (2000). Top 10 tips for successful grantsmanship. *Research in Nursing & Health, 23,* 91–92.

Kraicer, J. (May 5, 1997). In *The art of grantsmanship.* Retrieved August 22, 2001, from Health Scientific Frontiers Program Web Site: *http://www.hfsp.org/How_to_apply/Art_of_Grantsmanship/Art%20of%20Grantsmanship.htm*

Lone-Eagles.com. (2001). *Grantwriting tips.* Retrieved August 19, 2001, from *http://lone-eagles.com/granthelp.htm*

Lorian, R. P. (2000). Grantsmanship: A view from inside and out. In W. Pequegnat & E. Stover (Eds.), *How to write a successful research grant application: A guide for social and behavioral scientists* (pp. 39–45). New York: Plenum.

National Institute of Allergy & Infectious Diseases (NIAID). (August 30, 2001). *The original how to write a research grant application, amended, third edition.* Retrieved September 21, 2001, from *http://www.niaid.nih.gov/ncn/pdf/howto.pdf*

National Institutes of Health. (February 11, 1999). NIH Guide. In *Academic Research Enhancement Award* (PA-99-062). Retrieved September 15, 2001, from NIH Guide Academic Research Enhancement Award Web Site: *http://grants.nih.gov/grants/guide/pa-files/PA-99-062.html*

National Institutes of Health. (October 8, 1999). NIH Guide. In *Mentored patient-oriented research career development award (K23)* (PA-00-004). Retrieved August 23, 2001, from NIH Guide Web Site: *http://grants.nih.gov/grants/guide/pa-files/PA-00-004.html*

National Institutes of Health. (August 21, 2000). Policy, procedure & review guidelines. In *Review of new investigator RO1's.* Retrieved August 22, 2001, from NIH Center for Scientific Review Web Site: *http://www.csr.nih.gov/guidelines/newinvestigator.htm*

National Institutes of Health. (December 11, 2000). In *Research grants.* Retrieved August 22, 2001, from NIH Office of Extramural Research Web Site: *http://grants.nih.gov/grants/policy/emprograms/overview/resrchgrt.htm*

National Institutes of Health. (December 20, 2000). In *NIA pilot research grant program* (PA-01-037). Retrieved August 23, 2001, from NIH Guide Web Site: *http://grants.nih.gov/grants/guide/pa-files/PA-01-037.html*

National Institutes of Health. (February 22, 2001). NIH-Wide Programs. In *Minority Researchers' Training and Enhancement Programs*. Retrieved August 19, 2001, from National Institute of Allergy and Infectious Diseases Web Site: *http://www.niaid.gov/facts/mwhhp5.htm*

National Institutes of Health. (April, 2001). In *FY 2001 Investments*. Retrieved August 20, 2001, from National Institutes of Health Web Site: *http://www.nih.gov/news/BudgetFY2002/FY2001investments.htm*

National Institutes of Health. (April 9, 2001a). Press briefing FY 2002 President's budget. In *Press release for the FY 2002 President's budget*. Retrieved August 19, 2001, from NIH Office of Budget Web Site: *http://www4.od.nih.gov/officeofbudget/press.html*

National Institutes of Health. (April 9, 2001b). *NIH guide: Research supplements for underrepresented minorities*. Retrieved August 23, 2001, from PA-01-079 Web Site: *http://grants.nih.gov/grants/guide/ps-files/PA-01-079.html*

National Institutes of Health. (April 12, 2001). In *Data analysis and archiving in demography, economics, and behavioral research on aging* (PA-01-082). Retrieved August 23, 2001, from NIH Guide Web Site: *http://grants.nih.gov/grants/guide/pa-files/PA-01-082.html*

National Institutes of Health. (May 23, 2001). *Statement of the Director to the House Subcommittee on Labor-Education appropriations*. Retrieved March 23, 2002, from *http://www.nih.gov/about/director/fy02budreq.htm*

National Institutes of Health. (July 11, 2001). In *Referral & review*. Retrieved September 21, 2001 from Center for Scientific Review Web Site: *http://www.csr.nih.gov/EVENTS/AssignmentProcess.htm*

National Institutes of Health. (July 12, 2001). CSR Referral & Review. In *R01 reviewers' guidelines*. Retrieved August 19, 2001, from NIH Center for Scientific Review Web Site: *http://www.csr.nih.gov/guidelines/r)1.htm*

National Institutes of Health. (July 18, 2001a). CSR Referral & Review. In *Academic Research Enhancement Award (AREA, R15) guide for assigned reviewers' preliminary comments*. Retrieved September 19, 2001, from NIH Center for Scientific Review Web Site: *http://www.csr.nih.gov/guidelines/areaR15.htm*

National Institutes of Health. (July 18, 2001b). CSR scoring procedures. In *Referral & review*. Retrieved September 21, 2001 from Center for Scientific Review Web Site: *http://www.csr.nih.gov/REVIEW/scoringprocedure.htm*

National Institutes of Health. (August 24, 2001). A straightforward description of what happens to your research project grant application after it is received for peer review. In *Referral & review*. Retrieved September 21, 2001, from the NIH Center for Scientific Review Web Site: *http://www.csr.nih.gov/REVIEW/Peerrev.htm*

National Institutes of Health. (November 21, 1997). *NIH guide: Appeals of initial scientific peer review*. Retrieved December 30, 2002, from *http://grants1.nih.gov/grants/guide/notice-files/not97-232.html*

Ogden, T. E. (1991). *Research proposals: A guide to success*. New York: Raven.

Pequegnat, W., & Stover, E. (Eds.). (1995). *How to write a successful research grant application: A guide for social and behavioral scientists*. New York: Plenum.

Reif-Lehrer, L. (1989). *Writing a successful grant application* (2nd ed., Rev.). Boston: Jones and Bartlett.

Reif-Lehrer, L. (1995a). *Grant application writer's handbook*. Boston: Jones and Bartlett.

Reif-Lehrer, L. (1995b). Getting funded: It takes more than just a good idea. *The Scientist, 9*(14), 1.

The Foundation Center. (2001a). In *Your gateway to philanthropy on the world wide web*. Retrieved September 20, 2001, from *http://www.fdncenter.org*

The Foundation Center. (2001b). User aid: What is a foundation? In *Learning Lab*. Retrieved from Learning Lab Web Site: *http://fdncenter.org/learn/useraids/whatis.html*

The Foundation Center. (2001c). In *For grantmakers: How we can help*. Retrieved from *http://fdncenter.org/for_grantmakers/answers.html*

U.S. Department of Health and Human Services. (2001, January). Search our funding database. In *Office of Minority Health*. Retrieved August 23, 2001, from Office of Minority Health Web Site: *http://www.omhrc.gov/omh/fundingdb.htm*

U.S. Department of Health and Human Services. (2001, June). About OMH. In *Office of Minority Health*. Retrieved September 20, 2001, from Office of Minority Health Web Site: *http://www.omhrc.gov/OMH/sidebar/aboutOMH.htm*

U.S. Department of Health and Human Services Public Health Service. (August 8, 2001). In *PHS398 Grant Application*. Retrieved September 23, 2001, from the National Institutes of Health Web Site: *http://grant.nih.gov/grants/funding/phs398/phs398.pdf*

Wiggins, B. B. (2001, February). In *Funding and proposal writing for social science faculty and graduate student research*. Retrieved May 10, 2001, from University of North Carolina Odum Institute for Research in Social Science Web Site: *http://www.irss.unc.edu/irss/bwiggins/shortcourses/wigginshandouts/granthandout.pdf*

APPENDIX

This section identifies some major Internet and print resources that contain many grant-writing and related Web-based resources.

Internet Resources

- Centers for Disease Control Funding Opportunities
  http://www.cdc.gov/od/pgo/funding.funding.htm
- Community of Science Funding Opportunities
  http://fundingopps2.cos.com
- CRISP
  http://www-comons.cit.nih.gov/crisp
- Federal Information Exchange
  http://nscp.fie.com
- FirstGov—Official Website for Searching U.S. Government
  http://www.firstgov.gov
- Foundation Center
  http://fdncenter.org/index.html
- Foundations Online
  http://www/foundations.org

- Grants and Funding Opportunities Resources
  http://scilib.ucsd.edu/bml/grants.htm
- Grantsmanship Center
  http://www.tgci.com
- GrantsWeb International: Society of Research Administrators
  http://www.srainternational.org/cws/sra/resource.htm
- Health Resources and Services Administration (HRSA) Grants and Contracts
  http://www.hrsa.dhhs.gov/grants.htm
- Michigan State (MSU) Libraries: Grants & Related Resource Guides
  http://www/lib.msu.edu/harris23/grants/grants.htm
- National Institutes of Health Office of Extramural Research Funding Opportunities: Grants
  http://grants.nih.gov/grants/funding/funding.htm
- TRAM: Research Funding Opportunities and Administration
  http://tram.east.asu.edu
- U.S. Department of Justice
  http://www.nij.gov

Print Resources

There are also many books and articles about getting grants and writing grant proposals that you can purchase or find in most libraries. In addition, the following print resources may be helpful in finding information about granting agencies.

- Catalog of Federal Domestic Assistance (CAFDA)
  Superintendent of Documents
  U.S. Government Printing Office
  Washington, DC 20402
- Chronicle of Philanthropy (the newspaper of the non-profit world)
  The Chronicle of Philanthropy
  1225 23rd Street N.W.
  Washington, DC 20037
- Directory of Biomedical and Health Care Grants
  Oryx Press
  4041 North Central at Indian School Road
  Phoenix, AZ 85012
- Federal Grants and Contracts Weekly—Project Opportunities in Research, Training and Service
  Capitol Publications

   1101 King Street
   P.O. Box 1454
   Alexandria, VA 22313
- Federal Register
  Superintendent of Documents
  U.S. Government Printing Office
  Washington, DC 20402
- Foundation Directory and Supplement
  The Foundation Center
  79 5th Avenue
  New York, NY 10003
- NIH Guide for Grants and Contracts
  NIH Printing and Reproductive Branch
  Room B4BN23, Building 31
  Bethesda, MD 20892
- The Scientist
  The Scientist Inc.
  3600 Market Street
  Suite 450
  Philadelphia, PA 19104

3

Facilitating Passage Through the Institutional Maze

Joellen W. Hawkins, Cynthia S. Aber, and
Loretta P. Higgins

BACKGROUND

Launching a multisite study usually means negotiating the maze of the institutional review board not once, but many times. To illustrate the process and describe the pitfalls, we use our study of abuse during pregnancy.

In order to better understand abuse during pregnancy, our team of researchers designed a study to delineate the prevalence of intimate partner violence, using a diverse sample of prenatal care sites. The sites we sought were diverse in socioeconomic strata, ethnic and cultural backgrounds of the women served, and geographic locations. The specific aims of this study were: (1) to determine the prevalence of abuse during pregnancy in selected diverse prenatal care sites and to compare the birth outcomes for abused and nonabused pregnant women, taking into consideration other obstetrical and social risks; (2) to determine whether type and severity of abuse affect degree of impact of abuse on birth outcomes when controlling for preexisting risks; and (3) to determine whether pregnant women's appraisal of the risk associated with abuse and the women's self-care during pregnancy act as mediators of the effect of abuse on birth outcomes.

The study protocols included screening for abuse at all study sites using the Abuse Assessment Screen (AAS) (Parker, Ulrich, & Nursing Research Consortium on Violence and Abuse, 1990), chart reviews on all women enrolled for prenatal care during the study time period, and interviews with women who screened positive for abuse on the AAS during their current pregnancies.

The AAS developed by Parker, Ulrich, and the Nursing Research Consortium on Violence and Abuse (1990) has been used in a number of studies to identify abused women and has been found to be a more effective screening device than randomly asked questions on abuse (Norton, Peipert, Zierler, Lima, & Hume, 1995). The test–retest reliability was 100% for a sample of pregnant women queried twice in the same trimester (Soeken, McFarlane, Parker, & Lominak, 1998). Validity for the AAS was determined by comparing severity of abuse during pregnancy with scores on the Danger Assessment Scale (DAS) (Campbell, 1986), Conflict Tactics Scales (CTS) (Straus, 1979), and the Index of Spouse Abuse (ISA) (Hudson & McIntosh, 1981). Soeken and colleagues (1998) reported significant positive relationships with the DAS and the ISA. These data were important for institutional review board (IRB) approval because we were asking clinicians to screen with the AAS during prenatal intakes or at least one point in each woman's pregnancy.

For the interviews, we used the Severity of Violence Against Women Scales (SVAWS) (Marshall, 1992) to determine severity of abuse, and an adaptation of three scales from the Appraisal of Violent Situation (AVS) (Dutton, 1992) to determine the women's cognitive appraisal of the severity of abuse. The three AVS scales elicit a woman's rating of the severity of violence perpetrated against her by a spouse or partner, her ability to stop violence in the future, and the likelihood that the violence could lead to serious harm or death. The SVAWS, AAS, and AVS figured in the approval process for use of human subjects, but only the AAS was administered by staff members during the prenatal intake assessments at the study sites.

To answer the research questions, we needed as diverse a sample as possible to reflect a cross-section of abused pregnant women. In this chapter, we address the problems we encountered in navigating the IRBs, what we learned, and some of the solutions we came up with.

SELECTING STUDY SITES AND GAINING ACCESS TO SUBJECTS

In planning this research, our study team began to discuss prenatal care sites in the greater Boston metropolitan area that would yield a diverse sample. We had plenty of potential study sites from which to create our wish list. To access a diverse sample, we considered large tertiary care hospitals, community hospitals, community health centers, and managed care organizations.

Each study site had to have a large prenatal care clinic or service, in one or more ways contribute to the diversity of the sample, and have caregivers who showed at least some interest in the study. We used our many professional contacts at these potential sites. As Bossert, Evans, Van Cleve, and Savedra (2002) pointed out, personal contacts are the best method by which to identify potential study sites. Nurses in leadership positions in most sites under consideration had been students of members of the study team or were graduates of one or more of Boston College's programs. Interestingly, we encountered both encouraging strong support and stunning rejections. After months of negotiations and meetings, we were given support to proceed in two large tertiary care hospitals, several community health centers, three community hospitals, and one large managed care organization. Then the real work began: preparing materials for the IRBs. In all, we had to seek approval from two large urban medical centers with medical school affiliations; three community hospitals; two with their own IRBs; two community health centers; and a four-site, large managed care organization. In order to include students in the project, we also needed IRB approval from Boston College and the University of Massachusetts, Lowell. Thus, over the five years of the project, team members, but mostly the principal investigator (PI), interacted numerous times with five agency IRBs and two university IRBs. These interactions included annual renewals of IRB approval and the required reports to accompany the renewal applications. Annual renewals included reporting of any untoward effects experienced by subjects. We were fortunate that none occurred throughout the conduct of the study.

The first step through the IRB maze was getting accurate information about the chairperson of each IRB, copies of the appropriate forms to be completed, names of the IRB coordinators, and identification of the internal principal investigator, required in two of our sites. Simple as this sounds, it was an arduous process. Much misinformation was available and we found we had to check and double check before sending out any communications. Additionally, once we had submitted two of the IRB packets, we were told that the forms had changed and we would have to use the new forms and repeat the process. At two study sites, when the IRB process was almost complete, each hospital merged with another hospital. We then had to begin anew, because the newly created hospitals had new forms and processes for protection of human subjects, new IRB coordinators and chairpersons, and newly created IRBs. These mergers delayed approval for almost a year in one institution and for many months in the other.

Crucial IRB support often had to be negotiated through many bureaucratic levels: chief executive officers (CEOs), chief operating officers (COOs), physicians, research nurses, and IRB coordinators. Gathering support from so many parties with different levels of commitment to the project was one of the most frustrating aspects of the IRB process. Next in line for the title of most frustrating were the study obstructionists, described in detail in the paragraphs to follow. In some cases, letters of support were required by the chief of obstetrics and gynecology or the nursing administrator overseeing the prenatal care units. Approval from the nursing research committee, the medical research committee, and the grants office may also precede formal submission to the IRB (Bossert et al., 2002). We had to navigate through many of these committees and offices as well.

At most of the study sites, the principal investigator and other members of the study team had to appear one or more times before the IRB to discuss the study and its protocols. In the two sites requiring an internal PI, the person was designated by the institution for purposes of IRB approval only. For both sites, this person, in one case a physician, had minimal knowledge of the project and little or no vested interest in it, thus complicating communications. The physician PI changed several times over the course of the project without any notification to us. These experiences certainly confirmed the advice of Dibble, Bostrom-Ezrati, and Rizzuto (1990), who said that they carefully calculated the time they thought would be needed to proceed through each institution's review board and then they doubled it.

Even successfully traversing the many-obstacled path of an IRB did not guarantee that we could begin data collection. At one site, the new COO, a nurse, decided that she did not want any screening for abuse done throughout the multisite agency, effectively blocking implementation of the study. A physician at a teen pregnancy clinic decided unilaterally that he would not support the study, even though the clinic was part of a larger institution whose IRB had given us approval. At another study site, a key clinical person left her position, and it took months to renegotiate with the new clinical director before data collection could resume. During this time, the PI had to keep filing renewal applications for IRB approval. These, too, changed frequently over the course of the project. In some cases, the IRB coordinator sent us the renewal form and once we had completed and returned the form, this coordinator informed us that a new form had just been adopted and we would have to resubmit. Most, if not all, of the consent form requirements changed. Each study site had its own requirements for the consent form and some had to be on the study site's letterhead and have a stamp from the IRB. Not only did these complications cause delays, but they necessitated many complex visits to the study sites to pick up new forms, deliver as many as 25 copies of the IRB application, and secure the necessary internal signatures before the application for approval could be copied and go forward.

Eventually, approval was obtained from eight institutions for a total of 13 study sites yielding approximately 5,000 births per year. The study sites are located in Boston and in a 60-mile radius around the city. The socioeconomic mix ranges from low to middle income, with a strong representation of Hispanic, Brazilian-Portuguese, Southeast Asian, African-American, Haitian, and European-American cultures.

STUMBLING BLOCKS ALONG THE WAY

Over the course of the project, several high profile cases of alleged violation of the rights of research subjects occurred at other academic medical institutions (Putney & Gruskin, 2002). A "critical moment of heightened federal scrutiny" resulted and we were caught up in the concerns (Putney & Gruskin, 2002, p. 1067). What this scrutiny meant in concrete terms was training for all the study team members in protection of human subjects and revision of all the consent forms for the project. These consent forms were complex and detailed and we spent countless hours revising and faxing them to study sites, only to be told to revise or reword them further. The bump-down effect was a tremendous amount of coordination of the study packets for interviews to assure that the most up-to-date consent form was in each interview packet. Then we had to coordinate getting the latest version to the study team members and graduate student interviewers for the scheduled interviews with subjects.

We trained each interviewer in obtaining informed consent and truly protecting these vulnerable women. Bossert and colleagues (2002) suggested that a training manual be developed for all members of the study team. In this manual, the informed consent process should include the script for first contact with potential subjects; copies of the consent form for the study site; a script for presenting the consent form and study information, including questions that might arise; and instructions on how to obtain signatures according to the study site's policies.

IRB requirements changed as well, so new data were required to complete annual renewal applications, such as the number of subjects enrolled at each site, the ethnic breakdown of the subjects, and the number of subjects accrued during the previous 12 months. Since our data entry and the cleaning up of data from thousands of chart reviews lagged considerably behind the completion of those chart reviews, we were constantly struggling with producing different sets of requested information for each agency's IRB renewal. Additionally, we had to include a consent form signed by a participant with the application at a number of sites.

Personnel changes continued to plague us as we struggled to comply with IRB renewal dates. Sometimes the internal PI would have changed so the renewal applications would go undelivered and never eventually reach us. In other cases, the internal PI was so swamped with clinical responsibilities, that answering mail having to do with the IRB fell to the bottom of the priority list. Communicating directly with the IRB offices was very helpful in solving these internal problems.

Obtaining the requisite signatures prior to IRB submission for renewals also proved to be a challenge. Busy clinicians are hard to pin down, and many times we hand carried the paperwork, literally presented it with a pen for the needed signature, and then hand delivered the documents to be copied so that the renewal application would meet the deadlines.

Clinicians are highly protective of their patients for many good reasons. When the patients constitute a vulnerable population, clinicians are sensitive to the risks that may occur by participation in studies. As Demi and Warren (1995) have pointed out, researchers have exploited the vulnerable all too frequently in order to achieve research goals. Gaining the trust of clinicians, as Ebright (2002) noted, is key to having access to patients. Our study depended upon study site clinicians screening pregnant women with the AAS and referring those who screened positive for abuse and were willing to be interviewed to us for scheduling an interview. We also needed the cooperation of medical record room personnel in order to do chart reviews. Receptionists in prenatal sites helped us to find out when women's next appointments were scheduled, and to identify women when they came for those appointments. Nurses doing the prenatal intakes and screenings kept files of the AAS forms for us, as these did not become part of the patients' permanent medical records in any of the study sites. Sometimes, to our dismay, another researcher from a different project had scheduled an interview with a patient with whom we thought we had an interview.

An example of a major frustration we encountered at one of the study sites will serve to illustrate. Study team members assigned as facilitators at each site to enable compliance would carefully place the AAS forms in the prenatal patient charts to ensure they would be readily available for use by the clinicians who were doing the screening during prenatal intakes or routine prenatal visits. One study team member discovered, at a subsequent visit to her site, that the AAS forms had been removed from patient charts. One could only surmise that screening for abuse was not being done at that site and, if it was being done, results were not recorded in the patients' charts. What we did know was that the AAS forms supplied by the study team and placed in the charts had been removed by someone and for some reason unknown to us. This occurrence, which continued on and off throughout the study, was not only frustrating and demoralizing to the study team members, but bordered on being subversive to the study. All attempts to locate the AAS forms, or to discover why the forms had been removed from the charts and by whose authority, proved fruitless. Clearly, someone at that site was not interested in participating in this study and was willing to do almost anything to keep it from happening. One other consideration was that the abuse screening was actually being done albeit not using the AAS forms, but not being recorded anywhere on the charts unless there was evidence of abuse. Comprehensive prenatal care, as prescribed by the Joint Commission on Accreditation of Health Care Organizations (1996), requires abuse screening; standards were not being met at that site.

OBTAINING CERTIFICATES OF CONFIDENTIALITY

Our research required subjects considered to be very vulnerable. Battered women are at great risk and participating in research can increase that risk. As Parker and colleagues (1990) noted, fear of retaliation by the perpetrator of intimate partner abuse is an ever-present concern. Furthermore, there is the risk of subpoena of the research records by the perpetrator should a custody battle or property dispute arise, or if the woman tries to leave or seeks sole custody of minor children. Thus, we were advised by both the office overseeing research at Boston College and under federal directives to seek a confidentiality certificate for each study site.

The U.S. Public Health Service Act 42 U.S.C. 241 [d] (1998) authorized the issuing of certificates of confidentiality. The National Institutes of Health (NIH) recently issued a statement on certificates of confidentiality and has made the information available on-line (NIH, 2002). Researchers granted these certificates for their work "may not be compelled in any Federal, State, or local civil, criminal, administrative, legislative or other proceedings to identify [subjects] and may withhold subjects' identities from all persons not connected with the research" (Melton, 1998, p. 69). We applied to the Substance Abuse and Mental Health Services Administration (SAMSHA) which issues these certificates. Although the process is fairly expeditious, the many-paged application form is intimidating, so a member of the staff of the Boston College research office walked each study site through this process and worked closely with the study team. Obtaining the confidentiality certificates also delayed the process of IRB approval.

LESSONS LEARNED

For any project, especially one involving vulnerable subjects and anticipating use of two or more study sites, plan on 6 to 12 months minimum to achieve IRB approval and obtain certificates of confidentiality. Then double that time. The sooner you can begin the process, the sooner you can begin data collection. We began the process while preparing and submitting a proposal for funding, but did not have IRB approval for all study sites until well into the first year of funding. Personal visits by the PI to all the IRB offices might have expedited the process a bit, but team members did make personal contact with the IRB coordinators at the sites for which they were responsible and we still experienced delays.

Anticipate mergers, changes in personnel, dissolution of affiliations among agencies, and roadblocks thrown up in the process of access to subjects, even with IRB approval. Plan, if possible, on more sites than you need or substitutes you can invoke if you meet roadblocks in accessing subjects. In order to minimize the many possible frustrations that can occur in multisite research studies, all middle managers, nurses, and other health care professionals responsible for screening patients or in any way contributing to data collection or eligibility of patients for the study, as well as directors of services, must be on board and be agreeable to participating in the study. This is one strategy that will avoid or minimize potentially subversive tactics. The trickle-down effect from director to clinician level does not always occur. The intentions of and agreements made by administrators at a study site may not be congruent with what the rank and file clinicians at that site perceive as something they wish to participate in. This difference of opinion can quickly become a tug of war and/or battle of wits between management and providers. In the end, the study, as well as the patients at that site, will be the losers in the struggle. It may be more positive and satisfying for investigators to locate another study site, rather than continually play the detective role to ensure that the activities agreed upon in fact are happening.

Request that IRBs send renewal notices directly to the study's PI. We found that IRB coordinators were most understanding of the delays that could occur with an internal PI for IRB purposes only. Anticipate that forms may change often in this climate of heightened scrutiny and plan accordingly so as not to miss IRB meeting cycles. Create files for each study site just for the IRB processes, both paper and computer, so you can retrieve data quickly when dealing with questions that inevitably arise about the status of the project.

Keep a complete file of all presentations, publicity about the project, and publications. Several IRBs requested these as part of the renewal process. Of course you will also need them for any interim as well as the final report.

Listen to clinicians and heed their advice on protecting the subjects. All team members going into the study sites wore name badges identifying them as part of the Pregnancy Support Project (PSP) and carried bags with our interview packets with that logo on them. Our project business cards used the logo, and the study office telephone had a message in English and Spanish identifying the project. All persons answering the telephone or retrieving messages were prepared to protect the subjects by describing the goals as providing support during pregnancy.

Discuss with clinicians what you might provide for them so they, in turn, can better care for their patients. This is especially important when you are asking clinicians, as we were, to screen for a condition, in this case, abuse. We provided brochures with information about getting a restraining order, the laws pertaining to intimate partner abuse in our state, shelter and hotline numbers, and how to plan to leave a violent relationship. We also provided an annotated compendium of resources including all shelters, hot line numbers, and other resources for battered women and their children. This compendium included information on how to access the shelters, the rules and regulations governing guests there, access to translators, and how long one could stay. Posters with post-it tear-offs with abuse hot line telephone numbers were provided to each study site. To protect the women, sites requested rubber stamps with the acronym RADAR—Routinely screen female patients, Ask direct questions, Document your findings, Assess patient safety, Review options and referrals (Bureau of Health Professionals, 2002; Philadelphia Family Violence Working Group, 2002), so the person screening for abuse could indicate that the screening had occurred and could put the results of the screening on the medical record, but in a way that would not draw attention to it for the perpetrator.

The arduous task of seeking approval from many IRBs for multisite research continues to siderail projects. In the United Kingdom, an experiment has been underway for several years to create multicenter ethics committees. It will be interesting to follow this innovation with the hope that we in the United States might learn strategies for adequately protecting human subjects while streamlining the process for multisite studies (Tully, Ninis, Booy, & Viner, 2000).

Most of all, we learned patience through negotiating the IRB maze, and when to give up on a potential study site and move on to another. We also learned never to leave any agency with anything but friendly relationships, because we might be seeking cooperation for another project. When the National Institute for Nursing Research (NINR) funding for the project ended, we mailed a copy of the final report to each study site with a cover letter thanking the staff for their participation. These time-consuming but important communications may help us or other researchers in the future.

ACKNOWLEDGMENT

The authors gratefully acknowledge funding from the National Institute of Nursing Research, National Institutes of Health, AREA grant entitled "Abuse, Women's Self-Care and Pregnancy Outcomes" 1 R15 NR04246-01. Gratitude is also due to the study team members: Joyce Dwyer, RN, MS, MPH; Margaret Kearney, RNC, PhD; Deborah Mahony, RN, PNP-CS, Dr PH; Barbara Hazard, RN, PhD; Carole W. Pearce, RNC, PhD; Margaret Bell, RN, CS, MS, Project Director; Ursula A. Kelly, RN, CS-ANP, PhD (c); Sharyl Eve Toscano, RN, CS-FNP, PhD; Roseann Barrett, RN, PhD, and all the nurses at the study sites.

REFERENCES

Bossert, E. A., Evans, S., Van Cleve, L., & Savedra, M. C. (2002). Multisite research: A systems approach. *Journal of Pediatric Nursing, 17,* 38–47.

Bureau of Health Professionals. (2002). RADAR training. Retrieved July 28, 2002 from *bphc.hrsa.gov/mtw/mtwsh103.htm*

Campbell, J. (1986). Nursing assessment for risk of homicide with battered women. *Advances in Nursing Science, 8*(4), 36–51.

Demi, A. S., & Warren, N. A. (1995). Issues in conducting research with vulnerable families. *Western Journal of Nursing Research, 17,* 188–202.

Dibble, S. L., Bostrom-Ezrati, J., & Rizzuto, C. R. (1990). Developing multisite research in critical care. *Dimensions of Critical Care Nursing, 9,* 236–242.

Dutton, M. A. (1992). *Empowering and healing the battered woman.* New York: Springer.

Ebright, P. R. (2002). Learning "how to" conduct clinical research from others' experiences. *Clinical Nurse Specialist, 15,* 284–285.

Hudson, W., & McIntosh, S. (1981). The assessment of spouse abuse: Two quantifiable dimensions. *Journal of Marriage and the Family, 43,* 873–888.

Joint Commission on the Accreditation of Healthcare Organizations (JCAHO). (1996). *Accreditation manual for hospitals.* Chicago: Author.

Marshall, L. L. (1992). Development of the severity of violence against women scales. *Journal of Family Violence, 7*(2), 103–121.

Melton, G. B. (1998). Certificates of confidentiality under the Public Health Service Act: Strong protection but not enough. *Violence and Victims, 5,* 67–71.

National Institutes of Health. (2002). *NIH announces statement of certificates of confidentiality.* Retrieved March 15, 2002, from the NIH website *http://grants.nih.gov/grants/policy/coc/index/htm*

Norton, L. B., Peipert, J. F., Zierler, S., Lima, B., & Hume, L. (1995). Battering in pregnancy: An assessment of two screening methods. *Obstetrics & Gynecology, 85,* 321–325.

Parker, B., Ulrich, Y., & Nursing Research Consortium on Violence and Abuse. (1990). A protocol of safety: Research on abuse of women. *Nursing Research, 39,* 248–250.

Philadelphia Family Violence Working Group. (2002). *RADAR training.* Retrieved July 28, 2002, from *www.members.aol.com/psrphila/sufamily.htm*

Putney, S. B., & Gruskin, S. (2002). Ethics in public health research. *American Journal of Public Health, 92,* 1067–1070.

Soeken, K., McFarlane, J., Parker, B., & Lominak, M. C. (1998). The Abuse Assessment Screen: A clinical instrument to measure frequency, severity, and perpetrator of abuse against women. In J. Campbell (Ed.), *Empowering survivors of abuse: The health care system, battered women, and their children* (pp. 195–203). Newbury Park, CA: Sage.

Straus, M. (1979). Measuring intrafamily conflict and violence: The conflict tactics (CT) scales. *Journal of Marriage and the Family, 41,* 75–88.

Tully, J., Ninis, N., Booy, R., & Viner, R. (2002). The new system of review by multicentre research ethics committees: Prospective study. *British Medical Journal, 320,* 1179–1182.

U.S. Public Health Service. (1998). *Public Health Services Act 42 U.S.C. 241 (d).* Washington, DC: Department of Health and Human Services.

4

Utilizing Research Assistants

Ursula A. Kelly

Research assistants (RAs) are an integral part of the research team for any multisite research study. Roles can exist for RAs in every step of the research process, with RAs often serving as the direct link between the data and the investigators. Because the integrity of any research study relies on the quality of the data and the research process, RAs are critical to the success of the research endeavor. This point has been discussed in the literature as it pertains to maintaining research integrity and avoiding academic misconduct (Gift, Creasia, & Parker, 1991), intellectual property considerations (Oberst, 1996), and authorship credit (Hanson, 1988). However, there is scant discussion in the nursing literature and in research texts to guide nurse researchers in working with RAs. The purpose of this chapter is to review our use of RAs, to describe what worked, and to suggest strategies that may circumvent problems based on the lessons learned in our multisite quantitative research study of abuse during pregnancy.

The effective use of RAs requires focused attention to the details of hiring, contracting with, orienting, monitoring, mentoring, and evaluating RAs (Gift et al., 1991). These activities are used as the organizing framework for this discussion. While the activities are ultimately the responsibility of the principal investigator (PI), some of these components may be delegated to senior members of the research team or to a paid project manager. The responsibilities of research team members, including RAs, often shift over the course of a study, necessitating even greater attention to the details of each person's roles and duties.

THE PREGNANCY SUPPORT PROJECT: A STUDY OF ABUSE, WOMEN'S SELF-CARE AND BIRTH OUTCOMES (PSP)

The PSP is a multisite nursing research study conducted by nursing faculty researchers at a major university. The goals are to study the prevalence of intimate partner abuse in pregnancy and the effect of emotional and physical abuse on birth weight, gestational age, and Apgar scores. Additionally, interview data are used to study the influence of types of abuse, and women's appraisals of abuse severity, danger, and controllability on prenatal care attendance, weight gain, smoking, and alcohol and drug use.

Data were collected at 13 health care settings, involving nine agencies over a three-year period. Medical record reviews and structured interviews with pregnant women were the sources of the data. The research team during the funded period of the study included faculty from three universities, over 50 students (RAs) from three universities, and a paid half-time project manager. Nursing students from each educational level participated as RAs: undergraduates, graduate students, and doctoral students. The data collection involved close to 6000 chart reviews at agencies located from one to more than 50 miles away from the university. This phase of the study could not have been completed without the dedicated work of the RAs.

UTILIZATION OF RESEARCH ASSISTANTS

Hiring

There are many considerations that influence decisions about what type of RAs to hire for a given research project: qualifications, financial, educational, and institutional. Of course, the ideal scenario is to hire the person/s most qualified to meet the needs of the study. However, PIs in major university settings often utilize self-selected students as RAs, for both educational and financial considerations. Students may be involved for course credit, research fellowships, or as work-study students.

Involving students in research projects as RAs can be beneficial to the individuals involved, to the research study, to the academic institution, and to the nursing profession. Faculty researchers often enjoy the opportunity to mentor students as novice researchers (Gift et al., 1991). Students can experience the work as educational (Bostrom, Dibble, & Rizzuto, 1991), and as an opportunity for developing collegial relationships with faculty mentors. In addition, involving students in research as RAs can have a positive influence on their plans for research involvement in the future, contributing to knowledge development within the profession (Bostrom et al., 1991). Academic institutions benefit by having genuine research learning opportunities available to students.

The PSP Experience

The confounding influences of educational needs and finances contributed to the decision to use all levels of students as RAs in this research project. However, the project also hired paid consultants and a project manager to ensure that the needs of the study would be met. In fact, the decision to use students as the primary data collectors contributed to the need for a paid project manager to oversee them. Student RAs participated for course credit, as work-study students, as paid RAs, as volunteers, and as research fellows.

The roles and responsibilities of the students varied by educational level. Undergraduate students were utilized for data collection by chart review only. Graduate students were involved in data collection by chart review as well as by interviews with pregnant abused women. The doctoral fellows assigned to the project participated in both types of data collection, data entry and cleaning, and data analysis. After the funded project manager position ended, the fellows took on partial responsibility for overseeing the graduate and undergraduate level RAs, as well as general project management. The fellows were also provided the opportunity to participate in publishing and presenting the research findings with faculty members of the research team.

The recruitment process was relatively easy. All faculty in the sponsoring institution's nursing program were informed of the project, and the opportunity for involvement was announced in both graduate and undergraduate classes, as well as published as an option for the Master's level Research Practicum courses. The involvement of faculty from three universities provided a broad student base, quantitatively, geographically, and culturally/ethnically, from which to draw RAs. The variety of hiring arrangements provided the project with needed help and met the diverse needs (learning, course credit, income, altruism) of the students involved.

What We Learned

Patients' motivation to participate in research studies is influenced by their attitudes and opinions about research and health care, personal beliefs, and personal histories (Ellis et al., 2001). The same appears true for student participation as RAs in research studies. Articulated motivations among our students included academic requirements, interest in the research process, passion for the topic of domestic abuse, interest in women's health issues, and a desire to work with particular faculty members. Similarly, student qualifications for the position varied in terms of previous experience in research, organizational skills, and academic achievement. The variety in both the nature and the amount of motivation and the hired RAs' qualifications, compounded by external demands on them as individuals, influenced their effectiveness as RAs.

Contracting

The relationship with an RA should be formalized via a written contract. Specific details of the job requirements and responsibilities should be specified and agreed upon by both parties. Compensation and other benefits should be explicated, with particular attention to issues of data ownership, intellectual property, and authorship.

Published articles in many disciplines have addressed the issues of multiple authors and the responsibilities and ethics of authorship. Guidelines have been published delineating the level of involvement that any co-author, including RAs, should have in a particular publication (Gay, Lavender, & McCard, 1987; Hanson, 1988; Jones & Tilden, 1998; Nativio, 1993). Typical criteria include having significantly contributed to the manuscript itself, conception and design or analysis and interpretation of the data, and the ability to defend the publication if necessary. The issue of coauthorship should be discussed and guidelines agreed upon at all levels of the research team. This is particularly important in academic environments, where publications influence compensation, promotion, and professional recognition for faculty. Clarity in the relationship between the PI and the RA, as established early on by the contract, may prevent problems in the future.

The PSP Experience

Given the variety of working arrangements with RAs, several methods were used to clarify the specific details of the relationship, including job requirements, responsibilities, and the parameters of each individual's involvement in the research process. Contracting occurred both formally and informally.

For those RAs registered for the Research Practicum course, the syllabus for the course outlined their responsibilities, including participation in training, project team meetings (voluntary), data collection (at least 60 chart reviews), maintenance of a narrative log of activities, a signed contract for a minimum of 100 hours of work on the project, and weekly check-in with the site coordinator or the faculty of record for the course. Work-study students signed contracts with the administrative dean of the nursing program, and not specifically with the study PI. Virtually all paid RAs and volunteer RAs had functioned under another arrangement (course credit or work-study) prior to their work in these capacities, so no additional contracting was done. Doctoral research fellows were either assigned to or requested to work on the project. They signed contracts with the university for their research fellowships, which explicated compensation and responsibilities in terms of their time commitment.

In addition to the written contracts, verbal or informal contracts were agreed upon by most of the RAs and the PI. Issues of coauthorship, data ownership, and intellectual property were discussed in some detail, mainly with the doctoral fellows. For doctoral students who are both employees and students, there can be a cross-fertilization of ideas and a blurring of roles (Oberst, 1996). This can lead to confusion and potential conflict over data ownership and intellectual property. These discussions were intended to clarify, if only verbally, the parameters of the fellows' involvement in the project. The faculty members of the research team discussed coauthorship at team meetings throughout the project, and clarified the parameters of each publication with involved RAs.

Graduate students who participated in specific aspects of the project that were the subjects of publications were included in the writing and editing process, and listed as coauthors. Otherwise, verbal discussion of the guidelines for authorship and issues of data ownership, as well as the nuts and bolts of their involvement, were part of the orientation for all RAs to the project.

What We Learned

We have been lucky! With over 50 RAs involved in the project to date, there have been no significant conflicts or problems with performance or concerns about authorship or data ownership. However, the creation of written contracts specific to the project for students at different levels would likely have avoided confusion and hurt feelings. Problems of perceived performance or credit can plague even the most collaborative and mutually respectful relationships with RAs. At the same time, setting a tone of collegiality early on can enhance the relationships among all team members, including RAs.

Orienting

RAs should be fully oriented to the research study before any work begins. This may involve background reading as well as in-person training with the PI or his/her designee. RAs need to be familiar with the general topic of the research, the research protocol, and the specifics of their duties. The PI should meet regularly with the RAs during the period of orientation to discuss the project and to answer any questions the RAs may have. A formal means of communication should be established at this time, that is, electronic mail, a log book for questions or problems, regular meetings, and/or telephone contact.

The PSP Experience

With the exception of doctoral fellows, the majority of the RAs worked for one academic semester only. The number of RAs varied each semester, ranging from 0–12. One mandatory orientation session was scheduled at the start of each semester for all new RAs. Either the PI or a coinvestigator conducted these sessions, with the assistance of the project manager or a doctoral fellow. Students were given a general overview of the research study (purpose, funding, members of the research team), a copy of the entire AREA grant proposal, including bibliography and a brief overview of the project, verbal and video information about the role of health care providers in screening/intervention for domestic abuse, and instruction in the specific tasks involved in data collection. The two-page chart review form was reviewed item by item, with specific instructions.

While the chart review form was used in all sites, the procedures for accessing the medical records and the organization of medical records varied across sites. This variance in health care agency systems, procedures, and organization complicated the orientation process for RAs. Students were oriented in a second session to the particular site to which they had been assigned. These individualized orientation sessions were conducted either at the specific site or at the university by the project manager, a doctoral fellow, the faculty member responsible for the site, or a student previously at that site. Scheduling needs were the main determinant of the where and by whom of these sessions. Following these two sessions, students began data collection by medical record review.

Any student who was scheduled to conduct interviews was given another one-on-one training session on the interview process, the instrument, informed consent issues, and the legal and ethical requirements of conducting a research interview with a vulnerable subject. In particular, students were reminded of their status as mandated reporters of suspected child abuse and neglect, even while functioning as researchers. The ethical mandate to report any serious clinical or psychiatric symptoms to the participant's clinician was also discussed. In addition to the mandatory orientation session, the orientation for doctoral students consisted of several meetings with the PI and the research team, including the project manager and other doctoral students. This orientation provided the doctoral students with a rich understanding of the project, facilitating their involvement in many more aspects of the project than the undergraduate or graduate level RAs, such as data cleaning and analysis, site and project management, and copresentation and copublication of results. The doctoral students also were given a copy of the AREA grant, as well as related literature to review.

What We Learned

Scheduling challenges and time demands made scheduling the orientation sessions extremely difficult, particularly in semesters with many new RAs. Not all students attended the mandatory session, necessitating additional individualized orientation sessions. These were typically briefer than the formal sessions, with the student given responsibility for reading a summary of the project grant and independently watching the video on health care providers' response to domestic abuse. Students oriented in this manner seemed to lack an understanding of the role of their sometimes mundane data collection efforts in the overall scheme of the research project. Arranging for the second orientation session, preferably at the site, was very challenging. At various points, no one on the research team with direct experience with a particular site was available for the orientation of new RAs. This lack of continuity caused minor delays and confusion in data collection.

Monitoring

Monitoring of data collection and data management procedures is essential to maintaining the integrity of a research project. RAs need to be supervised to ensure that proper data collection procedures are being followed. This is particularly challenging and important in multisite research projects. Project site directors are considered essential in multisite research, playing the role of liaison between the investigators and the study site (Williams et al., 1999). The project site director monitors RAs by directly observing data collection procedures and maintaining communication between the investigators and the RAs. This direct supervision is often intermittent, and should involve both announced and unannounced site visits for observation (Gift et al., 1991). It is suggested that provisions be made for monitoring data entry as well by having a second person review entered data for accuracy.

The PSP Experience

This research project involved 13 sites. Faculty members of the research team were assigned the role of director for each site. After the departure of the project manager, doctoral fellows were also assigned as coordinators for various sites. Individuals varied in their direct and indirect involvement with sites, resulting in varying degrees of monitoring of RAs and data collection procedures. One faculty member was on site with her students on average eight hours per week during the data collection period. The most obvious result of this direct involvement was a high number of referrals for interviews. Chart reviews were completed promptly and with consistency among the RAs at that site. Sites in which there was less faculty or coordinator involvement had fewer interviews and more data collection errors. These errors included duplicate chart reviews, missing data, and procedural errors. RAs who performed data entry were self-monitored or monitored by another RA through systematic data checking. This process was very helpful in establishing consistency in data interpretation and data entry.

Given the high rate of attrition of RAs (a function of their student status) and staff (clinical, administrative, and medical records) attrition at the study sites, lack of direct and ongoing involvement of a site manager or coordinator at certain sites resulted in communication and procedural breakdowns. Situations arose in which study site personnel were unaware of the project, and site managers no longer had contacts at the site. This resulted in the need for reorientation to the project for site clinical staff. Similarly, data collection procedures were interrupted and potentially compromised because of lack of continuity in RA monitoring from semester to semester.

What We Learned

Communication is a critical element in multisite research. While much communication can occur via electronic mail, memos, and telephone calls, an on-site presence and in-person communication greatly enhance data collection procedures, and ultimately the reliability of the data. Optimal continuity in data collection procedures is dependent upon site manager presence and communication. Particular attention to the importance of this role should be given as decisions are made regarding research team members' responsibilities.

Mentoring

PIs and coinvestigators often serve as mentors for RAs working on research projects. Mentors provide support and guidance, fostering the intellectual and professional development of RAs. This may occur in the form of intellectual challenges, guidance in research skills, collaboration, coauthorship, and support and direction in research presentations. PIs serving as mentors also provide emotional and personal support to RAs, being sensitive to the challenges and stresses RAs face both in their research and academic endeavors (Gift et al., 1991). This is particularly important when the research involves a sensitive or difficult topic or subjects who have been victimized or traumatized. PIs have the opportunity to be role models in academic and research pursuits, including managing the stresses that can accompany these activities.

The PSP Experience

The PI embraced the role of mentor to RAs as well as to staff at study sites. Students were explicitly invited to participate as actively as they chose in research activities beyond data collection. Opportunities were presented for coauthorship, presentation at professional conferences, and involvement in other research projects. Students were also encouraged in their own research endeavors and professional development. This included networking, support for individual publications, and engaging intellectual discussions. Of equal import and benefit to students was the consistent and ongoing emotional support provided by the PI. An atmosphere of collegiality permeated the research project, activities, and relationships among all members of the research team, including RAs.

Mentoring also occurred between coinvestigators and RAs, and among the RAs themselves. As an example, the third-year doctoral student mentored the first- and second-year students; all of the doctoral students provided mentoring to the master's and undergraduate students. RAs were mentored formally via inclusion in training of site staff early in the project, site visits with the PI, and in meetings and seminars with the project consultant, Dr. Barbara Parker. Informal mentoring relationships were fostered via annual project celebrations and faculty site visits during data collection. Overall, the RAs involved with the project over the years reported very positive experiences. Many mentoring and collegial relationships have continued long after the RAs completed their work on the project. One clinician is involved in the next phase of the project. She was an RA during her master's program.

What We Learned

Mentoring activities can be tremendously beneficial to RAs, personally and professionally. Mentors derive satisfaction and enjoyment from their mentoring activities and the relationships they form. Overall, attention to mentoring RAs as part of the research endeavor benefits the project, as RAs are motivated in their work and in developing research skills.

Evaluating

Evaluation of RAs is necessary both for their own development and for quality assurance for the research project. Feedback should include areas of strength as well as areas for growth in their job performance. Evaluation should occur in an ongoing manner, and is often both formal and informal. The job description, contract, and orientation materials can serve as references for evaluating RAs. For RAs primarily involved in data collection, monitoring the accuracy of the data provides evaluative information. RAs should perform self-evaluations, and, with the PI, identify future performance-related goals.

The PSP Experience

The majority of RAs involved in the project were participating for course credit. As such, evaluation criteria were clearly outlined in the syllabus. Graduate students were required to submit research activity logs and reflective journal entries on a weekly or biweekly basis, in addition to completed chart reviews. Students were evaluated on their data collection and on accompanying writing and academic work. They were also required to maintain weekly contact with either the faculty of record for their course or the site manager, who were in most cases not the same individual. The timeliness and content of the weekly check-ins varied significantly by student. It was not always immediately clear who was in contact with individual students, if in fact anyone was. In addition, the timeliness of submission of the collected data varied. In some cases, students held their chart reviews for weeks prior to submission. This delay resulted in lost opportunities for evaluation and feedback prior to additional data collection. The result was repeated errors in data collection and duplicate chart reviews being conducted by the same or different students. Work-study RAs were monitored and evaluated by the project manager, who assigned them data collection or administrative support tasks. Without the project manager, these RAs left the project for other positions within the university.

What We Learned

The students and the research project would have benefited from closer RA supervision and evaluation. It is preferable to have one individual identified as the supervising contact person for each student. This would avoid the confusion that resulted from the faculty and the site manager each thinking that the other had contact from the student and that progress was being made. Similarly, the requirement of submitting chart reviews each week should have been enforced to provide timely evaluation and feedback and to avoid unnecessary data collection errors.

In hindsight, for those students engaged in the project for course credit, regularly scheduled mandatory seminar meetings (weekly or biweekly) would have facilitated both the conduct and the evaluation of the RAs' work. The contact that was left up to students to initiate could occur in the seminar time, with other students providing feedback and reflection as well. Students can benefit from the experiences and comments of each other, as well as from faculty. Materials would be submitted at each seminar meeting, allowing for timely feedback, for monitoring of individual students' progress, and for overall progress in data collection.

SUMMARY

Effective utilization of RAs in multisite research requires attention to several dimensions of the researcher–RA relationship. The issues involved in hiring, contracting with, orienting, monitoring, mentoring, and evaluating the RAs should be addressed during the planning phase of the study. Of course, there are several significant influences on these tasks, a few of which include personnel, research site variance, and the decision to use students as RAs.

These supervisory tasks require personnel. At a minimum, a multisite research project utilizing RAs requires a general project manager. This person is directly responsible for each of these tasks, in conjunction with the PI. Ideally, in addition, there should be a site manager at each site to oversee RA and staff activities throughout the research project. This person would have more direct contact with RAs in the field, and would provide continuity to the research process. The PI and other research team members also have roles and responsibilities relative to the RAs, depending upon the specific arrangements for the RAs' involvement in the research project.

More than anything, this requires time and energy on the part of the faculty, which may be very challenging, given other workload demands, especially when a project does not have funding for release time for the PI and other faculty investigators.

Variances across sites in organizational structure, policies and procedures, data information systems, and personnel all influence the work and supervision of RAs, especially in terms of orienting, monitoring, and evaluating their performance. Particular attention to these differences is necessary to facilitate the RA's work, and therefore to ensure integrity in the data and the research process. RAs working in cumbersome systems with layers of bureaucracy may encounter more problems and be less productive than those in well-organized, seamless systems.

Utilizing student RAs serves several educational, financial, and institutional functions, as discussed above. However, the consequent attrition rate of trained RAs adds additional challenges to the research project. Student RA attrition creates the need for continuous attention to the outlined tasks involved in RA utilization. With new RAs beginning every academic semester and some summers, hiring, contracting, and orienting are cyclical and repetitive tasks, as opposed to being time-limited activities early in the research process. The PI, coresearchers, and project manager must work harder to provide continuity in data collection in the context of such rapid turnover. Staff attrition at the research sites can provide similar challenges. Organizational support, research protocols, and individual staff members' personal investment in the project may need to be revisited as issues when staff familiar with the research project leave and new staff replace them.

Beyond these specific influences on RA utilization are two critical components of any research project: resources and communication. The need for adequate resources and effective communication is magnified by the nature of multisite research. Resources (personnel, faculty/researcher time, money) are necessary to first secure and then effectively use RAs working in multiple sites. The need for more costly in-person contact with RAs can be mitigated by carefully developed communication systems. Regularly scheduled contact (in-person, e-mail, telephone, log book) between RAs and the PI or project manager will enhance RA performance and therefore the research process and quality of the data.

CONCLUSION

While the tasks involved in utilizing RAs are primarily the responsibility of the PI, they will be best achieved through collaboration with coinvestigators and a project manager. A project manager and very involved coinvestigators can provide continuity and mitigate the effects of multisite variance in organizational structure, policies and procedures, and the high rate of student RA attrition. Adequate resources and well-developed communication systems are critical to the success of any research project utilizing RAs.

REFERENCES

Bostrom, J., Dibble, S., & Rizzuto, C. (1991). Data collection as an educational process. *The Journal of Continuing Education, 22*(6), 248–253.

Ellis, E., Riegel, B., Hamon, M., Carlson, B., Jimenez, S., & Parkington, S. (2001). The challenges of conducting clinical research: One research team's experiences. *Clinical Nurse Specialist, 15*(6), 286–292.

Gay, J. T., Lavender, M. G., & McCard, N. (1987). Nurse educator views of assignment of authorship credits. *IMAGE: Journal of Nursing Scholarship, 19*(1), 134–137.

Gift, A. G., Creasia, J., & Parker, B. (1991). Utilizing research assistants and maintaining research integrity. *Research in Nursing & Health, 14,* 229–233.

Hanson, S. M. H. (1988). Collaborative research and authorship credit: Beginning guidelines. *Nursing Research, 37*(1), 49–52.

Jones, K. D., & Tilden, V. P. (1998). Authorship issues in multidisciplinary research teams. *American Journal for Nurse Practitioners, 2*(5), 18–20, 25, 34.

Nativio, D. G. (1993). Guidelines for nurse authors and editors (Commentary). *IMAGE: Journal of Nursing Scholarship, 25,* 8.

Oberst, M. T. (1996). Student research assistants: An ounce of prevention (Editorial). *Research in Nursing & Health, 19,* 259–260.

Williams, A., Hagerty, B. M., Hoyle, K., Yousha, S. M., Abdoo, Y., Andersen, C., & Engler, D. (1999). Research from afar: Considerations for conducting an off-site research project. *Journal of Professional Nursing, 15*(5), 288–293.

5

Special Considerations for Multicenter Research

Joyce M. Dwyer

Few reports discuss the particular features of multicenter studies. The problems encountered during these studies are often viewed by investigators as deterrents to successful completion; however it is possible to surmount these obstacles.

Multicenter studies are usually time consuming. For this reason, serious consideration during proposal development should be given to the benefits of collaborating with several health care agencies or institutions. Gilliland (1994) pointed out some of the values inherent in multicenter research. Pohlman (1994) noted that multiple study sites enlarge the sample size, increasing the generalizability of research findings and decreasing the need for replicating studies. Multicenter studies also increase the social and cultural diversity of the subjects, as well as involving several specialized clinical settings, such as trauma centers, intensive care nurseries, transplant units, or spinal injury units. Time spent identifying potential settings is useful during the preliminary phases of proposal development. The feasibility of simultaneously guiding a proposal through several institutional review boards (IRBs) and implementing the data collection methods at each site needs to be carefully explored.

Preliminary consultations with agency administrations and the staff at each site are helpful in gauging the possibility of successful implementation. It is advantageous to have a completed proposal prior to beginning the search for potential sites. Accommodation may be possible in order to adapt to a given setting without affecting the proposal's design or methodology. A completed proposal allows investigators to consider the implications of suggested adjustments and make decisions about including a site.

PRELIMINARY CONSIDERATIONS

Potential Study Sites

It is helpful to identify possible agencies during the early phases of developing a proposal. Appropriate sites are essential to the successful completion of a project. Agencies are often selected based on proximity to the investigators and the fact that they service populations that meet the characteristics of the study's subjects.

Academic medical centers receive a large volume of proposals. They have stringent requirements for proposal preparation and submission. Submission dates are scheduled periodically during a given year. Managed care organizations may also be useful resources for multiple sites. The number and variety of ambulatory facilities scattered throughout a network and the association with many inpatient institutions make these organizations desirable. Free-standing community health centers generally have individual procedures and guidelines for utilization as research settings. Community hospitals may be valuable resources, welcoming opportunities to become involved in research. On-site studies provide opportunities for the staff to develop and maintain associations with urban, academic institutions, stimulating interest in advanced professional preparation and fostering cooperation between service agencies and academia.

Feasibility of Study Implementation

Implementing a study is largely due to the support received from an agency's administration. It is worthwhile to explore the educational and clinical preparation of key personnel at each site and their views about nursing research. Negative attitudes about studies including human subjects, the on-site presence of investigators, or hostility to academic pursuits does not create a suitable atmosphere for the successful initiation or completion of a study. Potential support from other disciplines such as social work and medicine should also be explored.

The complexity of conducting data collection at several sites requires organization skills. The number of research personnel necessary to service sites and maintain constant communication and collaboration should be anticipated. Strategies should be designed to ensure the integrity of the data collection process at all sites, and intervention should occur in any circumstance that may threaten ongoing research.

The Proposal

Preliminary exploration of possible clinical sites is enhanced by prior completion of a well-designed proposal explaining the study's design and methodology concretely and precisely. A study's impact on ongoing patient care and potential infringements on staff time and institutional resources are common concerns of administrators. Specific concerns should be addressed by the investigators at each site prior to submission of a proposal to an institutional review board. Discussion of any research-related responsibilities that may impinge on the workload of site personnel is critical. Resolution of concerns will facilitate the progress of a proposal through the review process.

Guidelines

Generally, each agency has specific guidelines for developing proposals and a process for submission to institutional review boards. Copies of the guidelines for each agency must be reviewed. They vary considerably. It is unlikely that a proposal can be submitted to several agencies in the same format; however often simple reorganization of a few paragraphs may be sufficient to comply with the various agency requirements.

Separate informed consent forms for each agency must be developed. They must comply with the specified instructions for each agency. A specific place will be designated in the form for including the standard statements required by federal law for the informed consent of all human subjects enrolled in research studies.

Individualized protocols for recruiting subjects and accessing patient information may also need to be developed. Information contained in a protocol is dictated in part by the procedures required at a given agency: for example, requiring a copy of the signed informed consent or screening tool in a subject's medical record or permitting only certain individuals to obtain informed consent.

The date(s) for the submission of proposals to institutional review boards are scheduled by each agency and are stipulated in an agency's guidelines. Because the submission dates will vary among agencies it is helpful to develop plans for coordinating deadlines and the scheduled dates for each individual review board meeting. The guidelines will also indicate the number of proposal copies necessary for each review board. It may vary from 2 to as many as 25 or more copies. The signatures required on the original proposal will also be designated. Requiring the signatures of both the Vice-President of Nursing and Medicine or the Director of Nursing and Chief Operating Officer is common practice.

Internal Principal Investigators

Investigators need to be apprised of the requirement by many large medical centers of the designation of a member of the agency's internal staff as a principal investigator. The staff member may either be recruited by the study's principal investigator or appointed by the administration and serves as a liaison between the institution's review board and the study's principal investigator. While this practice is perceived to be useful for review boards it is frequently cumbersome, causing delays in responding to requests for additional information and proposed revisions. Verbal and written communication occurs between the institutional review board and the agency's designated investigator, who notifies the principal investigator of the status of the study.

THE PLANNING PROCESS

Timing

O'Donnell, Ruhlandt, Roberts, and Baer (1998) described some of the steps included in planning their hospital-based cardiovascular study. These are useful to reiterate here. Because scheduling conflicts are inevitable in multicenter research, developing plans to coordinate the deadlines specified by the agencies for proposal submissions, revisions, resubmissions, and annual reviews is useful. Planning assists investigators in allocating work assignments to members of a research team and meeting targeted completion dates. The different timetables encountered in multicenter studies make a date for fully implementing an investigation imprecise. Data collection is frequently staggered due to different starting and completion dates at each site, thus prolonging the data analysis phase.

Meeting the specified dates for submitting a proposal to the various institutional review boards is mandatory. Failure to meet a deadline prevents the review's evaluation at the next scheduled board meeting, impeding the approval process and usually delaying implementation at one or more sites. Requests for resubmission following suggested revisions is not uncommon and should be anticipated when targeting start dates. Most agencies require a proposal's submission one month before a review board meeting. The average time for completion of the internal review process in multicenter studies varies from four to twelve weeks. Because more than one agency is involved, the approval process for initiating a study could require four to six months or more.

Adjunct Nursing Review Committees

Angetucci and Todaro (1993) indicated that some agencies may have a two-stage review process due to the addition of separate nursing review committees. Adjunct committees can add weeks or months to an already lengthy process. The purposes of these committees differs among agencies. They may be established to review the quality and scientific merit of proposals prior to submission to institutional review boards or may be charged with considering the feasibility of implementing studies, given the resources of an institution and the intended clinical setting. These committees generally require proposal submission up to four or more weeks prior to a scheduled meeting.

The role and function of these nursing review committees (NRC) is controversial and the relationship with institutional review boards (IRB) is unclear. They are frequently composed of nursing staff who have neither research experience nor expertise. Many competent, well-prepared nurse researchers, including Jacobson and Winslow (1993) and Nokes and Dolan (1992) believe that nursing research has been discouraged and impeded by the gatekeeping activities of these agency committees, adding further unnecessary obstacles to the approval process.

INSTITUTIONAL REVIEW BOARD SUBMISSION

Proposals must be written according to the individualized instructions of each agency. Each review process entails a heavy additional workload and time commitment by investigators. Oddi and Cassidy (1990) and Webber and Jenkins (1990) provided insight into the role and functions of institutional review boards. These authors suggested certain aspects of proposals that are closely critiqued by review boards and should be carefully developed. Compliance with federal law requires that these committees oversee the safety and well-being of subjects and minimize any potential risks. Additionally they must assure that there are adequate informed consent procedures and provisions for maintaining the security and confidentiality of research data. If vulnerable populations are involved, a certificate of confidentiality from the Substance Abuse and Mental Health Services Administration may be required. These certificates provide investigators with some protection from being required to identify subjects involved in criminal or legislative inquiries.

Consent Forms

Attention should be directed to devising informed consent forms that adhere to the strict instructions of each agency and to the ethical standards specified in the Belmont Report (1979). Agencies will require an individualized format. The instructions will stipulate the location for inserting the standard paragraphs regarding the confidentiality of data contained in a subject's medical record, the provision for necessary care if injury results from participation in a study, the freedom to withdraw consent and participation, and the availability of a copy of the signed consent form. Review boards will also focus attention on the explanations of the objectives of a study, the potential risks and benefits to subjects, and the research procedures involved. These statements must be written in language that can be easily understood by the subjects. Each review board may require different wording, resulting in different consent forms for each site.

Procedures for ensuring the confidentiality and security of research data, such as the coding of study instruments and screening tools, the facilities available for storing data, and the names of individuals who will have access to data, will be scrutinized. Protocols for agency personnel outlining how subjects will be recruited and how data will be collected are also of particular interest because of the potential for the intimidation and coercion of subjects. These will also need to be developed specifically for agencies and may vary slightly due to particular stipulations imposed by agencies. Potential interferences in the ongoing work of patient care and infringements on the time of an institution's staff will be examined.

Revisions and Resubmissions

One problematic feature of multicenter studies is the frequent request for different changes in a proposal by each of the institutional review boards.

Because conducting a study at several sites requires that a proposal be submitted to each agency's institutional review board, full compliance with all requested revisions can be troublesome. Members of various boards often have different interests and concerns. Requested changes can range from the simple rephrasing of an item on a questionnaire or interview scale to significant changes in research methods; for example, restructuring the sampling methods, removing content from a data collection instrument, or changing the use of standardized research instruments. Prudent consideration must be given to requests because it is essential that the design and methodology of a study remain intact at each agency. Smith, Salyer, Geddes, and Mark (1998) have emphasized that interference with standardized data collection procedures in multicenter research can threaten the internal validity of a study. Sometimes changes can be readily accommodated. However, once a proposal has been approved by one or more institutional review boards, changes in the study are not feasible. If negotiations with a particular agency are not fruitful the investigators may need to withdraw from a site.

Most requested revisions involve the format of an informed consent form, added security safeguards, or clarification of the instructions for subjects included on a research instrument. Other frequently sought revisions entail the procedures for obtaining informed consent, the location for interviewing or testing subjects, and the process for reviewing confidential medical files.

While revisions requested by review boards must receive careful deliberation, any change in a proposal will affect the conduct of a study at all agencies. Proposal changes require resubmitting to each institutional review board, essentially halting all progress in implementing a study. Investigators must consider whether requested changes will permit a study to be conducted at all the proposed sites; whether sufficient study staff, time, and financial resources are available to support the changes; or whether a given site needs to be dropped from further consideration.

CONDUCTING MULTICENTER STUDIES

Despite meticulous planning, problems arising during the early phases of multicenter studies are often due to the current upheavals in the health care system as well as to inadequate communication between investigators and the agency staff at each site. Unanticipated events occur frequently, especially sudden reductions of professional staff, changes in administrative personnel, reorganization or elimination of patient care services, institutional mergers, changes in computer systems and software, or new policies and procedures for accessing medical records or other critical data. Investigators should be prepared to devote resources to finding alternatives and solutions to unforeseen complications in order to facilitate ongoing studies at multiple sites.

Maintaining constant communication between investigators and key agency staff is essential. Coordination of multisite studies is helped immeasurably by the appointment of project directors when possible. The importance of coordination during these multicentered projects is emphasized in Cohen's (1997) nursing study of compliance in families with children with human immunodeficiency virus infection. Both Pohlman (1994) and Smith and colleagues' (1998) reports have stressed the importance of developing detailed and structured protocols for data collection, constant communication with agencies, on-site training of participating agency staff, and coordination to minimize the problems associated with multicenter studies.

Preparations for initiating multicenter studies should include familiarizing the staff at each site with the research plan, especially the data collection aspects. Separate orientation sessions conducted by the investigators at each agency are beneficial. The sessions enhance the collaboration between the investigators and the agencies. The valuable contributions of staff members to a study's success should be emphasized, and investigators must be committed to fostering collegial relationships throughout the duration of a project.

The odds of meeting the desired sample size are increased by initially enlisting the participation at more agencies than may be required. However, the number of projected enrollees may not be forthcoming at one or more sites due to unforeseen circumstances. Populations served by agencies may change as a result of variations in the demographics of surrounding communities or institutional mergers. The census of inpatient or ambulatory units may decrease following downsizing, the closing of aligned community health centers, or the combining of patient care units or clinical services. Conditions are seldom stable in health care and contingency plans are warranted.

Occasionally stipulations attached to approval of a study by an institutional review board cannot be met, forcing withdrawal from a site. Examples of stipulations include (1) prohibiting the review of medical records by investigators or research assistants who are not members of an agency's internal staff, and the lack of available staff necessary to provide the information about a potential subject's eligibility for participation; (2) requiring investigators to notify each potential subject's private health care provider prior to seeking participation and informed consent; (3) restricting the time during which investigators may have contact with subjects; (4) limiting the number of medical records that can be obtained for review during a given time period; or (5) prohibiting the use of graduate student research assistants on site. While intended to minimize disruptions or inconveniences to agencies, these and other similar restrictions may preclude investigators from proceeding at a site despite the considerable time and effort invested during the preliminary planning phases of a study.

CONCLUSIONS

The difficulties involved in developing and conducting clinical research are increased and magnified in multicenter studies. Nokes and Dolan's (1992) study of the experience of nurse researchers in gaining access to research subjects in health care agencies indicated that the problems included the necessity of completing lengthy and duplicate forms, the requirement of adding other investigators from the internal staff of the agency to a proposal, the excessive time frames required to gain approval, and discouragement from nursing administrators within agencies. While these problems continue to exist and can be particularly troublesome in multicenter studies, persistence and commitment to the research objectives will greatly contribute to successfully overcoming obstacles. The unique problems encountered involve increased time requirements; an additional need for organization and coordination; the ability to comply with the individual differences and stipulations of a number of agency institutional review boards, as well as administrators and staff; and vigilance in maintaining the integrity of the research design and methodology.

A heavy time investment is required to undertake these studies. The increased time allotment is largely due to the duplication of the planning and implementation phases for each collaborating agency. Coordination of the study sites, especially during data collection, adds to the need for increased time. The staffing requirements for multicenter research make it more suited to studies including teams of investigators. Individual investigators will find these studies very burdensome and labor intensive.

Organizational skills are essential to the coordination of all phases of these projects. Among the many tasks are the preparation of multiple variations of the proposal to meet the differing institutional review board requirements at several agencies, several different versions of the informed consent form and any protocols necessary for the study's implementation, and the annual reports and requests for institutional review board renewal at each agency.

Compliance with the many requirements of multiple agencies requires constant monitoring once a study is in progress. Careful monitoring is necessary to ensure adherence to the stipulations of several institutional review boards and the administrators and staff of cooperating sites. Effective communication and negotiating skills are advantageous in overcoming unanticipated obstacles.

Maintaining the integrity of a proposal's design and methodology is paramount in multicenter studies. Violations in the conduct of a study can result in serious and even fatal flaws in the data collection and analysis. Constant communication with agency staff, frequent on-site visits, and timely and appropriate problem solving are critical to sound study outcomes.

REFERENCES

Angetucci, D., & Todaro, A. (1993). An adventure in scientific inquiry: The development of a hospital-based nursing research committee. *Journal of Nursing Staff Development, 9*(6), 270–273.

The Belmont report: Ethical principles and guidelines for the protection of human subjects of research. (1979). Washington, DC: National Commission for the protection of human subjects of biomedical and behavioral research.

Cohen, H. L. (1997). Coordinating a large multicentered HIV research project. *Journal of the Association of Nurses in Aids Care, 8*(1), 41–50.

Gilliland, K. A. (1994). Why multicenter research? *SCI Nursing, 11*(2), 50–51.

Jacobson, A., & Winslow, E. (1993). The role of nursing research committees. *Nursing Research, 42*(3), 62.

Nokes, K. M., & Dolan, M. (1992). Experiences of nurse researchers in gaining access to subjects for clinical nursing research. *Journal of Professional Nursing, 8*(2), 115–119.

O'Donnell, L., Ruhlandt, R., Roberts, C., & Baer, L. (1998). The growth and development of a research study: Why stroke survivors wait so long. *Journal of Cardiovascular Nursing, 13*(1), 88–92.

Oddi, L., & Cassidy, V. (1990). Nursing research in the United States: The protection of human subjects. *International Journal of Nursing Studies, 27*(1), 21–34.

Pohlman, B. (1994). Multicenter research. *SCI Nursing, 11*(1), 19–20.

Smith, C. S., Salyer, J., Geddes, N., & Mark, B. A. (1998). Strategies to enhance internal validity in multi-center longitudinal research. *Outcomes Management for Nursing Practice, 2*(4), 174–179.

Webber, M., & Jenkins, N. (1990). The internal review process: Implications for the novice clinical researcher. *Progress in Cardiovascular Nursing, 5*(2), 59–64.

6

Managing the Multisite Team

Carole W. Pearce

W hen a multisite, multidisciplinary team is awarded funding for a research study, the initial reaction is euphoria, and then reality sets in (Minnick, Kleinpell, Micek, & Dudley, 1996). Disbelief may be the initial response, particularly when the news comes by telephone and there is no confirmation in writing for team members to see. Then, oh wow, now we really have to do this study like we said we would! Whoever thought it would actually be funded? This was true when the application for examining disparities in health care among health care workers we submitted was considered a long shot, and the multidisciplinary team was newly formed for the purpose of writing the grant proposal. Now the study has to be implemented and deadlines met. Any future funding depends upon successful completion of the current funded study (Minnick et al., 1996), and successful management of the many people involved.

DEVELOPING THE RESEARCH TEAM

Multidisciplinary, multisite research projects require careful planning, from developing the team, deciding on the research question, selecting the sites, carrying out a pilot study, writing a proposal for funding, collecting and analyzing the data, to disseminating the findings. There is no one way to plan and carry out a multisite research study. However, following certain guidelines can help make the process successful. The elements to enhance that success include commitment, communication, attention to logistics, contribution, consensus, compatibility, and credit. Real collaboration occurs when a unified projects results from the ideas and responsible behavior of many persons (Durham, 1998; Lancaster, 1985).

81

Membership

Every research team is unique. Each member of a research team should be carefully chosen for the contribution of that member's particular expertise, experience, geographic location, past funding, race and ethnicity, or location of primary employment (Grant et al., 1998). Team membership should represent all areas where expertise is needed and all sites (Nail et al., 1998). A team may also be assembled from a group of persons who wish to work together, who have a common interest, who know each other already, or who have worked together successfully before (Grant et al., 1998). Drawing on the strengths of the individuals will benefit the team in quality of the proposal, productivity, data collection and analysis, and dissemination of findings. It is also possible to seek funding for development of a research group (Grant et al., 1998).

Assembling a multidisciplinary research team necessitates consistency of the goals of individuals and/or institutions involved. The vision of the research team and the team members at the site must be congruent (Ingersoll et al., 1995). Researchers also need to be concerned about the design, implementation, and dissemination of the study. In nursing, assembling a team of faculty and clinicians is essential for research-based practice (Lengacher & Mabe, 1992). When collaborators are truly partners it is possible to plan and implement a multisite research project that has a unified conceptual and methodological framework.

Team Building

Every collaborative project needs a principal investigator (PI) who directs the project, and each site needs a coordinator or principal investigator responsible for that site. The site coordinator is crucial to the success of the project and serves as champion for the site, while developing and encouraging support from upper level administration (Durham, 1998). The PI brings the team of collaborators together, determines meeting dates, and serves as a liaison with administration. Although the most effective teams are democratic and share the responsibilities, the PI holds the ultimate responsibility for the research project (Stone, 1991).

The team building process begins with an initiation phase during which members express their individual identities and credibility and become connected as a team (Grant et al., 1998; Nail et al., 1998). Face-to-face meetings, group activities, and social opportunities are important, particularly if there are team members who do not know each other professionally. The opinions of each member must be respected (Nail et al., 1998) and objectives of the group, confidentiality, and authorship issues should be discussed (Grant et al., 1998). Meetings should be held monthly at rotating sites, enabling members to become familiar with each of the sites. The research process at each institution should be shared. Facility tours should be given, key personnel introduced, parking issues solved, and pertinent literature reviews begun (Grant et al., 1998).

Each investigator should share his/her expertise and expectations. Consultants on issues such as content, methodology, relevance, clinical issues, instrumentation, and other needs of the team should be brought in. During this time the team makes decisions concerning theoretical and project design issues, using data from literature reviews and data analysis. The potential number and variety of subjects are determined from individual site data, and the aims and methods for the proposal are chosen (Grant et al., 1998).

Definitions are finalized and the proposal is written. Each team member may be responsible for a section. The principal investigator combines all the sections, prepares a budget and time line, and modifies the proposal into a cohesive document. In a study of fatigue and quality of life, the team consisted of advanced researchers and clinical experts and included nurses, a public health specialist, a physician, an anthropologist, and a psychologist (Grant et al., 1998).

Communication

Regular communication is essential to developing a multidisciplinary team. Good communication within the team depends on building trust and taking adequate time for the process to develop; developing a cohesive research team can take up to a year (Grant et al., 1998). Communication should be early and frequent. Each member of the team, including investigators, students, agency administration, and agency staff must have ownership of the project—a stake in its success (Pieper, Dobal, Martin, & Balding, 1998). The appropriate methods of communication need discussion. How will communication happen? At meetings? On the telephone? By memos? E-mail? Website? Multiple modes of communication enhance interactions. Who needs to communicate with whom? Academic researchers communicate with their own department chairpersons, associate deans, or deans, and clinician researchers communicate with clinical nurse specialists, head nurses, directors, and vice presidents of patient services at the study sites (Stone, 1991).

The entire team must develop a plan that includes the frequency and content of the scientific exchanges, project logistics, responsibilities of each individual, time lines, milestones, and procedures for handling dis-agreements. Individual work styles need recognition or clashes may occur (Durham, 1998). Flexibility is needed to accommodate communication during periods of intense work as well as when the work is proceeding according to the plan (Nail et al., 1998).

The career interests and motivations of the individual members need to be clear from the beginning of the project. Motivation may be career and skill development, publication, clinical work release time, or increased quality of data. When a team member is unable to meet personal goals through the project, that member's interest may decline, deadlines may not be met, or the person may resign.

MULTIPLE SITES

Finding Appropriate Sites

All sites do not have to be identical in key attributes. The uniqueness of each site should be valued and the differences viewed as strengths, not weaknesses, of the project (Nail et al., 1998). Site selection for a study is crucial to obtaining adequate data in the expected time frame. The sites must be appropriate for the design and goals of the study (McGuire & Kirchhoff, 1991). Selection considerations include whether the site has adequate participants who meet the eligibility criteria for the study and whether there is institutional and nursing support (Dibble, Bostrom-Ezrati, & Rizzuto, 1990).

High staff turnover and new managers may be obstacles to the implemen-tation of a project. These issues should be examined before making final choices (Ingersoll et al., 1995). It is the responsibility of the investigators to keep track of these staff; this task is not likely to be very high on the priority list of administration (McGuire, 1991). To study heart/lung transplant patients would require sites around the country, whereas study-ing the effect of patient position on homodynamic changes would not (Dibble et al., 1990). When each site has a solid research infrastructure, the collaboration team benefits (Durham, 1998). Institutions may bargain with the team; they may want presentations from the researchers and/or questions added to the study in exchange for providing the site (Dibble et al., 1990). If a site is required to hire and supervise research staff, adequate funding from the project is needed, as site budgets rarely can support unfunded research (Durham, 1998).

Keeping the Sites

Communication is also crucial to keeping the sites. It is important to provide the opportunity for the sites' personnel to get together and for the researchers to clearly explain the expectations. Site personnel should be kept informed throughout the study. If communication is inconsistent and the staff's commitment is uncertain, valuable time and momentum may be lost early in the study. A newsletter can be an important tool to inform agency staff and administration of the progress of the project and problems that may be occurring; sites may also share highlights of staff involvement. Other ideas include holding monthly meetings for information sharing with executives and frequent planning and implementation meetings with staff directly involved in the project. Descriptions of the project and plans for implementation should be in writing for all sites. Ask researchers and site administrators to keep logs related to their implementation of the research project and to document research-related activities, including, of course, any events that are likely to influence the outcome of the research. They could document their individual perspectives on the progress of the project and their personal reactions to the project's demands (Ingersoll et al., 1995).

In their work, Ingersoll and colleagues (1995) found that managers and staff responsible for data collection wished that the principal investigator had been more visible. Staff members and site managerial staff must be given direct, positive feedback acknowledging their work, and provided with information about the progress of the project. It is important that site staff understand both the parts and the whole of the project, and how the roles they are playing fit into the larger picture. Use of examples can be helpful. Staff also need to know how the research and findings fit within their current work situation. Posters and/or videotapes can be used to convey these messages. If outside people are hired to facilitate the research, these people's roles must be very clear or role conflicts may occur (Ingersoll et al., 1995).

PLANNING THE PROJECT AND THE PEOPLE INVOLVED

If an investigator wishes to carry out a research project, s/he should first seek support from the home institution. Because the time needed to carry out a project takes the investigator(s) away from assigned obligations, administrators must see the proposed research as an asset, as a benefit to the institution, a good investment. Before writing the proposal, the investigator must be assured that the time and money needed for writing the proposal and carrying out the project are available. The money may come from the department, internal seed grant, or external grants. Starting with small grants gives the research group a chance to test the team and its members' ideas (Selby, Riportella-Muller, & Farel, 1992).

Proposal Development

The principal investigator is chosen by consensus and is the main person responsible for proposal development. If investigators lack experience, it is most helpful to contact more experienced researchers who are willing to share their expertise (Selby et al., 1992). A meeting with the entire team is needed to create work assignments, decide on the focus of the study, and designate leaders in areas such as instrumentation, process evaluation, and data analysis. As specific sections of the proposal are developed, they are sent to the PI and team members for revision and comment. The focus should be on presenting and firming up the strengths of the proposal and dealing with the weaknesses (Nail et al., 1998).

The proposal development stage is facilitated by the team members' familiarity with the diverse body of literature available, experience with previous proposal development, and prior grant-planning experience. Such a match among team members facilitates development of the proposal, and use of the fax machine enables them to have rapid delivery of written material (Nail et al., 1998). We have found that the use of e-mail is even better and that corrections can be made directly and returned very quickly.

Proposal writing competes with other preexisting demands and commitments and meeting deadlines is difficult. Just getting materials to all the sites for review can be overwhelming at times. When sites are in different time zones, the availability of a time frame in which to communicate is shortened (Nail et al., 1998).

At many institutions, any department that will be affected by the grant must send approval letters. Contacting the responsible individuals during the planning and grant preparation phase makes their approval more likely (Selby et al., 1992).

Budget Preparation

Most health care or academic institutions will help facilitate budget preparation; a specialist can make this time-consuming and confusing task easier. The budget process is more complicated for a multisite research project. Consultation and guidance from the home institution will help avoid serious miscalculations (Selby et al., 1992). The PI should prepare a preliminary budget and a proposed prototype budget for each site. Resources are often allocated primarily to data collection instead of investigator salaries (Nail et al., 1998). However, budgeting investigators' salaries enables them to have reduced workloads and thus to devote the time needed for the project.

Everything needed for a grant must be considered in the planning, including personnel, office space, office equipment with computers, phones, fax machine, and so on. Most funding agencies have restrictions on what they will and will not fund. Actual funding includes direct money (what the budget covers) and indirect money (overhead to cover those costs the direct money doesn't cover). If the grant will not cover costs, the contribution that is expected from the institution must be openly discussed (Selby et al., 1992).

Sample

The research questions and the number of variables will determine the sample size as calculated by a power analysis, and the number of sites needed will be determined by the number of participants available at each proposed site (Dibble et al., 1990). Site leaders and staff may have their own ideas concerning what the variables should be. Meeting early on and giving them an opportunity to be of help can minimize the possibility that certain data are unavailable (Ingersoll et al., 1995).

Final Details

The remaining details are who must be notified, at the funding agency, that the grant application has been sent, if the proposal can be routed to the appropriate study section, and who can make that happen (Selby et al., 1992). Early contact during the planning stage with the appropriate person at the funding agency can minimize the possibility that the application will go to the wrong study section, or that some expectation will not be met.

HOW TO MANAGE THE MULTISITE TEAM

Once a grant is funded, the team needs to have a planning meeting. The purpose of the meeting is protocol development and the processes for group decisions. The planning meeting can take up to three work days. Review of existing possible instruments, according to a specific format, can be assigned to members of the team. The results need to be collated by the study leader and presented to the team. Having a consultant present at the planning meeting is helpful (Nail et al., 1998), as this person has no vested interest in the project but does have expertise in the field of study. The expected outcome of the planning meeting must be predetermined and a strong commitment to meeting that objective should be a first priority. If a team member has expertise in team building, that expertise can be used to set the agenda. Accountability can be handled with a responsibility chart, grid, or matrix. The decision-making procedure must be defined and processes for those decisions decided upon. A responsibility chart can be designed to anticipate the types of decisions to be made and the role of each team member in those decisions. Necessary decisions vary widely, but may include protocol design, data coding, and allocation of resources (Nail et al., 1998).

The time frame of the research project should be realistic and followed as carefully as possible, keeping the investigator(s) aimed toward the milestones of the project. A good rule is to estimate the time needed and then double it (McGuire, 1991).

Minnick and colleagues (1996), who had the experience of a 17-hospital study, stated that any large-scale study requires careful coordination of the many research tasks. The PI needs to carefully read the proposal and draft a business plan for implementation of the study. The plan should outline the specifics of conducting the study at each site, including site-specific data collection requirements, human resources needed, storage of supplies, and their distribution and collection. The research must be carried out within the budget and on time. A business consultant may be useful.

Public Relations

Public relations are important for any grant and should be planned early on, before the media call. The grantor and the home institution's public relations or external relations staff need to be involved in handling media contacts and setting policies pertaining to public announcements. Advice on how to give an interview may be needed. Positive stories in the news are important for obtaining and maintaining support at participating sites and the interest of potential subjects. Interested staff at the sites may call and volunteer to participate in the study (Minnick et al., 1996).

Public relations are important with the PI's home site staff and colleagues, at all sites, and with participants and their families. It is likely that administrators wrote letters of support for the grant proposal; however, the PI must motivate the chief administrators to continue the participation of their institutions at a high level of support. Making sure they understand how they benefit from the research should not be overlooked. Ways to keep their continued support include personal phone calls, letters, presentations to executive committees and boards, informal visits, interim reports, and presentation of findings (Minnick et al., 1996).

Distribution of a fact sheet outlining the purpose and methods of the study (Minnick et al., 1996) and pertinent data is also important. In our abuse in pregnancy study we created a fact sheet with statistics about abuse in general and during pregnancy specifically and handed it out during our orientation sessions at each site. We also prepared and distributed a summary of the research study, including purpose and methods. Specific requests for assurances that disruption on the units will be minimal, meeting all data collectors, and knowing exactly when investigators and data collectors will be on site must be honored. Site staff need to know that their ability to do their jobs will not be disrupted; trust established between researcher(s) and staff is crucial (Minnick et al., 1996).

The data collectors and support staff can handle public relations with participants and their families for the most part, but the PI sets the tone with the data collectors and site leaders (coordinators). Obtaining informed consent is vital and necessitates information sharing for understanding of the study. Why subjects' participation is desired and the details of expectations of participation must be clear. Making follow-up as convenient as possible will yield a high response rate (Minnick et al., 1996).

Managing the Finances

Both the funding agency and the home institution have rules regarding how grant money can be spent. Generally, an account is created from which funds can be expended. The proposed budget, revisions, and spending guidelines should be examined. Either set up a meeting with budget officials or attend an orientation session if possible. The PI and staff must become familiar with budget issues, and staff must learn how to complete and process the accounting forms. A handbook or chart explaining all the various financial forms, with details for completion, is helpful both at the beginning of the project and when new personnel need orientation (Selby-Harrington, Donat, & Hibbard, 1993). How finances must be handled will vary; however, careful and accurate use of funds is of utmost importance.

The Principal Investigator

The PI has the overall responsibility for quality control of the project. The PI is responsible for identifying the skills needed to carry out the grant (Selby-Harrington, Donat, & Hibbard, 1994). The PI must be familiar with or learn the procedures and rules for hiring, promoting, paying, evaluating, giving salary increases, and terminating employees (Selby-Harrington et al., 1993, 1994). Positions need to be established, job descriptions determined, applicants recruited and interviewed. Training of personnel to meet the job expectations may need to be considered (Selby-Harrington et al., 1994). All staff must be oriented and trained to understand the importance of the extreme accuracy needed to maintain the integrity of the project, especially data verification and quality control (Selby-Harrington et al., 1993). Cross training enhances the value of staff and enables the work to continue in someone's unexpected absence (Selby-Harrington et al., 1994).

The PI also has overall responsibility for correspondence and reports, although other team members meet most of the ongoing routine needs and draft letters and reports. Final approval of all reports by the PI is necessary. All documents should be labeled and dated to avoid confusion, especially when there are multiple drafts before the final version (Selby-Harrington et al., 1994).

Keeping abreast of current research in the subject area is also important for the PI; grant staff, librarians, and others can keep the PI informed by summarizing or highlighting relevant literature. Professional meetings and conferences provide networking opportunities where preliminary findings, problems, and solutions can be shared (Selby-Harrington et al., 1994).

The Project Manager

A project director, manager, associate, or coordinator is responsible for the overall management of the study. Although the role can vary, overseeing and coordinating the project and organizing the staff are crucial to success of the project. Prioritizing; troubleshooting; maintaining communication with the PI, coinvestigators, site leaders and data collectors; and facilitating ongoing monitoring are all facets of the role (Minnick et al., 1996).

The Coinvestigator

Minnick and colleagues (1996) described the roles of coinvestigators, or co-PIs, in multisite studies as the persons who ensure adherence to protocols at the various sites, manage or analyze data, or serve as consultants or in an administrative roles. With multiple coinvestigators, each investigator may assume a different role.

The Site Leader

Each site needs a designated leader. The daily implementation of the project falls to the site leader, who represents the project to the data collectors, staff, and participants. The site leader is the "ambassador" for the project. This role requires coordinating the activities of all people involved in the grant, dealing with human resource issues, troubleshooting, determining whether needed decisions can be handled on site or at the main project office, and collecting data if a collector is absent (Minnick et al., 1996). A master's-prepared person with good experience in the field of the study and management is needed. This person is often the site representative or coinvestigator on the research team (Pieper et al., 1998). Training of site leaders is expensive, can take up to three days, and should include details of public relations, data collection, and personnel management. Site leaders need to know the research study objectives, time line, instruments, and protocols (Minnick et al., 1996). Site leaders need to meet periodically with central staff and with each other to share progress and helpful hints (Minnick et al., 1996).

The Data Collectors

The PI and project director must list the qualities they want in a data collector before they write the job description (Minnick et al., 1996). Data collectors can be recruited from the student population at a university, university affiliates, persons known to the site leaders, and the site itself

(Minnick et al., 1996; Nail et al., 1998). Data collectors who are staff members on one unit involved in a study should collect data on another unit or at another site to avoid role confusion. When collecting data, it is important that the data collectors wear a project lab coat an l/or name badge for identification. In addition to training for data collection, they also need to know the project objectives and details, organizational chart of the project, whom to contact in an emergency or for questions, public relations, and personnel information. They need to feel comfortable in the role, have ideas for decision-making situations, and feel empowered (Minnick et al., 1996). We have found that role-playing during training sessions is helpful.

The Project Secretary

When planning the budget for a multisite research project, it is important to consider inclusion of a project secretary to keep track of the details of the project. This crucial role calls for the organizational, computer, and interpersonal skills necessary for maintaining all project and data collection files, coordinating personnel schedules, monitoring time/attendance forms, directing work assignments to research assistants, ordering and monitoring of supplies, and meeting with the PI and manager for budget matters. In addition, the secretary may handle data collection returns, prepare staff training manuals, and make project name badges. The secretary must be oriented to purposes and objectives of the project, time line, and expectations of the role (Minnick et al., 1996). Minnick and colleagues (1996) found that having the secretary accompany the PI and site leader to their pilot site enabled that person to have a sense of the challenges facing the rest of the team. It is helpful if the secretary has experience with the same institution; if not, a lengthy orientation for the role is needed.

Personnel Policies

Personnel policies need to be clear to everyone working on the project. Do they need to attend the home institution and/or site for orientation? Do they need a badge both for the home institution and the site? How is an identification badge obtained and when? Do they need health screening and immunizations? What is their health and liability insurance status when working on the project? What is their job category (full-time, part-time, hourly worker, salary, temporary, permanent) and what are the benefits (if any)? Are travel time and mileage compensated for? How are expenses reimbursed? How are paychecks distributed? All of this information, plus the content of the training programs, what forms are available and where, how forms are processed and when, should be in the project manual (Minnick et al., 1996).

Morale

Attention to morale is crucial to the success of the project and all members of the research team, including investigators and hired personnel, must be considered when planning specific ways to foster enthusiasm. Establishing a sense of teamwork is important to accomplish that goal at the sites, between site workers, and within the management group. Expecting data collectors to help each other builds camaraderie. Giving positive feedback and keeping everyone informed of the progress of the data collection at the various sites are other ways to foster positive feelings (Minnick et al., 1996; Nail et al., 1998). The team is able to build on what is successful and change processes and procedures that are not meeting expectations. It is important to hold meetings with site leaders, project manager, and PI to review progress and acknowledge their accomplishments; holding informal social events and sending written humorous communications concerning the project are worth consideration (Minnick et al., 1996).

Data Collectors and Staff

Recruiting Data Collectors

Recruiting data collectors works best if nurses or other staff who are interested in the study are offered the opportunity for these positions. They may be interested because of the promotion possibilities in a clinical ladder-based nursing department, to obtain credit for school, or to earn extra money. During one study, the site coordinators were paid $500 a month and an additional $10 an hour for data collection (Dibble et al., 1990). In another study, where the nurses were the participants, those units that returned more questionnaires than they had for a previous study and the unit with the highest return rate were given $100 rewards (Ingersoll et al., 1995). Money for education or course vouchers can also be given.

Training of Data Collectors

All data collectors must be carefully trained and supervised to preserve the reliability of the data. A carefully planned training program near the actual time of data collection improves the quality of the data. Details concerning abilities and schedules of each data collector are needed for future reference. A schedule for data collection for the entire study should be available at the training program sessions, enabling these persons to schedule and plan their hours. A pilot study can be done to test the instruments for timing and ease of administration and to determine the actual feasibility of the collection procedures (Dibble et al., 1990). Changes are better made based on a pilot study, rather than midway through a project.

Orientation for Staff

All staff on units used for a study must be oriented to the details and should provide their ideas about the study. This groundwork planning is crucial to the success of any project; it takes multiple sessions to ensure that each staff member is included in an orientation session. The investigator responsible for that particular site handles the orientation sessions (McGuire, 1991). We have found that when all staff on a study unit are familiar with the research study, they are able to help with recruitment of participants, discuss the study with the clients/patients, and feel comfortable referring questions they cannot answer to the investigator. The staff need to know the site coordinators well enough to ask them questions.

Staff Turnover

The unexpected will always occur, so be prepared. Resignations of key staff or administrators, closing or moving of units, and failing to inform temporary help of the need to find participants are all problems that may cause delay and threaten the validity of the data (Dibble et al., 1990). Keeping staff interested in the study over time can be problematic, particularly when they see no direct benefit (Ingersoll et al., 1995). See chapter 3 for some solutions.

Storing Supplies and Equipment

Supplies should be stored in a safe and accessible location. They should be labeled to minimize loss that increases the cost of the project. Supplies must be checked and replenished regularly by the site coordinator or a designated person (McGuire, 1991); failure to do so may result in loss of opportunity to obtain data.

Data

Data Collection

Gathering data is an exciting time during a research project, and a venture into the unknown whether the researcher is a novice or an expert (McGuire, 1991). The principal investigator and coinvestigators can carry out data collection, research assistants can be hired to collect data at each site (Dibble et al., 1990), or staff can be recruited for that purpose. Alternately, a site coordinator, who is responsible for all the data collectors and the accurate and timely collection of data, can be hired for each site (Dibble et al., 1990). If the study takes place over an extended period of time, data collection can be difficult due to loss of site coordinators and data collectors (Dibble et al., 1990). McGrew, Bond, Dietzen, McKasson, and Miller (1995) found the clinical coordinator (site manager), who was an expert clinician, invaluable in their multisite study where they implemented an assertive community treatment program. The coordinator was able to train staff in critical skills, accompany team members on home visits, and be responsible for maintaining a proactive stance throughout the study.

The investigator should examine the data as they are collected to detect any problems. It is far better to correct problems before too many data are collected (McGuire, 1991). Any problems should be handled with extreme tact and understanding, or the investigator risks alienating the site and jeopardizing data collection.

Managing the Data

After the quantitative data are collected, they must be entered into the computer for analysis. This can be carried out at the individual sites if money is available to set up the computers and network system to do this; however, it is more likely for data entry to be centralized and handled by specific individuals trained for that purpose. Data entry can be simplified if the data can be read directly by the computer. Weekly return of data keeps those staff members consistently busy, detects problems of data quality as they occur, and provides the team with preliminary results. If data are missing, or additional data are needed, they can be obtained in a timely manner (Minnick et al., 1996).

Data management at each site includes checking the data entry for accuracy and completeness and reconciling questions. Accuracy depends greatly upon the skill of the person entering the data. Collecting data on a predetermined time frame may be difficult, even for a single site study; use of multiple sites often magnifies the difficulty (Nail et al., 1998). It is easier to solve problems during the project than at the end; periodic analyses help to track the variables and uncover problems (Selby-Harrington et al., 1993). Security procedures for the data must be in place to minimize the potential loss of data due to computer crashes or even theft. Who will have direct access to the data must also be determined.

Adhering to the Time Line

Expect to have difficulty meeting deadlines, particularly when relying upon multiple sites and a large multidisciplinary team of investigators. Remember, the management of a grant is judged partly by whether the specified time line is kept. Every team member and every site need to know the time line. Breaking it down into detail for the current period and posting it where completed tasks can be checked off is a concrete way of judging progress. Flexibility of assignments enables extra work to be carried out during slow times in anticipation of those unexpected events. If one site is consistently tardy with data, discussions with the personnel at that site may reveal ways this problem can be minimized (Selby-Harrington et al., 1993).

Analyzing the Data

Analyzing the data calls for creativity. Data analysis should be planned when the proposal for funding is planned and written. When no one on the team has the appropriate skill, consulting a statistician is important from the beginning. The design, research question and hypothesis(es), variables, and levels of measurement will dictate the appropriate statistical tests (McElroy & Gonyon, 1991). Today, analysis is accomplished with a computer. The details are not needed for this chapter and can be found in any good statistics textbook.

Data can be analyzed from a singular point of view or from multiple, often conflicting, views. Use of multiple or plural analyses calls for the researchers to reconcile the differences in the final results (Brown &

Lindley, 1986). In the case of disparities in our health care study, eight separate research teams were funded to study the same fundamental problem. Each will find different results. Together they will paint a picture of the disparities in health care in the United States that we anticipate will affect policy in the future.

Plural analysis can also be used within a single study. Of course, if this type of analysis is used, the answers are unlikely to be as definitive as we have come to expect. Procedures for resolving the conflicts are just beginning to become useful. Both pooling and reconciliation of data are used for this integration; neither would be possible without the use of computer algorithms (Brown & Lindley, 1986).

Finding meaning in the results is the challenging task for the research team. Investigators determine whether the research question is answered or not, and interpret the meaning of the findings (McElroy & Gonyon, 1991).

Reports and Next Steps

Formal reports are usually submitted to the funding agency yearly (McGuire, 1991). Less formal reports are equally important. These internal progress reports keep personnel and site staff up to date and aid in uncovering and solving problems. At the completion of the study, a final report is due to the funding source and all sites (McGuire, 1991). All equipment, property, and supplies must be disposed of or allocated in accordance with the rules of the grant, usually within a given number of days. The next grant application should be submitted during the final year of an existing one. Success on one grant will likely lead to another (Selby-Harrington et al., 1993).

Termination With Staff and Sites

When sufficient data are collected, the data collection ceases and participants need to be thanked both in person and by letter. Upper-level management persons should also be thanked in person. Information about the date of closure and a summary of findings should be shared in writing (Dibble et al., 1990). A debriefing meeting is an excellent idea and should be held shortly after the data collection is complete. Recommendations from site personnel can be very helpful in future projects (Ingersoll et al., 1995).

DISSEMINATION OF FINDINGS

In a multiple site research study, it is important to disseminate the progress and preliminary findings both during the study and after its completion, to share the findings relevant to each particular site and the overall research project findings relevant to all sites. Inservice educational programs can accomplish this goal; granting continuing education credits and serving refreshments increase the attendance. An alternative is to make a videotape that nurses can view individually; a videotape can be used along with a live discussion in a continuing education program (Dibble et al., 1990). An article in the newsletter is another vehicle.

Presentation of the research at regional, national, and international professional conferences is an excellent way to disseminate the findings, especially during the research process and after completion of the study. Publishing articles in peer-reviewed journals is always an expectation of any research project.

Erlen, Siminoff, Sereika, and Sutton (1997) recommended that the entire team become involved in discussions about dissemination and that the role of each team member be determined. The team decides the rules for authorship. A leader for each paper must be chosen. However, the process for choosing the leader and that person's role and responsibilities must be decided by the team. Often, the major paper is the responsibility of the principal investigator, and other papers are the primary responsibility of those with the highest interest in the subject. The process for resolving conflicts must also be determined early in the project (Erlen et al., 1997).

Publication and presentation credits and rights should be negotiated by team members from the beginning of the project (Erlen et al., 1997; Nail et al., 1998; Stone, 1991). There is no consensus concerning this process (Stone, 1991) and in nursing, there are no specific authorship guidelines that apply to all journals (Erlen et al., 1997). Problems that can occur with multiple authorship are numerous. The team must cope with different writing styles and work pace, compromise on philosophical views and article content, and determine leadership process and equal workload distribution (Nehring & Durham, 1996). Authorship issues may cause division in personal and professional relationships (Stone, 1991). As the research project progresses, input from all members should be sought to identify potential publications and presentations and the members' interest in participation. This must be a process that allows team members to change their interest or availability (Nail et al., 1998).

Issues surrounding inclusion, exclusion, order of authorship, and recognition of those who assisted on the project can all be sources of conflict

(Erlen et al., 1997). Huth (1986) recommended that authorship be limited to those team members who take public responsibility for the work, including both the data and conclusions based on those data. For example, questions may arise concerning a statistician who may have a minor role in the research project, and then be assigned credit instead of authorship. On the other hand, a statistician may have had a significant role in developing the paper, but not have contributed to the research project, or may have been a team member from the onset. In both of these instances, authorship is appropriate. The question of authorship for others participating in the research, but not as investigators, poses further dilemmas. Giving these persons credit is certainly important, but does that include authorship?

Knowledge of group dynamics and how they influence the team's work is important when negotiating authorship (Nehring & Durham, 1996). First author can be chosen by alphabetical order, drawing the names out of a hat, rotation for multiple publications, giving credit to the person who is responsible for the final presentation or article, mentoring those who are less experienced, and/or those who may need credit for tenure and promotion. Is it safe to assume the last author has made the least contribution to the manuscript, or is the last author a senior person who contributed conceptually more than the others (Digiusto, 1994), or is the last author the corresponding author? In the past, first authorship often was dominated by the male members of a research team. Bacher and colleagues (2000) examined 30 years of publications in psychobiology and found that the percentage of women first authors had increased over that time span from approximately 15% to more than 50%.

The responsibilities of first author include inviting and/or selecting a team to assist in manuscript preparation, and determining the overall time frame and deadlines. The first author develops the first draft and circulates it to coauthors; revises the manuscript, using their suggestions; follows the author guidelines for the journal of choice; sends the manuscript for review; revises the manuscript with the coauthors; gives copies of all submissions to coauthors; and sends copies of the published article to coauthors and PI (Erlen et al., 1997).

Topics, ideas, and outlines of manuscripts should be shared with the research team. Timely completions of first drafts of manuscripts are circulated to coauthors for editing and comments and then submitted for review. All manuscripts should be reviewed by the PI. If the PI insists on authorship of every paper, even if the PI has not contributed to the manuscript, the issue needs to be resolved (Erlen et al., 1997).

Erlen and colleagues (1997) developed guidelines for authorship that are worth considering. Each team member should be given the opportunity for first authorship of at least one manuscript. Others involved in the project should be included in writing manuscripts if at all possible, and those who contribute to a manuscript should be authors even if they are not project team members. Those who have not contributed to the manuscript, including staff members and data collectors, but have had a significant role in the research project should be acknowledged on each manuscript and presentation, as should research staff members. Funding sources are always acknowledged for presentations and manuscripts.

Digiusto (1994) proposed an interesting point system for determining authorship, in which points are assigned to team members depending upon their contributions to the overall project. Each team member's points can then be spent on the manuscripts, with the cost for various levels of authorship depending upon the total number of authors for that paper. Although the point system seems complex, it might be useful when the multidisciplinary research team is large, and hierarchical problems make fair distribution of credit difficult and frustrating to team members.

The greatest benefits of the multiple authorship process include improved quality of the writing and the contribution of more expertise into a single publication (Nehring & Durham, 1996). Opportunities for personal growth (Nail et al., 1998) can be fostered by senior experienced researchers mentoring the junior members of the team.

When the team is multidisciplinary, articles should be written to target the professional journals of the team members. Nehring and Durham (1996) carried out a three-round Delphi study to examine multiple authorship in nursing and came up with a long list of rewards and problems. In spite of the tendency toward multiple authorship (Bacher et al., 2000), the value a department, college, or promotion and tenure committee within the university places on first and only authorship may determine whether multiple authorship is valued and whether any credit is given for authorship other than first author. Those team members whose disciplines do not value multiple authorship will need consideration from the team; the issue must be negotiated to best serve the needs of each member. These hard realities in academic positions may preclude a faculty person from either becoming a member of a multidisciplinary, multisite team and/or contributing to an article where credit does not solely belong to that one person or does not include first authorship. A footnote can be used to give the specifics of contributions of each author to the manuscript and authorship order. Waltz, Nelson, and Chambers (1985) found that those in academic positions are more interested in authorship than those in nonacademic settings.

KEYS TO SUCCESSFUL COLLABORATION

Dibble and colleagues (1990) proposed two models for carrying out research. The first is the collaborative model and the second the alliance model. In the first model, there is collaboration among researchers (Bergstrom, Braden, Kemp, Champagne, & Ruby, 1984; Pender, Sechrist, Frank-Stromborg, & Walker, 1987; Singleton, Edmunds, Rapson, & Steele, 1982); between clinicians and researchers (Lengacher & Mabe, 1992; Loomis & Krone, 1980; Stone, 1991); and among sites (Alzola, Lynn, Wagner, & Wu, 2000; Bergstrom et al., 1998; Koehler, Muller, Vojir, Hester, & Foster, 1997; McGrew et al., 1995; Nail et al., 1998; Thompson, 1996). The alliance model takes advantage of needed sites without using staff at those sites, but instead uses paid research assistants for data collection. Many studies combine the two models successfully with fair distribution of research roles and responsibilities (Dibble et al., 1990).

Stone (1991) believes that successful collaboration uses the uniqueness of the individual team members. The characteristics necessary for success are (1) acceptance of new perspectives and ideas; (2) openness and the ability to tolerate challenges, critique, and review of each person's thoughts and beliefs; (3) willingness to compromise and negotiate to reach consensus; (4) independent and interdependent functioning; (5) follow-through in completing assignments; and (6) trustworthiness in past and current work.

For multidisciplinary, multisite research to be successful, resources and support are imperative. The federal government encourages and supports multidisciplinary research, but often faculty members do not. Multidisciplinary research is not easy, but when faculty members learn to trust each other's perspectives and value each other's contributions, they will learn from each other and will share resources (Mazure, Espeland, Douglas, Champion, & Killien, 2000).

The team needs to decide on the structure and decision-making processes of the project early on. One person is chosen as the principal investigator of the group and the remaining members serve as coinvestigators. Individual members may be responsible for tool development, a manual to facilitate use of the instruments, and standardized coding. Others may be responsible for data entry and verification of all data. The primary investigator is responsible for the budget. All grant money is received by the PI's institution; coinvestigators must generate their own budgets and receive subcontracts each year (Bergstrom et al., 1984).

MINIMIZING ATTRITION OF PARTICIPANTS

In longitudinal studies, minimizing attrition of participants is important to the validity of the findings (Given, Keilman, Collins, & Given, 1990). Maintaining participation is seldom a focus; however, losing participants can seriously affect meaningful outcomes (Weinert & Burman, 1996). To minimize loss of participants, data collectors must be carefully prepared and supervised. They must have commitment and enthusiasm for the project, excellent communication skills, knowledge and understanding of the importance of the project, consideration and concern for others, and the ability to increase the chances of potential subjects to participate (Given et al., 1990).

The participants need to bond with the study, to be committed and actively involved. Having a theme and using a logo on stationery, question-naires, newsletters, and all other forms of written communication with subjects will help form this bond. At the beginning of the study, clear communication informs participants of the expected duration, frequency, and degree of participation in the study, including time commitments. Continuity of interviewers who collect the data establishes trust between the data collector and the participants and enhances the completeness and quality of the data. Quarterly newsletters, a toll-free phone number, prompt responses to contacts from participants, and respect for their time all are ways to keep communication ongoing. Birthday and sympathy cards can be sent, as well as thank-you notes and small gifts at regular intervals to demonstrate appreciation for their participation in the study (Given et al., 1990).

Protocol booklets delineate the conditions for participation and strate-gies to maintain participation of subjects (Given et al., 1990). An even more lengthy study manual and thorough orientation, prior to initiation of the study, are very helpful (Salyer, Geddes, Smith, & Mark, 1998). Debriefing meetings should held regularly and each data collector should be assigned to work closely with a senior researcher for receiving feedback and for problem solving (Given et al.).

Weinert and Burman (1996) made suggestions to maintain the interest level of those who are enrolled in a research project: (1) make everything as hassle free as possible, (2) increase the rewards, and (3) follow up with the nonresponders. These researchers found that the most common reason for withdrawal, however, was that the participants were no longer qualified to participate in their study.

ACKNOWLEDGING CONTRIBUTIONS

Nurse managers, staff nurses, and coordinators are important people to communicate with, and the researchers must acknowledge the importance of their contributions. It is also important to express positive regard on all correspondence and share issues, concerns, suggestions, and successes. Bonding with staff persons can be accomplished by sharing the abstract with them, attending staff meetings, posting flyers to alert them of the next data collection (Salyer et al., 1998), sharing articles and posters pertinent to the study, and presenting continuing education programs. The researcher can show respect for their time and effort by acknowledging concern for the length of the questionnaires, being flexible with time lines if possible, and making sure the research packets are complete and placed in envelopes. A lottery for cash can provide incentive for staff participation in the study (Salyer et al., 1998). A letter in the employee file, items in the agency newsletter, inclusion at performance evaluations, a gift, and/or acknowledgment in presentations and publications are tangible rewards for participation in a research study (Pieper et al., 1998).

CHALLENGES OF MULTISITE RESEARCH

Challenges are inherent in any research study, but the potential challenges in multisite studies are even greater (Lindquist, Treat-Jacobson, & Watanuki, 2000). Once the challenges are overcome, the rewards for the multidisciplinary team are great.

Communication

Good communication among investigators is a key to successful multisite research. Ways to facilitate good communication include frequent meetings of all investigators. Meeting monthly is ideal; however, this may not be realistic if sites are distant from each other. Even meeting 3–4 times a year (Bergstrom et al., 1984) can be challenging if the sites are geographically far apart. Rotating sites for meetings enables each investigator to share the travel and gives team members the opportunity to see each site personally (Bergstrom et al., 1984). Meetings should not be overused, as each person has other responsibilities (Pieper et al., 1998). Frequent memos, telephone calls, conference calls, and individual site visits all contribute to a successful project (Bergstrom et al., 1984; Pieper et al., 1998). The responsibility for documenting the conference call and meeting content, and the decisions, can be rotated (Singleton et al., 1982). Although reports are the responsibility of the principal investigator, all team members can contribute by writing their own sections, offering suggestions to drafts written by others, or even taking turns in writing the actual reports (Singleton et al.).

Mandated Diversity

Diversity is mandated by federal funding agencies, and sites are often chosen for their uniqueness in their patient population: cultural and racial groups, gender, age, medical diagnosis, or level of acuity (Lindquist et al., 2000). Of course, there is also the need for site comparability for internal consistency. Multiple sites may be chosen geographically to meet the requirement for differences in racial and ethnic backgrounds and family cultures (Lindquist et al.). In our study of the reported incidence of threat of or actual violence against pregnant women, prenatal sites were chosen for differences in socioeconomic status (Medicaid vs. private insurance and managed care organizations), race (white, black, and Asian), and ethnicity (Hispanic, Portuguese, and Haitian).

Finding Suitable Sites

Sites can be chosen for patient heterogeneity and demographic characteristics. It may be challenging to find sites with a favorable attitude toward research in general and the specific project in particular, an organizational culture that supports research, and administrative support (Minnick et al., 1996). Administrators and staff are most likely to participate if they believe that a project is feasible and is likely to benefit their population. Good communication and careful planning are important for successful recruitment of sites and access to subjects at those sites (Lindquist et al., 2000). Geographic separation of sites can pose difficulty in holding team meetings, and reimbursement for mileage and travel time adds to the cost of the research (Grant et al., 1998). If costs such as nursing time and resources at the sites and costs to third party payers are involved, compensation should be arranged in advance, when negotiating the site (Lindquist et al., 2000).

Multiple Institutional Review Board Approvals

For each site in a multisite study, the individual institution needs to approve the study. This approval may come from a committee, an institutional review board, an administrator, the nursing administration, the medical director, and/or the nursing staff most directly involved with the potential subjects (Lindquist et al., 2000). Ideally, each site has a research committee that is knowledgeable about how to institutionalize research. This committee carries out an internal review process and critiques research proposals. It may also circulate relevant research articles, publish an in-house newsletter, offer research study groups, and sponsor research presentations (Rizzuto & Mitchell, 1988b).

The requirements at the agency may vary. Approval may take many months and numerous modifications may be needed before approval is granted. Generally approvals are renewed annually after the initial application. The more sites in a study, the more difficult this task is (Lindquist et al., 2000). We have found that either having the site coordinator or representatives from each university responsible for the renewal of the individual approvals (violence in pregnancy project), or making renewal the responsibility of the grant administrator (disparities in health care), seems to work fairly well. If the responsibility falls completely to an unpaid PI, it is indeed an undue burden. If a site review board is hesitant, a visit by the principal investigator can be helpful in facilitating the participation and/or approval (Bergstrom et al., 1984).

Access to Participants

Access to subjects is dependent upon the schedule of the unit, and researchers may need to schedule their access around the needs of both the subjects and the nursing and medical staff (Lindquist et al., 2000). With very busy schedules, this may be one of the most challenging aspects of multisite research.

Cost/Funding

Research grant money is not always readily available for all those wishing to pursue research. Small grants within universities and service organizations can make research that would otherwise be impossible, possible. Combining a number of small grants can make significant research possible. Combining the talents of academia and service serves both institutions well.

Usually funding is awarded to a single institution, that of the principal investigator (Bergstrom et al., 1984). Subcontracts add to the time and complexity of grant proposal preparation due to added budget details and the need for letters of agreement (Lindquist et al., 2000). Subcontracts can be awarded to institutions of the coinvestigators on a one-year contractual basis (Bergstrom et al., 1984), or in the case of multiple-year external funding, written into the original grant proposal. Financial limits and a list of reasonable allowable costs may enable subcontracts to be more easily negotiated. Subcontracts may have high indirect costs required by the subcontracting institutions and add to the overall cost of the project (Lindquist et al., 2000).

The costs for multisite research are not necessarily more than those for single-site studies. If research team members and staff are efficient and are used in the most advantageous manner, money can be actually be saved. For example, if one site has a low patient census, the researchers may be active at another during this drop in census. Sharing of equipment may also cut costs. If sites are scattered geographically, travel time and reimbursement can become expensive, as can telecommunication. Use of the Internet technologies such as e-mail and bulletin boards can save money (Lindquist et al., 2000).

Time Commitment for Researchers

A diverse group of researchers must take the time to establish an identity; the process for this to evolve requires much effort. It may take up to three years for a consortium to develop a group that supports, educates, and encourages implementation of research (Rizzuto & Mitchell, 1988a). Working with multiple sites takes more time than most research teams anticipate (Rizzuto & Mitchell, 1988a). One team member may have more time available to commit to the research project than another, possibly due to the emphasis or lack of emphasis on research at a given institution, faculty workload (Singleton et al., 1996), or concurrent research projects.

We have found, on two different multiple site research studies, that sites may be initially receptive, but either change their minds or create difficulties when the researchers begin the implementation phase of the project. Ongoing education at the sites, monitoring adherence to the protocols, and travel to sites all take additional time and effort.

Staff Turnover

With a large team of investigators at multiple sites, there is likely to be high turnover among the team members, and keeping all members interested and vested in the project becomes problematic (Rizzuto & Mitchell, 1988a). At this time, in our disparities in health care project, we have had three coinvestigators resign due to time constraints, conflicts with other responsibilities inherent in an academic position, and retirement, accompanied by moving out of state. In both our abuse in pregnancy and disparities studies, students working on the project and staff employed at the sites were continually changing. Turnover among site coordinators may also be high (Rizzuto & Mitchell, 1988b).

Increased Planning

Thorough planning is definitely necessary in multisite studies. Devising protocols for multisite research can be most challenging, and reaching agreement among sites difficult. Flexibility in design is needed, but it is also crucial to maintain the scientific integrity of the project (Lindquist et al., 2000). If new sites are added at a later date, the protocols need to be reexamined and fine tuned at a meeting with representatives from all sites present as soon as the new site is part of the project (Nail et al., 1998). Measurement of outcome variables must be standardized (Lindquist et al., 2000). Without strict written protocols to follow, sites may score instruments differently, leading to errors and minimizing the ability to draw conclusions (Bergstrom et al., 1998).

Standardizing Procedures

Carefully crafting protocols aids in implementing the same design and method at each site and ensures the consistency needed for pooling of the data for analysis. Standardizing procedures across sites is important for the internal validity of the study, while at the same time, these procedures may need to be controlled or modified for consistency. This may be a daunting task. An example is a study on the effect of relaxation on increased intracranial pressure in surgical patients after a craniotomy. The therapy needed to be standardized concerning when the relaxation therapy was given, the length of the therapy, and the timing of the measurements. Patient positioning and calibration of equipment had to be agreed upon and consistently implemented across all sites (Lindquist et al., 2000).

Sites may have differences the research team has no control of. The length of hospital stay at one site may be different from that of another, and the availability of staff to deal with psychological problems, discharge planning, and patient teaching may vary. One site may have an all-registered nurse staff, while another may have a mix of nurses' aides, licensed practical or vocational nurses, and RNs (Grant et al., 1998).

There needs to be a balance between uniformity, to protect the rigor and quality control, and flexibility, to accommodate the differences in the clinical practices at the sites. The uniformity in implementation of research protocols determine the quality control and scientific rigor of a study. When a study includes many diverse sites, with geographic distance between them, implementation is a great challenge (Lindquist et al., 2000). In one instance, a trainer from one site trained staff at another, using a videotape and return demonstrations on actual subjects at the second site. This was very helpful in maintaining interrater reliability in the study (Bergstrom et al., 1984). In another, the sites were given the choice of the exact month to implement the study (Pieper et al., 1998).

Differences Among Sites

When protocols are designed, the investigators must have knowledge of the differences among the sites in order to accommodate all sites, minimize attrition of participants, and avoid obtaining data that are not useful. Protocols that are clearly written and make allowances for flexibility in certain aspects are needed (Lindquist et al., 2000). For example, in our abuse in pregnancy study, exactly when the various sites screened for violence during pregnancy, how they documented the screening, where the completed screening tools were stored, and the manner in which new prenatal clients were tracked from admission varied greatly among the sites. On the other hand, the Abuse Assessment Screen (AAS) needed to be administered in its entirety and in the language of the subject. Initially, at some sites, the nurse or intake worker asked only the first of five questions on the AAS, or translated the English AAS into Spanish without using the Spanish instrument; both were not within our protocol. One site was very reluctant to screen using the AAS, after initially using it at intake interviews. When this difficulty could not be overcome, one of the investigators and students screened the women at that site as much as possible. The nurses preferred the single screening question on their standardized intake form and felt that the additional four questions were a burden. Validation can be an issue; Bergstrom and colleagues (1998) found that when sites handled the scoring of an instrument inconsistently, differences in the data made it impossible to draw conclusions concerning the tool being tested. However, it did demonstrate that the protocol for testing of the tool was inadequate.

Waiting for Funding

There is usually a time lapse between writing the proposal and the receipt of funding. Keeping the group active during this time is important; inexperienced researchers may have a particularly difficult time maintaining their interest when nothing is happening (Bergstrom et al., 1984). Keeping in touch by telephone or e-mail can help. Sites may also change their minds about participation in the study during this interval.

Maintaining Interest of Staff

Once the research begins, keeping the staff at the sites interested for the duration of the study may also be problematic. If research is valued in the institution, this may be less of a problem. Administering care is likely to be a higher priority than carrying out a research protocol (Lindquist et al., 2000).

In our abuse in pregnancy study, the investigator responsible for each site visited at least monthly. Pizza and salad were provided at the clinic every six months, and periodically the site investigator brought bagels or muffins for coffee break. The staff were encouraged to ask questions, and updates on the progress of the study and the comparison of that particular site with the other concerning rate of screening and rate of reported violence was given. Our emerging statistics were shared with one clinic coordinator when she was seeking additional funding.

Staff Training

Staff training must be carried on at each site for all people who will be involved in the research, either directly as a site coordinator or data collector, or less directly as staff who suggest possible participants, explain the study to a participant and/or family before or after data collection, and so on (Dibble et al., 1990; Minnick et al., 1996). During our abuse in pregnancy study, the initial training of all staff at the sites was carried out by two of the investigators at each site following a protocol for orientation. New personnel were then trained as they arrived at the clinic and the clinics were given copies of a videotape, posters, and pertinent literature. All students working on the project were trained by the same two persons at one of the universities throughout the study. Data collected by students were examined by an investigator, and missing or questionable information was investigated. This ensured standardization and interrater reliability of data and minimized missing data.

Mentoring students and junior faculty benefits all members of the team. Just having them on board makes the project easier to carry out, but it also helps academic programs and advances the discipline. The students and junior faculty acquire research skills and the faculty mentor is more productive. Doctoral students and junior faculty can mentor graduate and undergraduate students. Mentoring students and junior faculty educates researchers for the future and helps both junior and senior faculty with promotion and tenure issues. A nursing program with a strong research component attracts better students and helps in faculty recruitment (Morrison-Beedy, Aronowitz, Dyne, & Mkandawire, 2001).

Getting Behind Schedule

If data are collected more slowly than expected, the cost can escalate (Lindquist et al., 2000). Planning for already overworked nurses to be data collectors may be unreasonable. Instead, use of research nurses, whose primary goal is identifying participants and gathering data, enables the study to proceed according to its protocols (Dibble et al., 1990; Minnick et al., 1996). Subject identification depends on maintaining positive relationships with the clinical nurses at the sites (Lindquist et al., 2000). The effort needed to keep the study protocol viable when multiple sites are involved is great, but it is essential (Koehler et al., 1997).

Investigators need creativity in reaching goals and incentives for participation in studies (Lindquist et al., 2000). The researchers need to communicate effectively to promote positive relationships and sustain their commitment to the study. Throughout the project, recruitment, training, and supervision of data collectors are crucial to reliable and valid data (Dibble et al., 1990; Koehler et al., 1997; Minnick et al., 1996).

Integrity of Data

Even with a well-conceived idea and the best protocols, a project can be sabotaged if the protocols are not followed carefully. Close attention must be paid to protocol consistency, and correction of errors must be carried out with utmost tact so that the morale and compliance of the personnel will not be compromised. Effective communication among all persons involved in a study site is very important. Clear, simple methods of communication between investigators and site personnel lead to effective problem solving and keep misunderstandings at a minimum. The Internet, telephone, pager systems, beepers, and written memos are all ways to keep the communication channels open. Other technologies that can facilitate cohesiveness and familiarity between researcher and participants are regularly scheduled meetings, conference calls, or use of listserv (Lindquist et al., 2000). In our abuse in pregnancy study, we held yearly meetings where we invited all the participants to one of the universities for dinner and a related educational program that offered continuing education credits.

Leadership

The principal investigator and research staff on a multisite research project must demonstrate leadership. If they are personally effective, they are the "glue" that holds the project together (Lindquist et al., 2000). In any research project there are certain to be conflicts. Communication (Lindquist et al., 2000; Salyer et al., 1998), accommodation, responsiveness (Lindquist et al., 2000), collaboration, negotiation, and compromise (Hinshaw et al., 1981) are important skills for these roles and are the keys to a solution.

Developing and maintaining a positive relationship with the staff at the sites aids in settling difficult situations; recognizing their contributions and demonstrating appreciation of them are necessary to avoid or overcome challenges and barriers. Having an interest in the staff and building relationships should be ongoing. Some techniques include knowing each person's name and using it (Salyer et al., 1998); conversing with each individual and getting to know each staff member; or perhaps sharing articles not related to the research project, but pertinent to a special interest of the nurse/staff. Helping the staff to understand the project thoroughly enables them to carry out the protocols so that the project will be a success (Lindquist et al., 2000).

Bergstrom and colleagues (1984) stated that facilitating collaboration depends upon "(a) strong leadership, (b) willingness to share, (c) good communication, (d) an attitude of give and take, (e) built-in rewards, and (f) supportive institutional leaders" (p. 25).

SUMMARY AND CONCLUSIONS

The team wishing to carry out multidisciplinary, multisite research must plan to capitalize on the positives and provide support to overcome the disadvantages (Grant et al., 1998). Flexibility is one of the keys to success for multisite, multidisciplinary research. Expectations may need to change concerning obtaining participants, and resources may need reallocation if changes are made. Open-minded team members are willing to consider new proposals and shift the direction of the study if new information becomes available. Team members may need to shift locations, their positions, and their responsibilities (Nail et al., 1998). Compromise is a lesson learned early on in a multisite study. One role may shrink and another may expand; equality is not necessarily the objective. Deadlines may need to be adjusted due to unforeseen circumstances, without compromising the overall project. A sense of humor, the ability to laugh when the unexpected occurs, helps the team to move on (Singleton et al., 1982). The ability to continue to match resources available and objectives of a study are crucial to overall success (Nail et al., 1998).

Creating an integrated data system with access to data from the individual sites is often very difficult, if not impossible. Data warehouses need to be developed within and across organizations, enabling researchers to access specific data for a study where they are coinvestigators, or to carry out approved secondary analysis on data generated within the organization from patient and hospital records (Durham, 1998). Managed care organizations and third party payers have the most comprehensive databases today; however, these data need to be expanded, with the eventual goal of a national database (Durham, 1998).

Research in our rapidly changing health care industry will continue to focus on cost containment, mergers, and acquisitions. Research for the sake of science is not as readily funded by the health care industry as is research that gives one organization a competitive edge over another. Convincing health care organizations that research adds value to an organization requires researchers to share research findings with larger numbers of key customers such as the public, policy makers, scientific organizations, and our own health care organizations (Durham, 1998).

REFERENCES

Alzola, C., Lynn, J., Wagner, D., & Wu, A. W. (2000). Length of stay and therapeutic intervention allow estimation of in-hospital resource use independent of site and inflation. *Journal of American Geriatric Society, 48,* S162–S167.

Bacher, L. F., Romm, R., Spanier, H., Tellefsen, L., Yip, S., & Smotherman, W. P. (2000). Developmental psychobiology: A look back on 30 years. *Developmental Psychobiology, 37*(1), 1–4.

Bergstrom, N., Braden, B., Kemp, M., Champagne, M., & Ruby, E. (1998). Predicting pressure ulcer risk. *Nursing Research, 47*(5), 261–269.

Bergstrom, N., Hansen, B., Grant, M., Hanson, R., Kubo, W., Padilla, G., & Wong, H. (1984). Collaborative nursing research: Anatomy of a successful consortium. *Nursing Research, 33*(1), 20–25.

Brown, R. V., & Lindley, D. V. (1986). Plural analysis: Multiple approaches to quantitative research. *Theory and Decision, 20,* 133–154.

Dibble, S. L., Bostrom-Ezrati, J., & Rizzuto, C. R. (1990). Developing multisite research in critical care. *Applied Nursing Research, 9*(4), 236–242.

Digiusto, E. (1994). Equity in authorship: A strategy for assigning credit when publishing. *Social Science and Medicine, 38*(1), 55–58.

Durham, M. (1998). Partnerships for research among managed care organizations. *Health Affairs, 17*(1), 111–121.

Erlen, J. A., Siminoff, L. A., Sereika, S. M., & Sutton, L. B. (1997). Multiple authorship: Issues and recommendations. *Journal of Professional Nursing, 13*(4), 262–270.

Finklestein, J. W. (1998). Methods, models, and measures of health-related quality of life for children and adults. In D. Drotar (Ed.), *Measuring health-related quality of life in children and adolescents* (pp. 39–52). Mahwah, NJ: Lawrence Erlbaum.

Given, B. A., Keilman, L. J., Collins, C., & Given, C. W. (1990). Strategies to minimize attrition in longitudinal studies. *Nursing Research, 39*(3), 184–186.

Grant, M., Anderson, P., Ashley, M., Dean, G., Ferrell, B., Kagawa-Singer, J., Padilla, G., Robinson, S. B., & Sarna, L. (1998). Developing a team for multicultural, multi-institutional research on fatigue and quality of life. *Oncology Nursing Forum, 25*(8), 1404–1412.

Hinshaw, A. S., Chance, H. C., & Atwood, J. (1981, February). Research in practice: A process of collaboration and negotiation. *Journal of Nursing Administration,* 33–38.

Huth, E. J. (1986). Guidelines on authorship of medical papers. *Annals of Internal Medicine, 104*(2), 269–274.

114	Strategies for Implementation

Ingersoll, G. L., Brooks, A. M., Fischer, M. S., Hoffere, D. A., Lodge, R. H., Wigsten, K. S., Costello, D., Hartung, D. A., Kiernan, M. E., Parrinello, K. M., & Schultz, A. W. (1995). Professional practice model research collaboration. Journal of Nursing Administration, 25(1), 39–46.
Koehler, J. A., Muller, K. L., Vojir, C. P., Hester, N. O., & Foster, R. L. (1997). Multisite clinical research: A challenge for nursing leaders. Journal of Nursing Administration, 27(7/8), 42–48.
Lengacher, C. A., & Mabe, P. R. (1992). A collaborative process and framework for nursing research. Nursing Connections, 5(4), 59–66.
Lindquist, R., Treat-Jacobson, D., & Watanuki, S. (2000). A case for multisite studies in critical care: Heart & Lung. The Journal of Acute & Critical Care, 29(4), 269–277. Retrieved June 17, 2002, from http:gateway2.ovid.com/ovidweb.cgi
Loomis, M. E., & Krone, K. P. (1980, December). Collaborative research development. Journal of Nursing Administration, 32–35.
Mazure, C. M., Espeland, M., Douglas, P., Champion, V., & Killien, M. (2000). Multidisciplinary women's health research: The National Centers of Excellence in Women's Health. Journal of Women's Health & Gender Based Medicine, 9(7), 717–724.
McElroy, M. J., & Gonyon, D. S. (1991). Analyzing the data. In M. A. Mateo & K. T. Kirchhoff (Eds.), Conducting and using nursing research in the clinical setting (pp. 198–217). Baltimore: Williams & Wilkins.
McGrew, J. H., Bond, G. R., Dietzen, L., McKasson, M., & Miller, L. D. (1995). A multisite study of client outcomes in assertive community treatment. Psychiatric Services, 46(7), 696–701.
McGuire, M. A., & Kirchhoff, K. T. (1991). Implementing the study. In M. A. Mateo & K. T. Kirchhoff (Eds.), Conducting and using nursing research in the clinical setting (pp. 186–197). Baltimore: Williams & Wilkins.
Minnick, A., Kleinpell, R. M., Micek, W., & Dudley, D. (1996). The management of a multisite study. Journal of Professional Nursing, 12(1), 7–15.
Morrison-Beedy, D., Aronowitz, T., Dyne, J., & Mkandawire, L. (2001). Mentoring students and junior faculty in faculty research: A win-win scenario. Journal of Professional Nursing, 17(6), 291–296.
Nail, L. M., Barsevick, P. M., Beck, S. L., Jones, L. S., Walker, B. L., Whitmer, K. R., Schwartz, A. L., Stephen, S., & King, M. E. (1998). Planning and conducting a multi-institutional project on fatigue. Oncology Nursing Forum, 25(8), 1398–1403.
Nehring, W. M., & Durham, J. D. (1996). Multiple authorship in nursing. Nurse Educator, 11(1), 15–18.
Pender, N. J., Sechrist, K. R., Frank-Stromborg, M., & Walker, S. N. (1987). Collaboration in developing a research program grant. IMAGE: Journal of Nursing Scholarship, 19(2), 75–77.
Pieper, B., Dobal, M., Martin, N. C., & Balding, M. (1998). Developing collaborative multisite research in home care. Home Healthcare Nurse, 16(5), 311–318.
Rizzuto, C., & Mitchell, M. (1988b). Research in service settings: Part I—Consortium Project outcomes. Journal of Nursing Administration, 18(2), 32–37.
Rizzuto, C., & Mitchell, M. (1988a). Research in service settings: Part II—Consortium Project. Journal of Nursing Administration, 18(3), 19–24.

Salyer, J., Geddes, N., Smith, C. S., & Mark, B. A. (1998). Commitment and communication: Keys to minimizing attrition in multisite longitudinal organizational studies. *Nursing Research, 47*(2), 123–125.

Selby, M. L., Riportella-Muller, R., & Farel, A. (1992). Building administrative support for your research: A neglected key for turning a research plan into a funded project. *Nursing Outlook, 40*(2), 73–77.

Selby-Harrington, M. L., Donat, P. L., & Hibbard, H. D. (1993). Guidance for managing a research grant. *Nursing Research, 42*(1), 54–58.

Selby-Harrington, M. L., Donat, P. L., & Hibbard, H. D. (1994). Research grant implementation: Staff development as a tool to accomplish research activities. *Applied Nursing Research, 7*(1), 38–46.

Singleteton, E. K., Edmunds, M. W., Rapson, M., & Steele, S. (1982). An experience in collaborative research. *Nursing Outlook, 30*, 395–401.

Stone, K. S. (1991). Collaboration. In M. A. Mateo & K. T. Kirchhoff (Eds.), *Conducting and using nursing research in the clinical setting* (pp. 58–68). Baltimore: Williams & Wilkins.

Thompson, J. (1996). AORN's multisite clinical study of bloodborne exposures in OR personnel. *AORN Journal, 63*(2), 428–433. Retrieved June 17, 2002, from *//gateway2.ovid.com/ovidweb.cgi*

Waltz, C. F., Nelson, B., & Chambers, S. B. (1985). Assigning publication credits. *Nursing Outlook, 33*(5), 233–238.

Weinert, C., & Burman, M. (1996). Nurturing longitudinal samples. *Western Journal of Nursing Research, 18*(3), 360–364.

7

International Multisite Studies

Linda J. Mayberry, Anindya K. De,
Eleanor L. Stevenson, and Dyanne D. Affonso

International multisite studies have proliferated during the past three decades. Both the World Health Organization (WHO) and the Centers for Disease Control and Prevention have been instrumental in encouraging collaboration among scientists worldwide to study important questions related to high priority health problems such as AIDS, eradication of childhood illnesses, and pregnancy and infant health outcome improvements. Clearly, there are a multitude of complex elements that will need to be addressed in order to achieve successful completion of this type of research. Based on a review of the published literature during the past five years, we present a background on the most relevant issues tied to the conduct of international multisite studies. The issues cited most often pertain to human rights and informed consent mandates, subject recruitment, and data collection recommendations. Key data management and statistical analysis considerations are briefly addressed. A recent comparative survey study of postpartum depression involving seven countries is also discussed to illustrate some of the common design and implementation issues that arise in the conduct of international multisite research.

HUMAN RIGHTS AND INFORMED CONSENT

Human rights is an important issue in all clinical research and particularly so in international research. Clinical research conducted today can be viewed in terms of the evolutionary progress made from the earlier studies conducted only one half century ago. Scientists in the first half of the twentieth century witnessed a tumultuous period in research highlighted by the Nazi Medical Experiments from 1933 to 1945 and the Tuskegee Syphilis Study starting in 1932 in which major human rights violations occurred. Unethical events such as these sparked the movement to regulate research and protect humans participating in research trials. After the Nuremberg Code was adopted in 1949, based on the outcomes from the trials of those conducting the experiments in the Nazi Medical Experiments, the Declaration of Helsinki was adopted in 1964 by the World Medical Association (WMA). This declaration was subsequently amended in 1975, 1983, 1989, 1996, and 2000 (WMA, 2000).

The Declaration of Helsinki addresses three requirements: (1) the necessity for providing better protection of human subjects from harm in nontherapeutic research studies; (2) the existence of a significant, independent reason for exposing a healthy human volunteer to substantial risk of harm beyond the purpose of gaining new scientific knowledge; and (3) protection of the health and life of each research subject by the investigator. Although the Declaration of Helsinki provides a standard by which research should be conducted, ethical dilemmas concerning the investigative process continue to exist. These ethical debates called the Declaration into question due to ongoing controversy regarding use of placebo-controlled clinical trials in developing countries (Woodman, 1999).

While revisions to the document have been called for since 1997 by the American Medical Association, proposed amendments that would abolish the current distinction between therapeutic and nontherapeutic research were said to justify the conduct of placebo-controlled trials even when there is already a proven treatment. For example, there was heated debate surrounding the implementation of placebo controlled trials in such countries as the Ivory Coast, Uganda, Tanzania, Malawi, Ethiopia, Dominican Republic, and South Africa, particularly in relation to maternal-fetal HIV transmission prevention studies that have been occurring during the last decade. According to Bayer (1998), when the AIDS Clinical Trial Group (ACTG) Study 076 was interrupted because preliminary data showed a decrease in perinatal transmission of HIV from 25.5% to 8.3%, it was declared that the administration of zidovudine during the last two trimesters, intravenous bolus of zidovudine during delivery, and administration of zidovudine to the newborn for six weeks should become the standard of care. The issue quickly became a financial one, as this $800 regime was deemed not feasible in the aforementioned developing countries. The debate raised the issue of whether or not placebo-controlled trials should be continued in these countries, in the hope that alternative and more cost-effective treatments would be found. According to Annas and Grodin (1998), the World Health Organization (WHO) concluded in 1994 that the 076 regime was not a feasible option in the developing world. At issue was whether or not conducting research in these developing countries is exploitation, exactly what the Declaration of Helsinki tries to protect against. According to Angell (1997), placebos should only be used as an arm to a study in the absence of a known treatment to a disease (not the case with perinatal transmission of HIV) and subjects who are in the study's control group should be given the best treatment known to date.

In describing a different perspective, Bayer (1998) noted that David Satcher, former director of the Centers for Disease Control (CDC) and Harold Varmus, former director of the National Institutes of Health (NIH), argued that conducting placebo-controlled trials in these countries represented no additional risk to the populations beyond the standard practice, as they had been receiving no care before participating in the clinical trials. The WHO also seem to support this viewpoint, based on the following quote from a meeting that was convened to assess issues surrounding research on perinatal HIV in 1994: "Placebo-controlled trials offer the best option for a rapid and scientifically valid assessment of alternative antiretroviral drug regimens to prevent [perinatal] transmission of HIV" (Lurie & Wolfe, 1997, p. 854).

The questions surrounding use of placebo-controlled trials are not easily resolved, however, in the current version of the Declaration of Helsinki (WMA, 2000), the World Medical Association has attached a note of clarification to paragraph 29 that addresses the use of placebo versus treatment in studies where no proven prophylactic, diagnostic, or therapeutic method exists. In this note the following is stated:

> The WMA is concerned that paragraph 29 of the revised Declaration of Helsinki (October 2000) has led to diverse interpretations and possible confusion. It hereby reaffirms its position that extreme care must be taken in making use of a placebo-controlled trial and that in general this methodology should only be used in the absence of existing proven therapy. However, a placebo-controlled trial may be ethically acceptable, even if proven therapy is available, under the following circumstances:
>
> –Where for compelling and scientifically sound methodological reasons its use is necessary to determine the efficacy or safety of a prophylactic, diagnostic, or therapeutic method; or
>
> –Where a prophylactic, diagnostic, or therapeutic method is being investigated for a minor condition and the patients who receive placebo will not be subject to any additional risk of serious or irreversible harm.
>
> All other provisions of the Declaration of Helsinki must be adhered to, especially the need for appropriate ethical and scientific review.

From 1932 to 1972, the U.S. Public Health Service sponsored the Tuskegee Study of untreated syphilis in which over 400 African-American men who were infected with syphilis were observed over time for the purpose of understanding how the disease progressed. During the course of this now well-known study, penicillin became an effective and inexpensive way to treat syphilis. The participants were never made aware of this new treatment, and their disease remained untreated for years. The Nixon administration called a halt to the study once the public became aware of its existence (Angell, 1997).

One of the key points to remember from the Tuskegee example was that the men were never provided informed consent, and, in fact, were deliberately deceived. As the new treatment became available, this information should have been presented to the study participants so they could make appropriate decisions regarding the care of their disease. Providing this information would have put the "informed" in the process of informed consent.

In 1948, the Universal Declaration of Human Rights was adopted, which declared that all human beings have dignity and rights. Although we aspire to achieve this standard when implementing clinical research trials involving human subjects, this goal is not always met. Using the Tuskegee Study of untreated syphilis as a source for comparison, Annas and Grodin (1998) addressed the ongoing issue of placebo-controlled research on perinatal transmission of HIV in developing countries. Their contention was that local populations, particularly vulnerable ones (children, mentally impaired, poor), should not be used as research subjects unless the population would likely derive certain benefits from the research being conducted. Further, although it might be argued that HIV-positive pregnant women in developing countries could benefit from participating in trials, informed consent must always be obtained, even in situations in which this is inherently difficult.

Varmus and Satcher (1997) reinforced that the conduct of research trials by the NIH and the CDC in developing nations must meet the same requirements for informed consent as if the research were taking place in the United States. The Belmont report (National Commission for the Protection of Human Subjects of Biomedical and Behavioral Research, 1988), which emerged as a result of the unethical practices surrounding the Tuskegee Study of Untreated Syphilis, outlined three principles for the protection of human research subjects. These include: (1) respect for persons (persons have the right to exercise their autonomy); (2) beneficence (the least amount of risk to the research subjects with the greatest amount of benefits to the research subjects and others); and (3) justice (persons involved in research should not be of a group that will not derive any benefit from the research).

Angell (2000) described the responsibility that investigators have in protecting the rights of humans when research is conducted in developing countries. It was suggested that ethical standards of clinical trials in these nations might not meet the standards established in developed countries. A project conducted in Uganda in which investigators looked at the risk factors associated with the heterosexual transmission of HIV was discussed as an example. The study was conducted in 10 clusters of villages in which five villages were given antibiotics to reduce the prevalence of sexually transmitted diseases (hypothesized as a risk factor) while the other five villages were merely observed and not provided with antibiotics. Surveys about sexual practices and health histories were completed, and body fluids, including blood, were collected. For 30 months, the individuals within the 10 clusters were observed. The issue raised in this study (Angell, 2000) was that the group who did not receive antibiotics were never treated for any sexually transmitted disease they presented with, but were merely referred to free government clinics. The cluster already receiving antibiotics would have specific diseases treated, with medication such as penicillin G benzathine for a positive serologic test for syphilis. In addition, none of the partners of the HIV-positive subjects were informed of their partners' HIV status, even though they were often counseled together as couples by the research team. Angell (2000) stated that a study such as this would never be conducted in the United States, as it would be expected that both the HIV as well as the sexually transmitted diseases would be treated. Further, in many states in the U.S., caregivers would ensure that partners were made aware of their risk due to the study subjects' HIV status. The previous discussion should serve as a reminder to researchers that the ideals of informed consent should be maintained in all international research studies.

PHARMACEUTICAL MULTICENTER INTERNATIONAL CLINICAL TRIALS

A major source of information on issues related to the conduct of international multicenter studies is the pharmaceutical industry. Pharmaceutical industries will regularly conduct clinical trials on experimental and marketed drugs and devices throughout the world in order to satisfy governmental requirements that specific numbers of subjects are exposed to a given drug within a certain time frame. Often, very large clinical trials are planned, encompassing dozens of countries on several continents. These trials are coordinated by one central location, potentially creating a unique set of management problems and issues. Issues that need to be sorted out include government regulations, varying standards of health care among the different countries, importation laws, shipping issues, facility availability, and culture/language considerations. When a pharmaceutical clinical trial, either domestic or international, is being managed within the United States, the first step is to apply for a New Drug Application (NDA) that is granted by the Food and Drug Administration (FDA). Clinical centers conducting drug trials are expected to follow Good Clinical Practices (GCPs) that guide the FDA in tracking studies.

When a U.S.-based pharmaceutical company manages an international clinical trial for one of its compounds, the study must not only follow the guidelines of the FDA, but also the guidelines of the particular country in which there is a clinical site. Each country has its own unique set of governmental guidelines and restrictions that mandate how clinical trials will be conducted within that country. The European Agency for the Evaluation of Medicinal Products (2002) provides assistance to companies by monitoring current legislative and regulatory developments across Europe that impact research related to pharmaceuticals, including both human and animal studies. This agency also publishes procedural announcements and position papers based on information compiled from scientific advice committees, current regulatory obligations, and guidelines for statistical considerations in clinical trials.

The challenge for the management team of the clinical trial is to coordinate activities within each of the designated countries to optimize the recruitment efforts so that each site has equal opportunity to have subjects participate. Unfortunately, it is sometimes the case that the approval process of certain countries is dramatically longer than others, with some country sites not receiving the approval required to begin the trial until after the recruitment goals have been met by the sites within the other countries. In these situations, it will be the investigator's responsibility to assess and report on the impact of a time lag in interpreting study outcomes.

Standards of care and import laws are other considerations for U.S.-based pharmaceutical companies when conducting research trials in other countries. A common study design for drug trials is placebo-controlled blinded studies. Stipulations exist in some countries that will not allow this type of study design to be used and participation in a large proportion of pharmaceutical trials is therefore limited. In addition, import laws vary from country to country, making the planning phase of the trial critical in order to coordinate the receipt of study materials by the sites, including items such as study medications, laboratory kits, and data collection tools.

The use of a central laboratory has become increasingly common among pharmaceutical clinical trials. For example, the Schering-Plough Research Institute mainly uses central laboratories with 80% of their clinical trials (S. Hochberg, personal communication, November 15, 2001). Use of central laboratories versus locally run laboratories promotes consistency among data, allowing a more confident analysis of the study's results. The increasing use of central laboratories also raises complicated shipping issues. For example, it is not uncommon that ambient laboratory samples must be received at the laboratory within 48 hours to ensure stability. Many sites are located in areas that are not easily accessible by couriers and this can delay sample transport. When frozen samples must be stored in either −30 or −70 centigrade conditions and have to be packed in dry ice for shipment, it is often the case that many sites do not have the appropriate freezers or dry ice making/storage equipment. Finally, couriers need to be experienced with each country's laws on sample transport in order to minimize delay in the receipt of the laboratory samples. When choosing clinical sites, decisions must be made as to whether or not the sites will impede the overall trial or if it will be too complicated to provide a proposed site with the appropriate equipment necessary to satisfy the study protocol.

As technology has advanced, so has the sophistication of the conduct of clinical trials by pharmaceutical companies in multiple-country sites. Electronic data capture (EDC) is a data capture method that is becoming increasingly utilized, replacing the need for an employee of the pharmaceutical company to go to the clinical site, collect the data, and bring them back to the company for cleaning and analysis. At present, many international sites do not have the ability to participate in trials utilizing EDC methods simply because of the lack of necessary equipment. Companies will need to consider whether to provide the sites with the appropriate, and sometimes expensive, equipment in order to be able to allow the sites to participate. Often, the phone line capabilities in certain countries prohibit participation, presenting a further obstacle to the conduct of international trials.

One of the biggest challenges facing management teams of U.S.-based pharmaceutical clinical trials is cultural variation. When developing informed consent forms for a clinical trial run under a U.S.-IND (Investigational New Drug), teams must incorporate key elements. Two of these elements are the inclusion of all possible side effects of the study medication and the use of easily understood language. In a large part of the world, however, physicians administer consent verbally and may be opposed to the U.S. guidelines for informed consent. This opposition is based on the fear that subjects might decide not to participate in the trial if provided with clearly delineated potential risks.

The monitoring activities that help the trial sites maintain good clinical practice and ensure subject safety are essential to a pharmaceutical trial. The FDA requires that pharmaceutical companies send trained professionals to the sites to ensure that GCPs and subject safety are maintained and to collect the data for analysis by the pharmaceutical company. In the U.S., most clinical sites employ clinical coordinators who handle the data recording and data entry. In many countries, the principal investigators will oversee the data recording and data entry themselves, which often forces the company's monitors to assume some of the roles of the clinical coordinators.

Time lines are a critical component to the management of any clinical trial, but may be a more important issue in pharmaceutical studies. It is often essential to meet tight goals for data collection and data cleaning. In today's market, companies have competitive goals to meet new challenges when working with international study sites. The time differences between the U.S. and other countries can present a logistical issue when sites attempt to communicate. The management team must be aware of these differences and plan their communications accordingly. For example, the summer months are often difficult times to communicate with certain European countries, and problems may occur if a critical time line coincides with a summer month. It is common for people to take vacations of up to four weeks at a time that can interfere with many study activities, such as subjects attending scheduled protocol-mandated visits or investigators for the company being able to visit the sites to monitor and collect the data.

The final challenge common to the conduct of international pharmaceutical clinical trials is the consideration of language. Communication between the U.S. management team and the international sites has the potential to be limited due to language differences, although it is not uncommon for the clinical site's staff members to speak English. All relevant study documents, including data collection tools, informed consent forms, instructions for the study subjects, and subject diary cards must be translated into the countries' languages. Often, a country will have more than one official language, presenting additional considerations. Study documents, including the informed consent form, might need to be translated by a certified translator, adding additional cost to a study.

ADDRESSING CHALLENGES TO THE CONDUCT
OF MULTICENTER INTERNATIONAL CLINICAL TRIALS

Subject Recruitment and Data Collection

One of the challenges in the design process of international clinical trials
is ensuring proper representation of subjects from all countries being
studied to achieve adequate subject recruitment quotas through carefully
planned data collection strategies. The significance of meeting adequate
subject representation obviously varies among studies, however. Walker
and colleagues (2001) pointed out that when, for example, global HIV
surveillance studies are conducted, data from one or more countries are
often not included in the analyses. This is sometimes a result of variations
in the ability to access sufficient numbers, particularly in rural areas. Also,
these types of studies often encounter difficulty due to distinctions in the
quality of the data collected, as many countries may be working hard to
quickly improve their data collection systems in order to meet the study
demands but face problems of decreased quality due to financial hardships.
For example, good collection systems were in place in Madagascar and
Lesotho, but limited financial resources and other restrictions resulted in
no data being collected during the designated time period. For the same
reason, countries like Namibia and Zambia were reduced to collecting data
only every two years in the surveillance studies.

Ditunno (2001) discussed challenges to conducting multicenter trials
with the example of studies addressing spinal cord injuries. In the several
studies examined, it was noted that if the trial lasted longer than three
months, half of the study participants decided not to continue. Issues such
as the complexity of a trial and staff enthusiasm toward subjects in the
control group are influential in subjects' decisions to continue participation,
potentially leading to overrepresentation of one of the subject groups. In
addition, modifications in hospital procedures can occur that will have an
impact on the design of the trial. All of these issues must be taken into
account, if at all possible, during the planning phase for clinical trials.
Mechanisms also need to be developed for tracking these factors across
the length of the study, particularly in international studies in which the
impact could slow progress.

Torgerson, Arlinger, Kappi, and Sjostrom (2001) described the challenges of large-scale trials with reference to the XENDOS study, a multicenter Swedish study designed to evaluate a study drug used in the prevention

of diabetes and obesity. According to the investigators, meeting recruitment expectations within the planned time frame was one of the biggest obstacles. The investigators pointed out that it was often necessary to include plans to overestimate the number of subjects available, particularly if inclusion and exclusion criteria clearly limited the available pool of potential subjects. In the XENDOS study, the goal of recruiting over 3,000 subjects across the course of only a few months was achieved, in part by utilizing a centralized recruitment strategy, which included centralized advertising. Another identified limitation to this study included the necessity for manual rescheduling of subjects due to the lack of computer support. Again, strategies for obtaining the best results in terms of subject recruitment and data collection must be incorporated into the study design, with the goal of making the most of available local resources.

Financial Considerations

Without sufficient financial support, no clinical trial would be able to meet its research study goals. Conducting multicenter international clinical trials requires that certain financial considerations be addressed both before the initiation of the trial and throughout the study period. This is even a larger issue in trials specifically designed to evaluate financial implications of interventions. Sullivan and colleagues (2001) examined the cost effectiveness of an early intervention for asthma based on data obtained from a multinational clinical trial. To date, no consensus exists as to how economic data from a multinational clinical trial should be collected and analyzed. For example, one of the challenges noted in determining the cost effectiveness of a medical intervention is the decision of whether to aggregate the costs over the different countries, as relative costs will often vary from one country to another. Because unit costs for health care are likely to differ between countries, these authors recommend that complicated cost estimates be obtained as part of any preliminary analyses.

Dickert and Grady (1999) discussed the issue of payment for research participants and its ethical impact on clinical research. For many years, subjects have been paid for their participation in certain clinical trials; this was one way to recruit subjects to participate. To many, this may be seen as a coercive act that presents the risk of undermining the investigator–subject relationship. Therefore, it could be argued that under no circumstances should subjects be paid to participate in clinical research. If an investigator can reconcile this issue and chooses to provide financial compensation to subjects, three possible payment models have been recommended by Dickert and Grady (1999). The first is the market model, in which subjects would be paid a large sum of money for participation in trials in which no other benefit is expected to occur from study participation. In the wage-payment model, subjects would be paid a lesser amount, commensurate with a standard hourly rate, with some increases in money for procedures that are viewed as uncomfortable or burdensome. In the reimbursement model, a subject is only reimbursed for the expenses incurred by participating in the trial, such as travel and meals. When considering the payment of subjects on an international level, investigators must consider cultural norms, as money has different meanings in different parts of the world, particularly under the unique conditions of participating in clinical research trials.

Use of Surveillance Research Strategies

The purpose of surveillance studies is to gather information and make judgments about diseases in certain regions of the world, or in the entire world. Epidemiological surveillance has been defined by the WHO as "the ongoing and systematic collection, analysis, and interpretation of health data in the process of describing and monitoring a health event" (Walker et al., 2001, p. 1545). Investigators who embark on the conduct of an international multisite research study can gain key insights into the complexities involved by examining various examples of surveillance research studies.

Schwartsmann (2001) discussed the surveillance of breast cancer incidences throughout South America. Statistical analyses were conducted based on the division of South America into two geographic regions: tropical and temperate. The breast cancer incidence between the two regions varied considerably, which has major implications for determining priorities for designing subsequent phases of the research. In situations in which scientists are faced with competing financial priorities to develop studies pertaining to specific health problems, the implication of higher versus lower incidences based on geographic analyses could provide additional justification for where to focus initial work.

Another surveillance initiative is the current Pregnancy Registry for the purpose of monitoring outcomes of prenatal exposure to four drugs manufactured by a major pharmaceutical company (Glaxo Wellcome) throughout the world (Reiff-Eldridge et al., 2000). A pregnancy registry serves to provide registration and the availability of follow-up data to observe the teratogenicity of certain medications. Although overall management lies within the Worldwide Epidemiology Department of the company, each country utilizes local operating companies to help register and follow up with any exposure to these drugs during pregnancy that occurs outside the United States. It is important to note that as these pregnancy registries are designed, there are no control populations of women not exposed to the specific drugs (Reiff-Eldridge et al., 2000). However, the registries are useful for compiling safety signals contributing to the development of a broader safety monitoring program for use in subsequent studies. Viewing this benefit of surveillance studies as an interim step within a multiphase research agenda may be useful to those investigators engaged in studies in which prior knowledge of central safety issues is paramount. It should be noted, however, that while developing the registries is very labor intensive, subject participation is still completely voluntary, with missing information a common problem. How to make use of the data obtained while accurately acknowledging the relative impact of the missing data may well become a major challenge to investigators. Again, accounting for this reality at the onset is important for long-term planning of subsequent phases of the research program.

Another arena in which the conduct of surveillance studies can provide information applicable to other types of international multisite studies is in the research addressing management of world-wide infection. Masterton (2000) stated that this type of surveillance "really acts to monitor the progress of resistance genes as they are expressed in, and transmitted through, various populations of microbes" (pp. 53–54). In the long term, surveillance of antimicrobial susceptibility exists to improve treatment quality in the community and hospital, enhance the development of policies surrounding antimicrobial susceptibility, and provide education for those in the public who use antimicrobials. For these goals to be met, it is essential that communication among the surveillance networks at both the regional and national levels be effective. In addition, the surveillance program must incorporate quality assurance plans to ensure that the data will be accurate and of good quality. According to Masterton, the surveillance programs with the most overall benefit will be the ones that are well planned and integrated on an international, national, and institutional level, and that are completed in a timely fashion.

The concept of data safety and quality monitoring plans has moved to the forefront in the U.S. with all NIH grants requiring specific plans to accompany submission. All Phase III clinical trials require data management and monitoring boards. Institutional review boards throughout the U.S. have developed broad guidelines, but this remains a high priority design consideration dependent on level of patient risk and type of study variables, as well as differences in patient populations throughout various countries and regions in the world. Investigators from an antenatal WHO study involving 53 clinical units in Cuba, Argentina, Thailand, and Saudi Arabia described components that were viewed as important to monitoring a large-scale study that included logistics, protocol compliance, efficacy, and subject safety (Bergsjo, Breart, & Morabia, 1998). A committee composed of members with expertise in biostatistics, epidemiology, and the clinical field relevant to the trial (in this case, obstetrics), was assembled with the responsibility to obtain full access and review of interim trial data. The committee was responsible at the start of the study for determining with the investigators if there should be criteria for stopping the trial. In addition, the adopted data collection and management procedures were examined, followed by receipt and review of monthly reports of recruitment and individual summary reports of adverse events, such as maternal death, fetal death, and cases of eclampsia. Another important addition was a review of routines for shipping data from the study centers to the central unit to ensure that the information collected was sufficient for comparative purposes.

Data Management Issues

Like other aspects of an international multisite study, the data management system should be carefully planned before data collection commences. If possible, scheduled trial runs should be performed for streamlining of the system using at least one or more sites, with particular emphasis on those sites with the most complicated procedural issues. Broadly, two types of systems can be constituted: either a centralized or a decentralized system. In a centralized system, processing at the site level is minimal such that individual site coordinators are responsible for collecting data forms and ensuring completeness. A procedure for delivery of all data forms to a central data processing location is organized where forms are verified; data are recorded into proper databases; and validation, including an accounting of missing data, additions, and modifications, is performed. For the process to run smoothly, an effective communication system (electronic mail, scheduled mailings, or even hand delivery) should exist between the designated personnel at the sites and the central data processing center. In contrast, in a decentralized system, data are made ready for analysis at the respective sites. In international studies where forms are printed and coded in different local languages, a decentralized system can be useful. With this approach, the data conflicts can be resolved quickly, but there will still need to be a clearly understood and uniform standard among all the sites. Training prior to the start of the study is crucial to clarify these procedures and to teach the use of various computer software and hardware. All sites should conform to the same procedure.

Investigators from the WHO Antenatal Trial (Pinol, Bergel, Chaisiri, & Gandeh, 1998) highlighted their use of "country data coordinating centers (CDCC)" as part of a decentralized system in this large study (p. 143). All operations on data, including additions or modifications, were performed using transaction processing files sent to the trial coordinating center in Geneva. Transaction files were used in interim data entry involving a verification process, whereby the data were entered twice, and values not matching the values of the first entries were flagged for correction by the data entry operator. At the end of this process, the transaction files were validated following rules for acceptable ranges of values for variables and verification of consistency between variables. The stated advantages of a transaction-based system were considered twofold. First, all additions or corrections of data to a form master file could be documented. Second, when a serious computer hardware breakdown occurred, the system was reloaded onto a new machine and study master files were easily re-created.

Use of the decentralized data management model was recommended if the CDCCs had available competent and experienced staff. A useful strategy to ensure accuracy was to organize a workshop before the start of the trial to present the system to each of the four participating countries. Annual site visits were used to monitor progress and additional visits were made to satellite sites when major or critical problems could not be solved by the CDCC.

According to Pinol and colleagues (1998), an advantage of the centralized data management model might be minimization of costs. However, good communication between the different sites is considered essential. A decentralized model in developing countries could be possible, however, due to lower costs of running a CDCC. The benefits, risks, and requirements of the two systems should be thoroughly examined before adopting one or the other for a study. Special attention is to be paid at the site level to missing data and attrition. Regular assessment of these is needed and proper remedial measure is to be taken. For example, if some items are confusing to the participants at a particular site then they may be reworded for clarity and ideally this should be done at a trial run. Also, if there are some subjects who do not respond to certain items or who decline to participate, several types of action may be taken. If the problem can be identified by a set of demographic or social characteristics, special effort may be given to recruitment and interviewing procedures.

An option at the time of analysis is to impute the missing data using a modeling technique (Little & Rubin, 1987). If utilized, proper planning is needed. Additional items or information in the background question-naires or tracking system might have to be added to allow efficient use of those techniques.

Statistical Analysis Considerations

There are a number of very important statistical issues that need close consideration in a multisite project, particularly at an international level. Proper planning prior to the start of the study, from a general scientific as well as from a statistical standpoint, is crucial for successful and timely completion of the study. Coordination and monitoring are typically chal-lenging when sites are located across the globe. Weak or flawed designs can necessitate changes in the study plan. Such changes may not be imple-mented in a timely manner and are potentially disruptive and costly. A good statistical design will lead to an efficient analysis without the burden of additional strain on resources. Choice of design should depend on efficiency aspects, cost, and any other identified constraints. Investigators may try to maximize efficiency within a given budget or, given a minimum acceptable level of efficiency, try to minimize cost. For most situations, the latter approach is used because it ensures a minimum predetermined level of precision. For example, in an estimation problem, one can fix the maximum length of the confidence interval and then determine the design parameters.

As with any research study, but particularly in multisite designs with considerable site to site variation in data, researchers need to be aware of the underlying assumptions and limitations of statistical procedures. There are some actions one can take when there is an indication of departure from model assumptions. Remedial measures can be adopted. Robust statistical analysis can be used or a general procedure that does not require such assumptions may be sought. With the advent of economical, but powerful computing facilities, an increasing number of newer techniques have be-come available to accomplish this. One of the most common methods used to address pertinent research questions is classical linear modeling. However, violation of necessary assumptions in a linear model analysis can be a serious impediment to the validity of the inference. For multiple linear regression, there are well-known results that can be used as remedial measures. For example, if the error term is not normally distributed, one may try suitable transformation of the dependent variable using the Box-Cox procedure, use results from robust methods, or use a different distribution for the error term eg. Gamma. These options are available in some of the statistical packages, like STATA (Hamilton, 2002; Hardin & Hilbe, 2001; Neter, Wasserman, & Kutner, 1990).

During the exploratory phase of the analysis, all the diagnostic procedures should be conducted to detect any of the common violations. Investigators need to keep in mind that the very nature of international multisite studies will often result in problems related to statistical test violations. These include: heteroschedasticity (nonconstancy of error variance); presence of non-ignorable intra-class correlation; and nonconstancy of slopes in an analysis of a covariance-like setup. For example, study outcome variances are likely to vary across international sites with significant intra-class correlation. Fortunately, there are various methodologies available now that are equipped to deal with these types of problems and provide correct and efficient analysis. These have been implemented in various statistical software packages. However, in some cases, different terminologies are used. For example, SAS now has a well-developed procedure on Mixed Model Analysis. There are also some special software packages that were specifically developed for such analysis including MIXREG/MIXOR, computer program designed for mixed-effects linear/ordinal regression analysis (Hedekar, 1994) or hierarchical linear model (HLM), which can analyze continuous or dichotomous data, count data, multinomial data or ordinal data (Bryk & Raudenbush, 1992).

Multisite studies, like a single site study, will benefit from a good sampling plan composed of an appropriate group assignment system. Adequate information on sampling frame such as census tract information, for example, from which units are to be drawn, should be available for proper implementation of a sampling scheme. This can be challenging in international studies because information on frames may not be available or may not be comparable among sites.

Survey data need to be analyzed using special techniques because in general, simple random sampling based techniques will generally not be applicable. For example, it could be a multi-stage sampling with stratification. Sampling can occur without replacement and with equal, or even unequal probability. Variance expression for the estimates can be quite complicated and sometimes will require the use of computer intensive methods like bookstrap. Appropriate analysis programs for dealing with complex survey data are available in a statistical software package called SUDAAN. Few other general packages like, SAS and Stata (Hamilton, 2002) also contain some basic analysis for survey data.

Often, researchers are interested in stratified analysis to achieve proportionate representation from various groups to gain better generalizability of the findings. However, in some cases, investigators will need to take into account the necessity for oversampling in certain stratum to enable these analyses. Well-planned choices of site locations in a multisite study will, of course, be helpful in this regard and minimize the risk for selection bias. For example, in a heart failure study where race will be an important factor, sites can be chosen in a country or region based on census tract information providing racial breakdowns. Choosing tracts with a higher percentage of Blacks or Asians, for example, would then ensure more adequate representation.

Stratification is also a tool to manage the problem of confounding. It may be the case in a certain multisite intervention study that it is desirable to maintain the same proportions in the corresponding strata within the various intervention groups. Therefore, if there are two groups, control and treatment, and sex is a confounding variable, an appropriate randomization technique sample would ensure 50% representation from each sex category in the groups.

When there are several confounding variables or intervention groups in a multisite study, the randomization process can become more complex and a computer-based system will need to be developed to enable use of a minimization algorithm. For example, suppose a heart failure study has 6 sites and 3 stratification variables: a) sex (2 categories), b) age group (3 categories) and c) race (4 categories) within 2 treatment groups. It will be extremely difficult, if not impossible, to manually assign subjects in the two groups following a randomization algorithm such that the proportion of subjects in each strata adheres to a predetermined value. Since the system will need to be a real time assignment process, a centralized computer based system will be essential.

Some research questions need to be based on longitudinal or panel data. Longitudinal studies involving the conduct of multiple assessment with the same subjects over the study period often do no satisfy all conditions of repeated measures analysis of variance. In general, the number of time points and times of measurement can vary from subject to subject. Moreover, if data from multiple sites are collected, it is likely that assumptions of independent errors for any two subjects will be violated because of potential intraclass correlations among the site members.

Computer-based methods are now available for conducting general longitudinal analysis (Diggle, Liang, & Zeger, 1994) or for studies with more than one site (Murray, 1998). Investigators should take advantage of these recent developments that are now part of many common statistical software packages such as Statistical Analysis System (SAS version 8) (Hamilton, 2002) and need not feel restricted by the conditions of classical linear models. In addition, if considered important, information on geographical distribution of the sites can also be considered using an appropriate spatial statistics model (Christensen, 2001). In spatial models, correlation between the two units depends on the physical distance between them. These models have wide application in epidemiological, ecological, and geological studies.

Statistical study designs can be relatively flexible, but attention needs to be paid to various design aspects before the study begins depending on the analysis to be conducted. In a longitudinal study, for example, if it is important to investigate the individual trend for an outcome, even in case of a linear trend, the outcome should be measured at a minimum of three time points in order to meet the conditions of a general hierarchical linear model (HLM) analysis (Bryk & Raudenbush, 1992). This is due to the fact that direct modeling of individual change is done at the lowest (person) level requiring at least two measurements. If there are only two observations per subject, there will be no degrees of freedom left to estimate intra-subject error variance for the linear model at the subject level, even in the simplest cases where a common variance is assumed for all subjects. So, if the study design does not have at least three time points, an HLM analysis is not possible without additional assumptions or imposing some constraints. In many instances, for example, a simple linear trend model with constant variance will not suffice. It would then be possible to incorporate various complex structures into the error variance.

Various forms of error structures that can be specified include the determination of person specific variances or the errors, autocorrelation, or the error variance can depend on a group characteristic such as age. In these cases, even more time points per subject will be needed. Judicious selection of the observation time points can lead to an increased efficiency in analysis which may be of great importance when conducting time-consuming and expensive international multisite studies. For linear individual growth models with a common error variance, four or more outcome measurements per subject are desirable and for polynomial growth curve model or for complex individual level error structures, time points per subject will have to be increased accordingly. It should be noted that when it is also possible to select the intervals between time points, that is, how far apart the observations for each individual will be, there can be some added benefit to the analysis (Diggle et al., 1998). Suppose, for example, that there are 3 time points in the study plan over a 3-year period. A typical choice for the time intervals might be: baseline, 1-year and 2-year with an equal amount of time gap (1 year) between each consecutive assessment. However, there may be some advantages in terms of statistical efficiency if the time points are chosen as baseline, 1-year and 2 years provided that this approach does not hinder any other aspect, scientific or administrative, of the study (Diggle et al., 1998).

As with all studies, another important step in the statistical planning process, is the assurance of adequate power to perform the designated statistical tests in the proposed analysis. Attrition can be particularly problematic in longitudinal study designs with several time points. Power analysis involves determination of the sample size, while estimating possible attrition, so that all the hypotheses can be tested for effect sizes chosen a priori, with sufficient level of power (Hedeker, Gibbons, & Waternaux, 1999). It is not possible to draw any inferences if a testing procedure with inadequate power fails to reject a hypothesis. On the other hand, although it may be tempting to oversample in the presence of a large and available subject pool, extremely high levels of power are also undesirable. Tests detecting small effect sizes with no practical or clinical significance can be misleading. A commonly accepted norm is to select the minimum sample size that is sufficient for at least 80% and not more than 95% power to detect the desired effect size.

Attention should be given to correlation among error terms and to any potential intraclass correlations. For longitudinal studies, observations on an individual subject will generally be correlated and there are several ways in which the variance structure can be modeled. Compound symmetric (covariance matrix with equal variances and equal covariances) or autoregressive (covariance matrix with equal variances and geometrically diminishing covariances depending on the difference between the time points) techniques serve as a reasonable choice in many situations, but other forms are also available. Tests can fail to attain the minimum detection power if the presence of intraclass correlation is ignored. When division by groups is used, subjects from the same group may have some degree of intraclass correlation. For example, subjects from the same site may share some common characteristic and their responses can be more similar than those of subjects from a different site. Even the presence of apparently small intraclass correlation can necessitate a substantial increase in the sample size. For example, consider a simple prepost study of the proportions of drug users in the treatment group (5% projected) versus the control group (10%). Investigators will want to know how many sites and subjects will be needed. If intraclass correlation is assumed to be 0.01, then 8 sites with 300 subjects will be required. However, if the intraclass correlation can be assumed to be 0.001, only 4 sites with 300 subjects will be needed. The number of subjects required will, therefore, be reduced by half depending on if the level of intraclass correlation is 0.01 or 0.001. Whenever possible, the number of subjects predicted per site and the number of sites in the study should always be predetermined to maximize power (Murray, 1998).

EXAMPLE OF AN INTERNATIONAL MULTISITE COMPARATIVE DESIGN STUDY

The purpose of this study was to explore the differences in postpartum depressive symptomatology (PPDS) among nine different cohorts of women to comprise an international sample from selected countries on five continents (North America: United States; South America: Guyana; western Europe: Italy, Sweden, Finland; Asia: Korea, Taiwan, India; and Australia) (Affonso, De, Horowitz, & Mayberry, 2000). Three research questions were addressed: (1) What differences, if any, in PPDS level existed among the selected country samples? (2) What degree of change in PPDS level occurred from 4–6 to 10–12 weeks postpartum? (3) What degree of concordance existed between the Edinburgh Postnatal Depression Scale (EPDS) and the Beck Depression Inventory (BDI) in measuring levels of PPDS? (Beck, Ward, Mendelson, Mock, & Erbaugh, 1961; Cox, Holden, & Sagovsky, 1983). The research team viewed this study as an opportunity to expand on the numerous international single-site studies that have resulted in published data on this phenomenon, and to obtain a global comparison of outcomes using a combination of quantitative and qualitative methods in one multisite study within the constraints of a limited budget.

Convenience samples of postpartum women were recruited from each country at a hospital, clinic, or home setting where women received standard postpartum care. With the wide variations in the type of care during the early weeks of postpartum in different parts of the world, the decision to open recruitment and encourage participation from women receiving care in either clinic or home settings increased the likelihood of accessing subjects. As with any study, the investigator needs to balance the impact of dissimilar data collection settings versus other factors that could have the potential of significantly affecting the study outcomes. For a study of this type designed for the primary purpose of obtaining comparative data across diverse populations, a convenience sample using this approach was considered appropriate.

The designated sample size from each country site was to include a minimum of 50 and a maximum of 100 women to participate in initial assessments, and to acquire a minimum of 50% sample returns for the second assessment. Since analyses were contingent upon a minimum total sample size of 450 women in the first assessment and 225 in the second (power analysis of analysis of variance [ANOVA] procedure demonstrated that a sample of 225 would be adequate to reveal a moderate effect size (f = 0.263) at a .05 level of significance and power of 0.8), recruitment of subjects allowed variations in the nine cohorts of women from the different country sites. We anticipated the difficulty in obtaining large samples, given the restricted time period allowed for the conduct of this study (approximately 36 months) and minimal financial resources available for investigator and subject incentives to participate. In particular, certain countries relied on mail returns of the questionnaires, and thus had lower sample cohorts at the second assessment than those that included personal contact with women at both assessment times.

Subjects completed the EPDS and BDI questionnaires initially at 4–6 weeks and again at 10–12 weeks postpartum. Each woman completed the same questionnaires twice, providing a total of four sets of scores per subject. Site investigators in each country were nurses, psychologists, or social workers and were responsible for recruiting subjects, obtaining informed consent, and administering questionnaires by mail or in person. Frequent communication among site coordinators is an important strategy for problem solving, but investigators also need to consider what level of professional should be involved as a site coordinator. We accepted a wide variation, based on the unusual circumstances for choosing the sites. Countries were selected based on two factors concerning the site investigators: (1) they had participated in a biennial International Conference (Fifth International Conference of Maternity Nurse Researchers, 1994) that focused on maternity-nursing research inclusive of PPDS, or (2) they had prior collaborative research encounters with one of the study's authors. Researchers from 15 countries indicated interest in participating. All potential sites were evaluated according to the following criteria: (1) availability of a qualified nurse or other researcher to serve as the country's site investigator to oversee the study, (2) ability of the site investigator to recruit the designated subjects, and (3) access to obstetrical services and resources necessary to fulfill the goals of the study. Nine countries met the criteria with sites at Boston and San Jose, United States; Georgetown, Guyana; Rome, Italy; Stockholm, Sweden; Helsinki, Finland; Seoul, South Korea; Taipei, Taiwan; Calcutta, India; and Queensland, Australia.

Key issues that must be addressed in designing and implementing multisite international studies that were presented earlier in this chapter and in other chapters in this book, also applied to this study. These include clear preplanning with generous time lines built in whenever possible in anticipation of delays, a designated communication structure between the principal investigators and all the individual research site coordinators, and approval of protocols and consent mechanisms by institutional review boards. Investigators should keep in mind that other issues can also have an impact on the data collection procedures. For example, variations in recognition of a health care problem among country sites can occur, particularly when the goal is to measure psychological variables such as depression symptoms. Explanation of the study's potential significance may therefore require more preparation in some settings than in others. Obtaining demographic information is typically viewed as straightforward, but with international studies in which multiethnic and multicultural subjects are involved, certain factors need to be examined more closely. Standard categories such as marital status may not be adequate in depicting the full range of possible relationships and partnerships that should be delineated in the study. In this study, for example, Sweden had more than one category for cohabitation.

Managing distances is not always easy. Not everyone has electronic mail access. It is easier if someone on the central team is familiar with the site. For example, in our study we found it helpful for one of our coinvestigators, who was a native of India, to be responsible for all direct communications with the site coordinator from Calcutta because he was familiar with typical health care system issues and cultural mores. Investigators need to be aware of the variations in local communities, particularly when the frequency of potential subject contacts can change considerably, even from day to day. Capturing unique features of these settings and, with permission, the subjects themselves, through photo images, is recommended and may be particularly important when interpreting and presenting study results from multiethnic and multicultural populations.

Initial and ongoing communications with the site coordinators were maintained through written (procedural tasks delineated in written documents) and verbal-electronic (telephone and e-mail) communications with each site investigator primarily addressing interpretation of written instructions, answering questions pertaining to each country site in the monitoring and tracking of procedures for data collection, and explaining preparation of data files that were sent directly to a designated team member for data analyses. We learned that having the same contact was important, but a designated back-up person, so that someone was always available on demand, was helpful, particularly for those sites in which this was the first collaborative research project. If a site coordinator had a question, we made the assumption that others might be similarly perplexed by the content of written correspondences, so we often passed the question and answer on to each of the other site coordinators as follow-up. This strategy served to increase the number of contacts with each individual site coordinator and helped to set the tone for the high level of responsiveness from the central team members that we wanted them all to anticipate.

In terms of continuity in data collection methods, specific variations among sites may be acceptable. For example, in our study, the interview method was adopted in Guyana and India to obtain participants' responses to the questionnaires because this approach was judged by the respective site investigators to be the most reliable and efficient way of collecting data. The other sites relied on questionnaire mail returns after the initial informed consent was obtained. At all but two of the sites (United States and Australia), questionnaires were translated from English to the dominant language spoken at those sites. If a translated version was not available, site investigators followed a process of translation and back translation, that is, from English to the local language and from the local language back to English, to ensure proper translation of the questionnaires. At selected sites, translated versions of the tools existed where BDI or EPDS use was common. We relied on published findings that demonstrated validity of these two questionnaires in eight of our designated country sites.

In multisite comparative studies, we also recommend consideration to developing a qualitative arm of the study as an important approach toward gaining a broader understanding of the full cross-cultural context underlying certain phenomena. In each of the original nine countries, focus groups were convened for the purpose of eliciting categories of depressive symptoms and their perceived meanings through content analysis of the dialogues (Horowitz, Chang, Das, & Hayes, 2001). Instead of sending the U.S. principal research investigators to the sites (desirable, but cost prohibitive), we found that involving native group leaders as facilitators turned out to be a clear strength of the study because of their ability to secure access to potential participants. In addition, the group leaders were integral both to the initial coding phase of the content analysis, in which key words and phrases were interpreted, and to the final level of coding, in which verification of category labels was achieved with one of the principal investigators.

Finally, we recommend that attention be paid early on to the potential long-term benefits to on-site research coordinators or coinvestigators of participating in an international multisite study. We organized a conference in the United States as a follow-up to the study so that site coordinators had an opportunity to meet and discuss the findings with each other. Future collaborations were discussed and linkages formed among those interested in sharing in the publication process both at the local and international level.

THE FUTURE

As communication and free trade continue to explode during the twenty-first century, countries around the world will become more and more dependent upon each other, both socially and economically. We are becoming a global and technological society that is ever expanding. Researchers are being challenged to develop and implement research projects on a larger scale and across international lines. As technology advances, researchers will have to be flexible, as these new technologies will be the key to the efficient management of clinical trials on an international plane. Pharmaceutical research studies are likely to continue playing a vital role in fostering the type of relationships required to develop complex research studies among countries (Shih, 2001).

It is clear that the study of populations in developing countries has become a heated issue, one that needs constant revisiting. In particular, multisite clinical trials designed to study HIV can be seen as a new frontier in research, as this disease process is quite young in both the medical and research areas. Researchers will need to become ever more sensitive to the ethical considerations that arise from such a pervasive and worldwide health/illness phenomenon.

Davidoff and colleagues (2001) stated: "Clinical trials are powerful tools; like all powerful tools, they must be used with great care. They allow investigators to test biological hypotheses on living patients, and they have the potential to change the standards of care" (p. 1178). With the advent of increasing numbers of international studies, attention to the various aspects of conducting well-designed multisite projects, as presented in this chapter, will be essential to changing and improving health care around the world.

REFERENCES

Affonso, D. D., De, A., Horowitz, J. A., & Mayberry, L. J. (2000). An international study exploring levels of postpartum depressive symptomatology. *Journal of Psychosomatic Research, 49,* 207–216.

Angell, M. (1997). The ethics of clinical research in the third world. *The New England Journal of Medicine, 337,* 847–849.

Angell, M. (2000). Investigators' responsibilities for human subjects in developing countries. *The New England Journal of Medicine, 342,* 967–969.

Annas, G. J., & Grodin, M. A. (1998). Human rights and maternal-fetal HIV transmission prevention trials in Africa. *American Journal of Public Health, 88,* 560–563.

Bayer, R. (1998). The debate over maternal-fetal HIV transmission prevention trials in Africa, Asia, and the Caribbean: Racist exploitation or exploitation of racism? *American Journal of Public Health, 88,* 567–570.

Beck, A. T., Ward, C. H., Mendelson, M., Mock, J., & Erbaugh, J. (1961). An inventory for measuring depression. *Archives of General Psychiatry, 4,* 561–569.

Bergsjo, P., Breart, G., & Morabia, A. (1998). Monitoring data and safety in the WHO antenatal care trial. *Paedatric and Perinatal Epidemiology, 12*(Suppl. 2), 156–164.

Bryk, A. S., & Raudenbush, S. W. (1992). *Hierarchical linear models: Applications and data analysis methods.* Newbury Park, CA: Sage.

Christensen, R. (2001). *Advanced linear modeling: Multivariate, time series, and spatial data* (2nd ed.). New York: Springer.

Cox, J. L., Holden, J. M., & Sagovsky, R. (1983). Detection of postnatal depression: Development of the 10-item Edinburgh Postnatal Depression Scale. *British Journal of Psychiatry, 150,* 782–786.

Davidoff, F., DeAngelis, C. D., Drazen, J. M., Hoey, J., Hojgaard, L., Horton, R., Kotzin, S., Nicholls, M. G., Nylenna, M., Overbeke, A. J. P. M., Sox, H. C., Van Der Weyden, M. B., & Wilkes, M. S. (2001). Sponsorship, authorship, and accountability. *Archives of Otolaryngology—Head & Neck Surgery, 127,* 1178–1180.

Dickert, N., & Grady, C. (1999). What's the price of a research subject? Approaches to payment for research participation. *The New England Journal of Medicine, 341,* 198–203.

Diggle, P., Liang, K. Y., & Zeger, S. L. (1994). *Analysis of longitudinal data.* Oxford, UK: Clarendon.

Ditunno, J. F. (2001). Multicenter clinical trials to establish the benefit of early intervention in spinal cord injury. *American Journal of Physical Medicine & Rehabilitation, 80,* 713–716.

European Agency for the Evaluation of Medicinal Products. (2002). Retrieved August 23, 2002 from *http://www.emea.eu.int*

Fifth International Conference of Maternity Nurse Researchers. (1994). *Vision of Childbearing Women's Health.* Waikoloa: Hawaii.

Hamilton, L. C. (2002). *Statistics with stata: Updated for version 7.* Duxbury, MA: Duxbury.

Hardin, J., & Hilbe, J. (2001). *Generalized linear models and extensions.* College Station, TX: Stata.

Hedeker, D., & Gibbons, R. D. (1994). A random-effects ordinal regression model for multilevel analysis. *Biometrics, 50,* 933–944.

Hedeker, D., Gibbons, R. D., & Waternaux, C. (1999). Sample size estimation for longitudinal designs with attrition: Comparing time-related contrasts between two groups. *Journal of Educational & Behavioral Statistics, 24,* 70–93.

Horowitz, J. A., Chang, S., Das, S., & Hayes, B. (2001). Women's perceptions of postpartum depressive symptoms from an international perspective. *International Nursing Perspectives, 1,* 5–14.

Little, R. J. A., & Rubin, D. B. (1987). *Statistical analysis with missing data.* New York: Wiley.

Lurie, P., & Wolfe, S. M. (1997). Unethical trials of interventions to reduce perinatal transmission of the human immunodeficiency virus in developing countries. *The New England Journal of Medicine, 337,* 853–856.

Masterton, R. G. (2000). Surveillance studies: How can they help the management of infection? *Journal of Antimicrobial Chemotherapy, 46,* 53–58.

Murray, D. (1998). *Design and analysis of group-randomized trials.* New York: Oxford University Press.

National Commission for the Protection of Human Subjects of Biomedical and Behavioral Research. (1988). *Belmont report: Ethical principles and guidelines for the protection of human subjects of research* (GPO 887-809). Washington, DC: U.S. Government Printing Office.

Neter, J., Wasserman, W., & Kutner, M. H. (1990). *Applied linear statistical models: Regression, analysis of variance, and experimental designs.* Homewood, IL: Irwin.

Pinol, A., Bergel, K., Chaisiri, E. D., & Gandeh, M. (1998). Managing data for a randomized controlled clinical trial: Experience from the WHO Antenatal Care Trial. *Paediatric and Perinatal Epidemiology, 12*(Suppl. 2), 142–155.

Reiff-Eldridge, R., Heffner, C. R., Ephross, S. A., Tennis, P. S., White, A. D., & Andrews, E. B. (2000). Monitoring pregnancy outcomes after prenatal drug exposure through prospective pregnancy registries: A pharmaceutical company commitment. *American Journal of Obstetrics & Gynecology, 182,* 159–163.

Schwartsmann, G. (2001). Breast cancer in South America: Challenges to improve early detection and medical management of a public health problem. *Journal of Clinical Oncology, 19,* 118s–124s.

Shih, W. J. (2001). Clinical trials for drug registrations in Asian-Pacific countries: Proposal for a new paradigm from a statistical perspective. *Controlled Clinical Trials, 22,* 357–366.

Sullivan, S. D., Liljas, B., Buxton, M., Lamm, C. J., O'Byrne, P., Tan, W. C., & Weiss, K. B. (2001). Design and analytic considerations in determining the cost-effectiveness of early intervention in asthma from a multinational clinical trial. *Controlled Clinical Trials, 22,* 420–437.

System 2000 Software. (2000). *Product support manual, version 1* (1st ed.). College Station, TX.

Torgerson, J. S., Arlinger, K., Kappi, M., & Sjostrom, L. (2001). Principles for enhanced recruitment of subjects in large clinical trials: The XENDOS study experience. *Controlled Clinical Trials, 22,* 515–525.

Varmus, H., & Satcher, D. (1997). Ethical complexities of conducting research in developing countries. *The New England Journal of Medicine, 337,* 1003–1005.

Walker, N., Garcia-Calleja, J. M., Heaton, L., Asamoah-Odei, E., Poumerol, G., Lazzari, S., Ghys, P. D., Schwartlander, B., & Stanecki, K. A. (2001). Epidemiological analysis of the quality of HIV sero-surveillance in the world: How well do we track the epidemic? *AIDS, 15,* 1545–1554.

Woodman, R. (1999). Storm rages over revisions to Helsinki Declaration. *British Medical Journal, 319,* 660.

World Medical Association. (2000). Declaration of Helsinki: Ethical principles for medical research involving human subjects. 18th World Medical Assembly, Helsinki, Finland. Retrieved August 23, 2002 from *http://www.wma.net/e/policy/17-c_e.html*

II

Lessons Learned From Specific Research Projects

8

Challenges of a Multisite, Multicultural Collaborative Research Endeavor: The Birthweight Study[1]

Jacquelyn C. Campbell, Doris Campbell, Sara Torres, Josephine Ryan, Christine King, and Patricia Price Lea

In October 1985, former Surgeon General C. Everett Koop convened a workshop to address family violence as a health problem. This was the first declaration of what now seems an obvious fact: violence in general (and intimate partner violence particularly) is a health care problem that needs to be addressed by health care research. Of the 62 invited participants at that 1985 workshop, 21 were nurses. Starting at that conference and the first Nursing Network on Violence Against Women International (NNVAWI) conference organized by Christine King later that same year, a small group of beginning nurse researchers began to share ideas. Barbara Parker organized us formally into the Nursing Research Consortium Against Violence and Abuse (NRCVA). There are now 18 members from 16 different universities all over the United States and Canada.[2] The goals of the NRCVA are as follows:

[1]Birth Weight and Battering During Pregnancy: Nursing Analysis of Cultural Influences, National Institute of Nursing Research R01NR02571, J. Campbell, PI.
[2]Current members: Linda Bullock, U Missouri; Doris Campbell, U South FL; Jacquelyn Campbell, JHU; Mary Ann Curry, OHSU; Faye Gary, UFL; Angela Henderson, UBC; Janice Humphreys, UCSF; Judy McFarlane, TWU; Christine King, U MASS Amherst; Karen Landenburger, UWA; Josephine Ryan, U MASS Amherst; Barbara Parker, UVA; Phyllis Sharps, JHU; Daniel Sheridan, JHU; Rachel Rodriguez, U WI; Janette Taylor, U Iowa; Sara Torres, UMDNJ; Yvonne Ulrich, UWA.

- Enhance nursing science on violence against women
- Decrease violence against women and children and/or the deleterious health effects from abuse
- Collaborate with shelters, other organizations, other disciplines, and health care settings in research
- Increase recognition of nursing contributions to science on violence against women
- Conduct culturally competent research
- Include battered women's voices in research
- Use both quantitative and qualitative methods (separately or in combination)

The birthweight study was one of four federally funded (Centers for Disease Control and Prevention [CDC], National Institutes of Health [NIH]) NRCVA research projects (J. C. Campbell, Ryan, et al., 1999). So no one thinks that the group has not had its frustrations, the consortium also submitted two major proposals that have not (yet) been funded. We have tried to include the other NRCVA members informally in the planning and writing of each grant proposal and formally as a named consultative group. We have also tried to increase the cultural diversity of the group; to have a truly collaborative and mutually enhancing work and discussion process; to promote each other's well-being in a variety of ways, including having fun together, writing letters of support, nomination, and recommendation for each other; and to forgive each other's occasional lapses from productivity, meetings, graciousness, and cultural sensitivity. We have not always been successful at either our stated goals or our group process and friendship endeavors. However, we definitely respect each other's work and commitment to the health and safety of women and children and basically like each other a whole lot.

In this chapter, the five coinvestigators on the birthweight study outline what we found to be three of the major challenges of the project: (1) cultural competence in research, (2) multisite research management, and (3) collaborative processes with hospitals and domestic violence shelters. We also outline the major strategies we used to address these challenges and what we found to be most successful.

CULTURAL COMPETENCE IN RESEARCH

In this study it was assured that a culturally sensitive design, data collection, analysis, and dissemination of research were all put into action. We included ethnic/minority researchers in the design, implementation, analysis, and dissemination of research. Sara Torres and Doris Campbell, of Puerto Rican and African-American descent respectively, challenged all of us to make sure that the study would both advance the knowledge related to abuse during pregnancy for women of color and would be culturally sensitive in its conduct. Cultural competence in the conduct of research is crucial if the outcome is to lead to knowledge that guides the provision of culturally competent care.

Investigators need to give serious consideration to the role of cultural factors and avoid assuming that identity with the minority culture is defined by the person's race or surname. Some reliable and valid means of assessing subjects' degree of identification with their own culture greatly enhances the research. Assessing the role of factors such as assimilation, country of origin, and migratory status is important. Equally important to us were our consideration and inclusion of numerous environmental and contextual factors that influence cultural differences and similarities in response to abuse during pregnancy. Dr. Torres was adamant that the sample would not lump all women of "Hispanic" descent together as is so frequently done in research. Based on this premise, we resolved to purposively sample for equal groups of African-American, Anglo, Cuban-American, Mexican-American, and Puerto Rican women. If we had not done so, we would have missed one of the most important findings of our study. The prevalence of abuse during pregnancy was significantly higher for Puerto Rican women than for those of the other Latina ethnic groups (Torres, Campbell, Campbell, Ryan, King, Price, Stallings, Fuchs, & Laude, 2000). We also resolved that there would be enough women in each of the five ethnic groups to do some within group analysis as well as across group analysis. The heterogeneity *within* ethnic groups is as important to explore as any differences related to ethnic group membership.

We discovered the cultural competence framework by Orlandi (1992) (Table 8.1), which was developed for social work practice, but could be adapted for research. Using that as our framework, along with the emancipatory research principles that have been outlined by Henderson (1995) and the goals of NRCVA, we tried to develop and apply tenets of cultural competence in research (Campbell & Campbell, 1996). We resolved that cultural competence had to be part of the entire research process, not just applied to heterogeneity in sampling as required by NIH.

Cultural Competence in the Research Team

In order to achieve cultural competence, the research team must be culturally diverse. There are no strategies that we can think of to substitute for

TABLE 8.1   Cultural Competence Framework

Domain	Culturally Incompetent	Culturally Sensitive	Culturally Competent
Cognitive	Obvious	Aware	Knowledgeable
Affective	Apathetic	Sympathetic	Committed to change
Skills	Unskilled	Lacking some skills	Highly skilled
Overall effect	Destructive	Neutral	Constructive

Adapted from Orlandi, M. A. (1992).

this requirement. This does not mean just hiring research assistants or interviewers of color, although this is part of the process. It is equally important that culturally competent researchers be available to help during the development of culturally appropriate research questions, sampling plans, interviews, and instruments, as well as during the data collection process, and to ensure that data analysis is conducted in a culturally sensitive way. Members of the team have to be full partners and fully qualified researchers (Campbell, Dienemann, Kub, Wurmser, & Loy, 1999). If such persons cannot be recruited, they need to be trained.

One of the strategies we used to increase the diversity of the team was to apply for a minority supplement from the National Institute of Nursing Research (NINR) as soon as the grant was funded. These grants are obtained through the NIH Institute that supports a project and can be used for salary support for a doctoral student or "new" (not more than five years since most recent research training) investigator of minority ethnicity on the project. It is a wonderful mechanism not only to provide research training for a developing nurse-scientist but to enhance the cultural sensitivity of the project in its conduct and interpretation of results and thereby improve the science. The developing scientist also provides needed training in another culture for the other researchers on the project. Additionally, the mechanism adds another brilliant mind and pair of hands to help get the work completed! The coinvestigator we were fortunate enough to recruit to the project using this mechanism was Patricia Price, then a doctoral student at Wayne State University College of Nursing. She provided training in the African-American culture and how it can influence women's responses to battering to the investigators and the research assistants we hired in each site. Dr. Price also helped in every other aspect of the research process from start to finish and was able to use the data collected from African-American women for an independent analysis for her dissertation.

The next major step is for the entire research team to gain in-depth knowledge of the cultures to be included in the research. It is not the responsibility of the members of the research team who belong to a particular culture to provide the knowledge of that culture for the entire team. It is up to each member to search out and find the information from books, videos, training programs, and so forth. The members of the team from that culture can help with complex understanding, but the other members must do the work.

The insights of Patricia Collins (1995) are always useful on this point. She has noted that the majority culture generally knows little about minority cultures, but that members of "minority" ethnic groups have always had to learn carefully about the majority culture in order to survive. We put quotation marks around "minority," recognizing that Anglos are no longer the majority ethnic group in California and will soon no longer be the majority ethnic group in the United States. Another useful insight for members of the majority culture to keep in mind is the extent of their privilege by virtue of the color of their skin and the advantage of their birth. The extent of this privilege is generally invisible to them; rather than recognizing that they were born "on third base," they think they got there by their hard work or by their other attributes. The responsibilities of members of the minority versus majority culture team members are summarized in Table 8.2.

Cultural Competence in Each Stage of the Research Process

The first step in the research process is usually to conduct a literature review. A culturally competent literature review includes examining and critiquing prior research in the area for sample ethnic heterogeneity, ethnic/cultural differences and similarities, and findings relevant to race, ethnicity, and culture. In articles where there are no reported findings related to race, ethnicity, and culture, or the findings are inappropriately analyzed or interpreted, the research needs to be critiqued appropriately. There also needs to be hand searching in journals specific to culture and ethnicity (e.g., *The Journal of the Poor and Underserved* or the *Journal of the National Medical Association* or the *Hispanic Journal of Behavioral Sciences*), which are often not included in electronic databases.

TABLE 8.2   Cultural Responsibilities of "Minority" and Majority Culture
Team Members

"Minority" Culture Team Members	Majority Culture Team Members
• Continue the struggle	• Look for and identify racism when we see it; challenge and educate colleagues
• Recognize good will and excuse well-meaning errors	• Recognize our privilege—that we got to "third base" by way of our birth advantage rather than by virtue or work
• Collaborate when asked, if the collaboration will be with total parity	• Ask for help—for collaboration with respect
• But insist on empowerment as an outcome, remembering the bottom line	• Learn at least one other culture well, including the language (e.g., "Black" English), and customs

Culturally relevant theory and concepts are needed as the theoretical base for the research. Culturally specific theory (such as Leininger's) can be used, or other theory can be made relevant to culture and ethnicity. Culturally relevant concepts such as ethnic identity can be incorporated into other theory.

A careful sampling plan with purposive sampling for diverse ethnic representation is needed for qualitative as well as quantitative studies, although there is a need for some studies within minority cultures in order to make up for prior lack of information within those cultures. It is also necessary to oversample among minority ethnic groups in population-based studies, so that there is sufficient ethnic minority group representation for appropriate analysis. There need to be culturally congruent techniques and settings for sample recruitment.

All instruments to be used for data collection must be carefully evaluated in terms of ethnic and cultural psychometrics including content validity, empirical reliability, and validity evaluations specific to each ethnic group to be surveyed (Porter & Villarruel, 1993). For example, we used the Index of Spouse Abuse (Hudson & McIntosh, 1981) as a measure of physical and emotional abuse. However, we also conducted a study of the reliability and factor structure of this instrument when used with African-American women (D. W. Campbell, Campbell, King, Parker, & Ryan, 1994) because validity and reliability studies previously reported did not include ethnic minority women in the samples, or did not report the race and ethnic makeup of the sample during analysis.

Translation of instruments in populations and languages other than those for which they were developed is based on the assumption that the concepts to be measured are constant, or at least very similar between cultures. Based on this assumption, an instrument could be used just as well with one population as with another. However, that assumption may be faulty. It is important to recognize that the list of symptoms on a self-report instrument and interpretations associated with it are attempts to capture and categorize the ways that people experience or report their experience. The experiences on which most instruments are based are usually of individuals of Euro-American origin. However, different experiences and different languages may engender different manifestations of distress or wellness. The culturally restricted descriptions of a concept represented in self-report instruments severely constrain the ability to recognize that concept in cultural populations other than the one for which the instruments were developed.

Problems in using instruments cross culturally could be due to education, incorrect translation, irrelevant content, lack of semantic equivalence, the different character of social interactions in various groups, or the nature of the response required. One study showed that Hispanics interviewed in Spanish responded differently to some items than Hispanics interviewed in English, and that those differences affected the conclusions.

Intracultural diversity makes the process of culturally meaningful translation even more complex. At present there is discussion regarding the appropriateness of any single Spanish language translation of material intended for use with such culturally diverse groups as, for example, Mexicans, Cubans, and Puerto Ricans. Considerable care must be taken in order to assure that any translation, whether culturally specific or not, achieves a level of language usage that is equivalent to the original source. Without such assurances, cross-language studies will be subject to the threat that between-group differences are an artifact of differences in the adequacy with which different languages are used. No cross-language survey should be fielded without the assurance of language equivalence offered by the blind back translation technique. Translation techniques need to be the most sophisticated available (Marin & Marin, 1991).

The same kind of process is needed for qualitative interview schedules. Nonhierarchical and culturally sensitive interview techniques are needed using carefully trained and selected interviewers. Although interviewers from the same ethnic/cultural group as the participants is often optimal, some participants may be uncomfortable talking with members from the same community about sensitive subjects. If possible, a choice should be given to participants, especially if the research is of a sensitive nature or in depth.

Data analysis beyond differences between ethnic groups is necessary. There must always be strategies to control for income and education level when conducting quantitative racial or ethnic comparisons. There needs to be analysis with each ethnic group separately as well as across groups in both qualitative and quantitative analyses. There are newer, innovative analytic techniques that are extremely useful to uncover important issues related to culture, such as analysis by neighborhood characteristics (O'Campo et al., 1995; Sampson, Raudenbush, & Earls, 1997), and various nested designs.

Data analysis strategies for the birthweight study were designed by the entire research team and focused specifically on answering the research questions and interpreting results within the context of study implications for the entire sample, but also for various cultural subgroups participating in the study. The diversity of researchers on the team assured that we were able to appropriately consider the unique cultural variations across the participants but also to examine social, economic, environmental, and other contextual factors within groups that influence the perception and response to abuse during pregnancy.

Interpretation of the results needs to be within a culturally specific context. Socioeconomic data were collected so that analysis and interpretation of minority data can be placed in the context of larger social issues. The entire team needs to grapple with the cultural interpretation and get help from the research participants or the community from which they come.

Our research team discussed and reached consensus on how findings from the study would be disseminated. Some team members participated in quantitative data analysis while others focused on qualitative analysis; each had full access to both. Based on specific interests, all team members were encouraged to take the lead in writing articles for publication. Each member of the research team contributed to and was a coauthor on each publication. A number of presentations at major conferences on domestic violence and abuse during pregnancy were made. We understood that validation and dissemination of the findings need to go back to the community or affected group in a user-friendly format, and that the results must be used for improvement of the condition of the cultural group affected.

MULTISITE MANAGEMENT

The two keys to multisite management are communication and trust. Regular e-mail, conference calls, and on-site meetings are essential. In the birthweight study, the original team members had known each other and had worked together over time, but in-person meetings were needed with new members in order to begin to form trust. We tried to put our competing agendas on the table and negotiate according to each person's priorities.

Working With Hospitals: Managing Many IRBs

At the time of grant submission, the University of the Principal Investigator provided a review and clearance from their Human Subjects Review Committee. Wayne State's name carries considerable weight. Once the study was funded, all members of the research team negotiated the Institutional Review Board of the hospitals where they would be collecting data. In every case the study was approved, but it was a lengthy process, sometimes taking up to three months. In the case when new data collection sites were needed, the IRB process had to be repeated, again with significant delays in data collection. Institutional review boards are given discretion to interpret and apply the federal regulations governing the protection of human subjects in research and may also vary in their approved research practices and informed consent forms (Silverman, Hull, & Sugarman, 2001). Having the approval of Wayne State on record made negotiating with the hospitals somewhat easier, as did the federal funding for the study. It is important to recognize and plan for these challenges when multisite designs are used and to be aware of site-related adjustments that might be necessary when data are analyzed (Russell, Berlin, Ten Have, & Kimmel, 2001).

Necessity for a Multisite Design

In order to enroll sufficient numbers of ethnically diverse participants it is usually necessary to use a multisite design. A multisite design is also useful in getting at diversity within an ethnic group. For instance, southern African Americans may be very different from northern African Americans in the same way that southern Euro-Americans will be different from northern Euro-Americans. A multisite study enhances the possibility of obtaining sufficient participants and allows for diversity within groups. However, even within the same state, a multisite study is difficult to manage while maintaining fidelity of data collection. The following sections describe the training and continued management of research assistants in a large multisite study conducted at two sites in two different states. We hope to provide some strategies for maintaining good fidelity of data collection in a complex, multicultural, multisite study.

Training the Trainers

This section is about maintaining control of data gathering at the multiple sites of this study, which involved four self-administered instruments and one semistructured interview. Some data were collected from medical records. These data collection sheets varied from site to site but were designed to collect exactly the same data. The research team met for several days to refine the semistructured interview to ensure that the posed interview questions and responses from all five ethnic groups would yield the best possible data. The team developed a protocol for data collection that incorporated a script to be used by all data collectors and included the invitation into the study, information to obtain consent (both oral and in writing), the exact order of instrumentation, and an advocacy protocol for use if the participant revealed abuse. If the participant did not reveal abuse, a briefer advocacy protocol was employed. All participants were provided with information about resources in the community specifically for domestic violence.

Preparing the Data Collection Sites

Control over data collection also involves ensuring that there are no threats to internal validity resulting from extraneous variables being introduced to the study by health personnel within the sites. Therefore the researchers obtained the support of the hospital administration to do a two-day training on the nursing role in intervening with women who are abused for health personnel in the maternity department within the sites. At these trainings, members of local shelter organizations presented the sessions and included African-American and Puerto Rican domestic violence experts. This increased the visibility of local support networks for abused women and provided an opportunity for hospital community links. Securing interest and cooperation of nurse directors, unit managers, and nursing staff for the research can result in rewards for the hospital and improved services for abused women. The final outcome at one site was that the researchers helped to create a hospital task force on domestic violence (at Baystate Medical Center, Springfield, MA).

Training the Research Assistants as Data Collectors

With this work done, the researchers then recruited their data collection teams. All data collectors were nurses. We were careful to select graduate research assistants who had a women-centered philosophy and were interested in conducting research in this area. Some data collectors were staff nurses at the sites but many were nurses enrolled in a nursing master's program. Major efforts were taken to recruit data collectors from the ethnic groups under study. However, given the nature of the nursing profession, most data collectors were Euro-American, although we successfully recruited both Hispanic and African-American data collectors at all sites. The training of research assistants as data collectors not only included study methods but also specific readings on domestic violence and discussions on culture and culturally appropriate interactions in the research environment. African-American and Puerto Rican domestic violence experts presented information at the training on ethnic differences in response to intimate questions. Research assistants also participated in an educational program on domestic violence and attended seminar discussions led by ethnic minority shelter staff to increase their cultural knowledge and competence.

These data collection teams were then trained in the protocol. The training included provision of literature about culture, and research on violence against women and advocacy for women. The instruments were explained and all data collectors completed each instrument. Each data collector was given a protocol, which was then explained. Emphasis was placed on fidelity to this protocol. Then each collector participated in at least one role rehearsal with a researcher playing the part of the research participant. Special care was taken with rehearsing the open-ended interview and the advocacy protocol if the woman revealed abuse. Data collectors then observed the researchers collecting data from participants and, after an opportunity to debrief as a group, began their own data collecting. They were provided with the research protocol, research packets for each participant in English and Spanish, money for the participants, a tape recorder, batteries, and a calculator. They were also supplied with information for turning in the research packets in a way that maintained confidentiality.

Maintaining Data Collection Fidelity

Ongoing monitoring and processing during data collection were critical to the integrity of the protocol. Interim training and debriefings were conducted during the study to ensure maintenance of adherence to the protocol and to allow the interviewers to discuss their feelings about difficult situations. Approximately every month the data collectors met with the researchers at each site to discuss how the project was going. Problems or issues were discussed and resolved. The discussion and resolution of data collection issues or problems were then relayed to the research team either in a face-to-face meeting or by telephone. The data collectors kept field notes after each data collecting session. These served both as material to be discussed at meetings and as a method for the researchers to maintain supervision. Also at these meetings the issues of cross-cultural data collection were raised in instances where none of the data collectors were African American or Hispanic. Nurses from the African-American and representatives of the Hispanic cultures were invited to these meetings to discuss interviewing and communication tips. As data collectors left the team they were replaced by new nurses who were trained and maintained in a similar fashion.

Finding Sufficient Subjects

The original study required data to be collected from 1200 women (600 cases abused during pregnancy, and 600 nonabused controls). We planned data collection from three Hispanic groups (Puerto Rican Americans, Mexican Americans, and Cuban Americans), African Americans, and Anglo-Americans. Co-investigators (2) at each site, research assistants, and staff nurses were data collectors. Women were recruited into the study four hours or more following delivery during a period in which the postpartum hospital stay had decreased from 72 hours to 24–48 hours. This left women with very little time, energy, or privacy for completing research questionnaires and interviews. In the middle of the study it became evident that not many Cuban-American woman were having low birthweight babies. First the data collection site was changed to another hospital that catered to more Cuban-American women. Even then there was great difficulty finding enough mothers of low birthweight infants for the study. Eventually the research team decided to change the subject eligibility and collect the remaining data from Central and South American mothers of low birthweight infants and their case controls. This was a difficulty of a multicultural study that we had not anticipated and therefore had not planned for.

WORKING WITH DOMESTIC VIOLENCE ORGANIZATIONS AND SHELTERS

In conducting multicultural research in the area of domestic violence it was essential that relationships be forged with the community agencies that provide services for abused women and their children. In every state there are a number of organizations and agencies that provide counseling, shelter, and advocacy for women who are experiencing violence and abuse. Frequently known as "Battered Women's Shelters," these domestic violence organizations and agencies are instrumental in addressing the needs of abused women in the community. These agencies are most often nonprofit and largely staffed by volunteers, of which a significant number are formerly abused women. Most agencies espouse a feminist philosophy and seek to empower women to make decisions and to take charge of their own lives. Principles of equity, justice, and cultural relevance are hallmarks of most of these agencies. The staff is frequently multicultural and its missions reflect a commitment to multicultural awareness and praxis. Not only did these agencies serve as referral sources for women who participated in our study, they were also an invaluable source of culturally relevant knowledge about domestic violence and its effect on women. During the course of this study, relationships were developed with a number of domestic violence organizations and shelters that were located in the communities where data were collected. The staff of these shelter organizations provided training support in preparing data collectors and hospital staff. They also served as referral sources for women who enrolled in the study. Informational pamphlets outlining the services of local organizations were distributed to all study participants. Interest and commitment to the study was obtained from the organizations and shelters in the study communities. Their support was invaluable and their contributions to enhancing cultural knowledge in the area of women and abuse was essential in the training of data collectors and hospital staff.

CONCLUSION

Conducting a multisite, multicultural, collaborative research project is not without challenges. Unanticipated delays in completing our study related primarily to additional time required to complete IRB approvals at the various hospitals, having to hire and train replacement research assistants and staff nurses as data collectors, and having to change from one data collection site to another in the middle of the study. We were fortunate to have an exceptional research team that was culturally diverse and culturally competent, who worked diligently to assure a high level of cultural sensitivity in our data collection teams throughout the study. We were also able to maintain a highly collaborative working relationship with hospital administration, nursing staff, domestic violence shelters, and advocates at multiple sites over the several years of data collection. Despite its challenges, more research of this type is necessary if we are to become culturally competent in nursing research. We certainly remain committed as members of the Nursing Research Consortium Against Violence and Abuse (NRCVA) and the Nursing Network on Violence Against Women International (NNVAWI) to continue our efforts to contribute to the development of knowledge essential for the practice of culturally competent care of abused women.

REFERENCES

Campbell, D. W., Campbell, J. C., King, C., Parker, B., & Ryan, J. (1994). The reliability and factor structure of the index of spouse abuse with African-American battered women. *Violence and Victims, 9,* 259–274.

Campbell, J. C., & Campbell, D. W. (1996). Cultural competence in the care of abused women. *Journal of Nurse-Midwifery, 41*(6), 457–462.

Campbell, J. C., Dienemann, J., Kub, J., Wurmser, T., & Loy, E. (1999). Collaboration as a partnership. *Violence Against Women, 5*(10), 140–156.

Campbell, J. C., Ryan, J., Campbell, D. W., Torres, S., King, C., Stallings, R., & Fuchs, S. (1999). Physical and nonphysical abuse and other risk factors for low birthweight among term and preterm babies: A multiethnic case control study. *American Journal of Epidemiology, 150*(7), 714–726.

Collins, P. H. (1995). *Race, class, and gender: An anthology.* Belmont, CA: Wadsworth.

Henderson, D. J. (1995). Consciousness raising in participatory research: Method and methodology for emancipatory nursing inquiry. *Advances in Nursing Science, 17*(3), 58–69.

Hudson, W. W., & McIntosh, S. (1981). The assessment of spouse abuse: Two quantifiable dimensions. *Journal of Marriage and the Family, 43,* 873–888.

Marin, G., & Marin, B. V. (1991). *Research with Hispanic populations*. Newbury Park, CA: Sage Publications.

O'Campo, P. J., Gielen, A. C., Faden, R. R., Xu, X., Kass, N. E., & Wang, J. F. (1995). Violence by male partners against women during the childbearing years: A contextual analysis. *American Journal of Public Health, 85*(8), 1092–1097.

Orlandi, M. A. (1992). Defining cultural competence: An organizing framework. In USDHHS: *Cultural competence for evaluators* (OSAP Cultural Competence Series). Washington, DC: Public Health Service.

Porter, C. P., & Villarruel, A. M. (1993). Nursing research with African American and Hispanic people: Guidelines for action. *Nursing Outlook, 41*(2), 59–67.

Russell, L. A., Berlin, J. A., Ten Have, T. R., & Kimmel, S. E. (2001). Adjustments for center in multicenter studies: An overview. *Annals of Internal Medicine, 132*(2), 112–123.

Sampson, R. J., Raudenbush, S. W., & Earls, F. (1997). Neighborhoods and violent crime: A multilevel study of collective efficacy. *Science, 277*(5328), 918–924.

Silverman, H., Hull, S. C., & Sugarman, J. (2001). Variability among institutional review boards' decisions within the context of a multicenter trial. *Critical Care Medicine, 29*(2), 235–241.

Torres, S., Campbell, J. C., Campbell, D. W., Ryan, J., King, C., Price, P., et al. (2000). Abuse during pregnancy: Prevalence and cultural correlates. *Violence and Victims, 15*(3), 303–321.

9

Testing the Efficacy of an Intervention Directed Toward Family Caregivers of Cancer Patients: The Family Care Research Program

Sharon L. Kozachik, Barbara A. Given, and Charles W. Given

Approximately 1.3 million persons will be diagnosed with cancer in the United States in 2002 (Jemal, Thomas, Murray, & Thun, 2002). Due to the ongoing shift of cancer care from the inpatient to the outpatient setting, greater numbers of family members are becoming involved in the ongoing and day-to-day care of their loved ones in the home. The family caregiver role is multifaceted, incorporating hands-on direct care skills to provide personal and medical/nursing tasks of care, monitoring for and managing the symptoms and side effects of cancer and its treatment (Bakas, Lewis, & Parsons, 2001; Given & Given, 1998a, 1998b; Mor, Masterson-Allen, Houts, & Siegel, 1992; Siegel, Raveis, Mor, & Houts, 1991; Stommel, Given, & Given, 1990), ensuring that instrumental care needs are met and administering medications (Krach & Brooks, 1995; Oberst, Thomas, Gass, & Ward, 1989), and providing emotional support to the person with cancer.

In essence, the family caregiver is an informal extension of the formal oncology care team operating from the home setting; coordinating care to facilitate continuity; providing early detection and timely reporting of symptoms, side effects, and adverse health events to the oncology care team; monitoring and supervising care that may be delivered by professional caregivers; and supporting the patient to implement the oncology plan of care (Kozachik, Given, & Given, 1999; Schumacher, Stewart, Archbold, Dodd, & Dibble, 2000). The cancer caregiver's role and the demands of care are fluid and not always amenable to structure or predictability. The role evolves as patient care needs and treatment change (Schumacher, 1996). Patients' abilities to assume greater or lesser self-care responsibilities may be influenced by treatment and stage of disease, symptom experiences, and/or emotional or physical functioning. Caregivers for cancer patients must be vigilant for subtle cues signaling changes in their loved one's status to either foster optimum levels of independence or supplement self-care abilities on behalf of the patient to ensure that requisite care needs are being met (Given & Given, 1998b). The family caregiver role involves activities 24 hours a day, 7 days a week, and may last for weeks, months, or even years, depending upon the disease, treatment, and location in the cancer trajectory. Since cancer is a chronic disease, it is noteworthy to mention that the role of family caregiver is not a developmentally normative experience; no one plans for the care of a spouse, sibling, child, or parent who has been diagnosed with cancer. Therefore, it is often the case that a family member is thrust into the caregiver role at the point of diagnosis and initiation of cancer treatment, and because of the timing and lack of forewarning, education, and training, is ill-prepared to assume this role and provide the requisite tasks of care (Schumacher et al., 2000). Additionally, family caregivers are often overcome with shock, sadness, and anger over their loved ones' cancer diagnosis, which may interfere with their capacity to make decisions or to be objective about care.

It is within this context of an integral and lengthy involvement in home cancer care that the family caregiver is considered as a focus of health care research. Increasingly, family caregivers have been included in research endeavors, with earlier studies focusing on the unique needs of family caregivers of patients with dementia. Family caregiver research has subsequently evolved to examine those family members who are caring for patients who have other chronic disease states, such as cancer (Given & Given, 1994a, 1994b; Given, Given, Helms, Stommel, & DeVoss, 1997; Given, Given, Stommel, & Azzouz, 1999; Jansen, Halliburton, Dibble, & Dodd, 1993; McCorkle & Pasacreta, 2001; Northouse, 1995; Schumacher, Dodd, & Paul, 1993).

The purpose of this chapter is to introduce the reader to the challenges of accrual and retention of patient–family caregiver dyads into randomized clinical trials (RCTs) designed to test the efficacy of behavioral interventions, especially nursing interventions, involving family caregivers in caregiving that improves the outcomes of patients. Included is a discussion of the additional time demands placed upon caregivers when they agree to participate in a longitudinal, randomized clinical trial of a behavioral intervention.

In this chapter, we discuss caregiver characteristics such as sociodemographics, caregiver workload, and tasks of care delivered in the home setting, and how these, together with competing role obligations of the caregiver and the characteristics of their patients, may interfere with caregiver participation in randomized trials. We also discuss study design issues, including selection of recruitment sites, eligibility criteria, data collection, and intervention protocols as potential barriers to caregiver participation. These barriers may impede accrual and subsequent retention of caregivers in longitudinal RCTs of behavioral interventions. Finally, we present exemplars of mechanisms for accruing and retaining patient–caregiver dyads into multidisciplinary, multisite, longitudinal, randomized clinical trials designed to test the efficacy of specialized nursing interventions to improve patient and caregiver outcomes following a cancer diagnosis. These exemplars are drawn from the experiences of the Family Care Research Program (FCRP) team that has conducted a number of RCTs designed to test the efficacy of a nurse-delivered intervention directed toward patient–caregiver dyads involving education on cancer and cancer treatment, symptom monitoring and management, mobilizing community and family resources, emotional support, and caregiver preparedness.

BARRIERS TO FAMILY CAREGIVER PARTICIPATION IN RCTS

Gender

Studies of the experiences of caregivers for cancer patients have demonstrated that women assume the caregiver role more often than men (Emanuel et al., 1999; Kozachik et al., 2001). Women probably are more apt to assume the caregiver role because its nature may be perceived as a natural extension of the traditional socialized female caring role (Robison, Moen, & Dempster-McClain, 1995). Wives or daughters/daughters-in-law are more likely to assume the caregiving role over husbands or sons/sons-in-law. The reasons male caregivers are not participating in clinical trials that test behavioral interventions have not been fully explicated in the literature. The Family Care Research team has had male caregivers refuse, citing privacy reasons, not wanting to share their experiences with interviewers or intervention nurses.

Cultural Characteristics

Our society is composed of many different cultural groups, and as such, awareness of the unique cultural lines of familial authority, that is, who assumes the role of the family spokesperson and/or gatekeeper, is necessary for successful accrual into a research study. Certain cultures defer all family decisions to the eldest male child, and other cultures do not allow their females to interact independently with male figures outside of their family structure (Josipovic, 2000). Thus, they may be unwilling to participate in caregiver research.

Cultural sensitivity—understanding and appreciating cultural health beliefs and perceptions of the formal health care system and demonstrating a willingness to embrace other cultural traditions—may foster rapport between the patient and/or caregiver and the researcher based on trust and mutual respect (Josipovic, 2000). Maintaining participants from varied cultures in a longitudinal study requires the research team to recognize holidays and high holy days that impose restrictions on participation. Although time lines are a necessary component of research endeavors, there may be times in which intervention encounters or interviews for data collection will need to be delayed on behalf of a participant's unique cultural or religious practices. Knowing whether there are particular days of the week, or times in the day, in which the patient and/or caregiver engage in spiritual or meditative practices will help to cue the research team about times when participants should *not* be contacted so as to respect these special times. Cultural and religious differences need to be considered during the planning of research endeavors to facilitate family caregiver participation.

Specific groups, such as African-American, Native American, Hispanic/ Latino, and Asian/Pacific Islander populations can be difficult to accrue into studies because of geographic location or recruitment strategies that may not be sensitive and relevant to those cultures. Because access to the full sociodemographic spectrum of potential cancer patients is not realized in most studies, study samples are homogenous; lack racial, ethnic, and cultural diversity; and produce results that are not generalizable to the population of cancer patients at large. Thus, it is imperative that research teams employ recruiters, data collectors, and interveners who are racially and ethnically diverse to facilitate comfort of minority groups.

Socioeconomic Characteristics

The lack of access to treatment centers that offer clinical trials of behavioral interventions may be a challenge in soliciting caregiver and patient participation in research. Most comprehensive cancer centers are in large metropolitan areas, readily accessible to middle- and upper-class patient populations. Access to comprehensive cancer centers may prove to be challenging for patients of lower socioeconomic status due to referral sources, transportation and/or financial constraints. Studies conducted solely within comprehensive cancer centers may not have access to patients and family caregivers across the full range of socioeconomic status. Unless specifically targeted, patients who qualify for Medicaid, or those who are uninsured, are generally not approached to participate in clinical trials involving behavioral interventions. Many patients and family caregivers who are covered by Medicaid simply do not have access to behavioral trials in the settings where they receive their usual health care. Additionally, many individuals of lower socioeconomic status may either not have the skills to negotiate the complexities of a comprehensive cancer treatment center, or may be intimidated by the system if they attempt to participate. In the latter case, researchers need to examine ways to make their trials less intimidating and more user friendly.

Emotional Status of the Caregiver

In addition to cultural and socioeconomic considerations, approaching caregivers to solicit their participation in a longitudinal study requires sensitivity not only to their emotional state, but also to their readiness to hear what the study would entail, including the duration and intensity of their participation. The introduction of a cancer diagnosis into a family imposes emotional trauma not only onto the patient, but also the family caregivers. Fears for the patient's physical decline and debilitation, pain and discomfort, and the potential for death weigh heavily on family caregivers. They may be emotionally overwhelmed and unable to develop or implement adequate coping mechanisms. During the phase immediately following diagnosis and prior to the initiation of adjuvant therapy, caregivers are overwhelmed by the decisions they have to make and the information that is provided, both in content and volume. Patients may rely heavily on their caregivers for emotional support at this time, which may further compromise the caregivers' capacity to tolerate any more influx of information or need to deal with any decision making. Participating in a research study, which is an additional activity, may be beyond their capacity at this time.

Aged Family Caregivers

It is noteworthy to mention that cancer is often a disease of aging and that an estimated 1 in 3 men and 1 in 4 women between the ages of 60 and 79 years were diagnosed with cancer in 2002 (American Cancer Society, 2002). If the elder cancer patient has a spouse, that person, who is also most often elderly, may be enlisted to assume many of the day-to-day cursory tasks of care. Aging caregivers experience normative physical changes, such as decreases in visual and hearing acuity, lean body mass, and physical functioning, as well as their own chronic illnesses (Kart, Metress, & Metress, 1992) that may interfere with their ability to participate in a longitudinal clinical trial. Many elders have decreased capacity to drive to treatment centers. These normative aging changes and chronic illnesses may impede the elder caregiver's desire or ability to participate in the study.

Workload and Tasks of Care

As indicated previously, being a cancer caregiver is not a developmentally normative experience. Often, caregivers are thrust into the caring role with little forewarning, education, or skills acquisition. They are called upon to provide various aspects of care, including assistance with personal care, administering medications, performing dressing changes, and monitoring for and managing symptoms and side effects of cancer and its treatment. Family caregivers may be physically, as well as emotionally, overwhelmed by the demands of care they may be asked to meet.

Stommel, Given, and Given (1993) examined the home-care costs for a patient with cancer, including the indirect costs of family labor in the delivery of home cancer care, and found that the average home-care costs for cancer care were not much lower than the costs of maintaining the cancer patient in a nursing home. This study took into account not only the caregiver's lost wages caused by the patient's care needs, but also the cost of care provided by those caregivers who were not gainfully employed, based on the average hourly wage for a local home health aide. Intangible costs and demands of care to caregivers of cancer patients in the home setting include loss of personal or respite time, decreased nocturnal sleep, inadequate nutrition, and mental and physical fatigue, all of which may result from performing the caregiving tasks. Additional intangible costs to caregivers include the likelihood that they may forego their own health care needs in favor of meeting their loved one's needs first. These care demands and intangible costs may pose barriers to a family caregiver's desire to participate in research studies.

Given and Given (1998a, 1998b) found at 6–8 weeks following initial treatment for an incident diagnosis of breast, colon, lung, or prostate cancer, family caregivers were providing, on average, 2 hours of assistance with activities of daily living (ADLs; range 0–23 hours), 10 hours of assistance with instrumental activities of daily living (IADLs; range 0–48 hours), and about 1/3 hour of assistance with health care procedures (HCPs; range 0–16 hours) each week. At one year following initial treatment, these family caregivers were providing, on average, 3 hours of assistance with ADLs (range 0–18 hours), 4 hours of assistance with IADLs (range 0–31 hours), and about 1/10 hour of assistance with HCPs (range 0–21 hours). In some instances, these caregivers were providing the equivalent of full-time care to ensure that their loved ones' needs were being met, in addition to attending to other role demands that were competing for their time.

Competing Role Obligations

Although many family members are motivated to assume the caregiver role due to the love and sense of obligation and commitment they feel toward the patient, many family caregivers must adjust, reassign, and relinquish familiar and/or other roles in order to provide care to a loved one at home (Given & Given, 1994a, 1994b). Additionally, family caregivers who are employed outside the home as the primary or secondary breadwinner, or those who provide insurance coverage for their family, must mold the caregiver role so that it introduces the least impediment to their employment obligations. Integrating the caregiver role may require that family members alter their work schedules by changing shifts, taking paid or unpaid time off, or reducing the number of days worked (Stommel, Given, & Given, 1993). Caregivers who also have school-aged or younger children in the home feel the impact of their children's needs for nurturing, guidance, care, schedules, and transportation with concomitant obligations to the cancer patient.

Young adults who are tenured into the caregiver role often have other competing roles (spouse, parent, employment) that demand their time and attention (Brody, 1981; Penning, 1998). These may further impede the ability of researchers to solicit these younger caregivers' participation in randomized clinical trials. Younger adults have many other role obligations and the addition of the family caregiver role may overwhelm them. Once a young adult is enrolled in a longitudinal trial, the multiple role obligations may have an adverse effect on the caregiver's ability to complete the study.

Cultural affiliation, socioeconomic status, age, the sheer volume of the requisite tasks of care being provided by the caregiver, and other role demands that compete for the caregiver's time can all affect a family member's willingness to consider participation in a longitudinal clinical trial. Health beliefs, access to comprehensive cancer centers, the nature of the tasks of care, and overall workload can also sway a family caregiver to forego participating in a longitudinal clinical trial.

REASONS FAMILY CAREGIVERS DO, OR DO NOT ELECT TO PARTICIPATE

Keeping in mind the nature, complexity, competing roles, duration, and costs associated with the caregiver role, how is it that some family caregivers feel able to carve out time from their schedules to participate in behavioral research? Often the research focus is bifurcated, incorporating both the cancer patient's and family caregiver's perceptions of and involvement in cancer care in the home setting. Generally it is the cancer patients who are most interested in and most value participating in a research study. Some family caregivers agree to participate in behavioral or psychosocial studies to please their loved ones, while recognizing this participation as an additional role they must assume. This situation presents a challenge to investigators in that caregivers may not fully commit themselves to the study process (telephone interviews, intervention sessions), a situation that may hinder timely completion of the study.

Caregivers who do not fully embrace a longitudinal, randomized clinical trial may not agree to participate in a study, while those who elect to participate may decide to withdraw prematurely from the study for a variety of reasons. These reasons may include lack of interest, frustration with the time commitment involved, the imposition of fitting the study into their already overextended lives, and the lack of discretionary time available for their own respite and rejuvenation. Participation in a longitudinal clinical trial is a role that family caregivers can easily relinquish because it is not tied to their own well-being or the well-being of their loved one.

Some caregivers, however, participate because they want assistance and see the study as potentially beneficial with respect to the care that they are providing to the cancer patient. This is especially true if the interventions have an assistive role to help the caregiver acquire knowledge or skills to provide care, critical thinking skills to assist with problem solving or decision making, or if the interventions provide the caregiver with social or emotional support (Given, Given, Champion, et al., 1999; Kozachik et al., 2001; Pasacreta & McCorkle, 2000).

Caregivers are very sensitive to their patients' physical and emotional stamina and ability to tolerate demands on their time. Because of this, they may decline participating in an effort to protect their loved ones from the demands of a research study. By declining participation, the caregiver is also extracting the patient from the pool of patients who meet eligibility criteria for the study. The extent to which this situation occurs is not documented in the literature.

Anecdotally, cancer caregivers often report a keen interest in contributing to the advancement of science or improvement of future cancer care to others as the main reason they consent to participate in research studies. This altruistic participation has been noted across a number of our studies. Regardless of a caregiver's willingness, this new role of research participant must be integrated into the caregiver's other existing roles, including the demanding role of cancer caregiver, further limiting leisure and respite time.

What we do not yet fully understand are the research implications that result from patient and/or caregiver refusal to participate. Motzer, Mosely, and Lewis (1997) reported an overall 30.7% refusal rate for their multisite randomized clinical trial of a nursing intervention for recently diagnosed, early-stage breast cancer patients and their spouses/male partners. Kozachik and colleagues (2001) reported an overall 44% (n = 100) refusal rate for a similar study. Of the 100 refusals, only 12 (12%) were caregivers who reported that they were not interested, too busy, or too ill to participate. What is not known from either study is how the results were biased due to the nonparticipation of self-selected patient–caregiver dyads. Many researchers do not report the number of eligible persons approached for recruitment who refused to participate and their reasons for refusal. The impact of the soon-to-be-implemented Health Insurance Portability and Accountability Act (HIPAA) on access to potentially eligible patients and caregivers remains questionable at this time. Thus, future caregiving research is at a marked disadvantage by the lack of information about the family caregivers who refuse to participate in longitudinal clinical trials, the reasons they refuse, and how those who refuse differ from those who elect to participate. It is possible that those family caregivers who stand to benefit most from participating in a clinical trial of behavioral interventions are those who decline participation.

PATIENT CHARACTERISTICS AND ELIGIBILITY ISSUES

In order to be able to participate in research projects, a patient must first meet the list of inclusion criteria and not meet any of the exclusion criteria. Studies may limit patient eligibility by age, cancer site and/or stage, whether this is an incident or recurrent diagnosis, the treatment modality and/or point in the treatment trajectory, and presence of preexisting comorbid conditions. Caregivers for these patients may want to participate in a randomized trial but not be able to do so because their patients do not meet the eligibility criteria.

When eligibility criteria include capturing cancer patients by a specific time frame within their treatment protocol, such as within 60 days of initiating chemotherapy, timely enrollment is critical. Beginning a treatment protocol can be a stressful and frightening time for newly diagnosed cancer patients and their family caregivers. In addition to feelings of uncertainty about the outcomes, cancer patients and their caregivers are often overwhelmed by the information they receive and are not ready to hear about how they could participate in a longitudinal behavioral study. They may not understand the purpose of the study or what their role in the study would be, and they are not encouraged to participate in behavioral intervention trials by their oncologists or the infusion nurses. Recruiters must balance the need to expedite the recruitment process with the cancer patients' and family caregivers' emotional states. For those cancer patients and family caregivers who are ready and willing to learn about the availability of a study, recruiters must be aware of the patients' chemotherapy start date, try to approach the patients and family caregivers at a time that is most compatible with the treatment schedules, and advise them of the date by which their signed consents must be received in order to be eligible to participate in the study. The timing of patients' chemotherapy or radiation therapy can also hinder caregivers' ability to participate if it conflicts with caregivers' work schedules or other obligations.

Patients can hinder the accrual of family caregivers into studies based on eligibility criteria established by the research team, the point in their treatment trajectory in which they are identified as being eligible for the study, and their physiological and psychological hardiness. Many patients are too ill to participate in research studies due to the adverse effects of chemotherapy or the progression of their cancer. Patients may be referred to Hospice care or have lengthy hospitalizations, leaving them unable to participate in studies. Family caregivers from this subsample may most benefit from a behavioral intervention incorporating both social and emotional support.

STUDY CHARACTERISTICS THAT CAN POSE BARRIERS TO PARTICIPATION

Recruitment Sites

Family caregivers become enrolled in a study through a variety of mechanisms, primarily when their loved ones are receiving chemotherapy and/ or radiation therapy at a treatment site in which research is ongoing. Comprehensive cancer centers, university-affiliated cancer treatment centers, or National Cancer Institute designated Community Clinical Oncology Programs (CCOPs) are those treatment sites most likely to offer opportunities to patients and their family caregivers to participate in randomized clinical trials testing behavioral interventions. Although some community-based treatment centers participate in studies, such as clinical trials to test new drug protocols, there may be neither the interest in participation in research nor the requisite infrastructure established to support the needs of a behavioral intervention trial. Because cancer treatment centers, both community based and CCOPs, are focused on the patients and their adjustment to their cancer diagnosis and treatment, little attention may be placed on the family caregivers. Hence, unless the oncology team perceives that the patient would benefit from participating in a longitudinal clinical trial to test a behavioral intervention, the patient–family caregiver dyad may not be referred to the research study, even though the family caregiver may derive tremendous benefit from participation.

Study Design

Longitudinal studies, as the name implies, can be lengthy and may require a time commitment anywhere from a few months up to a year or longer in order to demonstrate efficacy or sustained effects of a behavioral intervention. In addition to the duration of participation, data collection for outcomes measures will need to occur, at the very least, both pre- and postexperimental manipulation. Time points for the collection of these data may arise at any point in patients' disease and treatment trajectories, including their nadir in response to therapy. Patients may not feel well enough to participate in telephone interviews at the nadir; thus, their family caregiver may wish to skip that data collection point or withdraw from the study completely.

Families may express unwillingness to commit to a longitudinal study involving a number of data collection points upon learning that they have a 50% chance of being randomly assigned to either the group that receives the extra nursing intervention or the group participating only in the outcomes data collection. Due to the design of a longitudinal study, patient–caregiver dyads are asked to commit their free time to facilitate data collection. Many have stated they do not wish to give up their time if they perceive no personal benefit from their participation. This research team has experienced refusals for both reasons: some did not wish to be involved in the special nursing intervention, and others would participate only if they were assigned to the group that received the nursing intervention.

Another situation that challenges researchers is cancer patients with many family caregivers who assume specific tasks related to the patients' care, such as transportation to treatment and physician appointments, performing hands-on tasks of care, or housekeeping and other home maintenance tasks. In these cases, there is no one person who assumes the primary family caregiver role. The data are intended to be collected from the *same* person at a number of different points in time. When one specific person cannot be identified as the family caregiver, these families are ineligible to participate in the study.

Longitudinal studies are designed to capture data at specific, multiple points in time, generally anchored to a pivotal point in the disease or treatment trajectory, such as date of diagnosis or date that treatment either began or was completed. Cancer patients may have treatment delays or stoppages due to toxicity or disease progression. Patients and caregivers may elect to withdraw in these instances. In the event that ongoing receipt of adjuvant therapy with curative goals is a criterion for participation in the research study, other plausible effects from treatment stoppages may include having the research team attrit the patient and family caregiver from the study.

The questions posed in telephone interviews can be of a personal and sensitive nature to both patients and caregivers. These interviews can also be lengthy in order to fully capture the experiences of the patients and family caregivers. Because of the nature of the study design, the same questions are asked at multiple data collection points; this can frustrate caregivers. "Why do you keep asking me the same questions?" may be their response.

Caregivers with low literacy may not have verbal skills sufficiently developed to comprehend some of the questions in standardized instruments or the subtle distinctions being queried for in questions that seem similar. In addition, many standardized instruments have five response categories, so beyond having to listen to and comprehend a query, they also must be able to select the response category that most accurately or closely represents their experience.

OTHER ISSUES THAT CAN HINDER FAMILY CAREGIVER ACCRUAL

Oncologists and nursing staff must be convinced of the value of behavioral oncology research and articulate their support to the patients and families who seek treatment at their practice sites. Many treatment centers have ongoing clinical trials for drug protocols. The introduction of a behavioral study into a site that has ongoing drug trials adds the challenge of competing for the pool of eligible patients and family caregivers. This problem is compounded because behavioral studies are often given low priority in cancer treatment centers. Although behavioral interventions rarely introduce confounding into a drug trial, many oncology teams are reluctant to involve their patients in more than one study. Oncologists and infusion nurses may not market a behavioral study to their patient population because the financial incentives for accruing patients into drug trials motivate them to concentrate on recruiting patients for the drug trials. The primary reasons patients and family caregivers participate in *any* cancer clinical trial, be it to test the efficacy of a new drug protocol or a behavioral intervention, are physician or infusion nurse endorsement or recommendation. Although some infusion nurses are interested in and supportive of nursing research in their clinical settings, many are indifferent to or uninterested in nursing research. For effective studies, oncology care teams must value the role of behavioral oncology in the ongoing care of the cancer patient and encourage their patients to participate in research studies whenever health permits.

STRATEGIES TO ENHANCE ACCRUAL AND RETENTION

Accrual

Successful accrual is paramount to the success of any trial. Recruitment protocols must be developed to take into account the diversity of the patient–caregiver population from which the study sample will be obtained. There is so much intra- and interracial cultural diversity that recruiters cannot assume all Caucasian people share the same belief patterns, or that all persons of any other racial/ethnic group share the same set of cultural beliefs. Multisite research needs to involve personnel from all sites in developing a recruitment protocol that is standard across all sites, yet provides the flexibility essential to address the special needs of diverse populations. The recruitment protocol needs to be flexible enough so the study investigators can be assured of having the access and time to recruit a diverse population without compromising the study design.

The Family Care Research Program (FCRP) routinely asks consented participants to disclose the best day of the week and the most convenient time of the day for the study personnel to contact them so that cultural practices, such as spiritual or meditative time, are not interrupted by telephone calls from the team. This inquiry helps to foster patient–caregiver dyad retention in the study and assure participants that the research team will respect their cultural rituals.

Accrual of dyads into the study is the primary *initial* focus and goal of the investigators. Before a caregiver can be approached to participate in a study, the patient's medical record must be screened to ensure that the established eligibility criteria are met. These eligibility criteria vary from study to study and are often specific to age, treatment and/or cancer site, as well as general health conditions. Ensuring that patients *and* their caregivers meet the eligibility criteria for the study requires extra work from the research staff.

Because both patient and caregiver must agree to participate as a dyad, extra communication may be required between the two to discuss the time commitment required (each contact as well as number of contacts) and negotiate other obligations that must be altered in order to participate in a behavioral trial. However, the patient and caregiver may not be together when the initial contact for study participation occurs. Additionally, the clinical study site may be busy, making it difficult to speak privately with the patient and caregiver.

The logistics of meeting with the patient and caregiver to discuss participation in the study become particularly challenging when either the patient or caregiver is a young adult with multiple role obligations (employment, child care, parental care). If the caregiver is employed outside the home, the patient will often need either to transport him/herself to treatment appointments or arrange alternative transportation. This scenario necessitates initial contact with family caregivers by telephone. This might be a cold call, as caregivers may have no prior knowledge of patients' expressed interest in participating in a study that involves their participation as primary caregivers.

Recruiters from the FCRP projects have reported that they used active listening skills when approaching patient–caregiver dyads to participate in the study, monitoring not only what the dyad said to them, but also looking for nonverbal cues, such as body language and eye contact, before they provided much information about the study. In the event that a dyad appeared overwhelmed or anxious, the recruiters provided them with a study brochure for review so they could consider participating without the pressure of making a decision. The recruiter would then ask permission to telephone them at home during the next week to discuss the study further and answer any questions that they might have about participation. One recruiter made it a habit never to approach a dyad until after completion of the first cycle of chemotherapy. Her rationale was that she wanted the dyad to see that in spite of the side effects experienced from the chemotherapy, the patient would feel better after a few weeks. Another recruiter discovered that some patients seemed much more excited about participating than their identified caregivers. In these situations, the recruiter asked the dyad to go home and discuss the pros and cons of participating in a longitudinal study, emphasizing the time commitment required of both, and that they telephone her with their decision after this discussion.

Retention

Once accrual of a patient–caregiver dyad occurs, retention of the family caregiver in the study is the next goal of the research team. Attrition from a study, either patient or family caregiver, can introduce bias that jeopardizes the internal validity of the RTC if the attrition is differential. For example, those who leave the study prematurely may differ from those who complete the study. Attrition can also affect external validity by compromising the study's capacity to demonstrate statistical significance through the loss of power and findings that are generalizable to the target population (Fogg & Gross, 2000; Polit & Hungler, 1999). Cancer does not occur in a vacuum; other significant life events arise that make continued participation in a study difficult. Patients succumb to their disease, and family caregivers also die or become ill while participating. Caregivers may have their own health deficits precluding them from being able to fully participate in a longitudinal study. The stress of a serious illness such as cancer can also test the bonds of marriage; some patients and caregivers divorce or separate while participating. We are a geographically mobile society; job transfers and geographical relocations occur due to family or financial needs. All these factors have an impact on sample retention.

Attrition may also occur because cancer patients themselves are assuming caregiver roles for their aging parents or have additional child care demands and they no longer have the time to participate in a study. In our case, in order to accommodate patients and caregivers to the fullest extent, the team examined each special need on a case-by-case basis to determine the degree to which we could relax the protocol without compromising the intent of the study. As an example, in the event that caregivers were unable to accompany their patients to the in-person nurse visits, the nurse was allowed to conduct the caregiver portion of the protocol by telephone. Previous work had shown that this modification did not compromise the content of their participation. One caregiver in the study was so grateful for this option that he telephoned the intervention nurse from whatever city he was in at that time just to continue participating.

This research team has experienced instances in which caregivers have had serious health events (strokes, heart attacks, cancer diagnosis, open heart surgery), have died, or have filed for divorce or separated from the patient. When caregivers leave a study, all attempts are made to afford patients the opportunity to complete the study if they so desire.

Caregivers may wish to participate in a study but subsequently withdraw for a variety of reasons, including efforts to conserve and preserve the patient's energy. If the patient–caregiver dyad interview or intervention encounter coincides with the patient's nadir, or if patients' physical conditions continue to deteriorate, with little change in their tumor burdens, it may be difficult to follow through with the study's protocol. In addition, caregivers may project their frustration, anger, and/or sadness onto the study, refusing to complete observation periods or withdrawing from the study. This research team has had instances in which caregivers have refused interviewers access to patients, saying that they don't want to participate in the study any longer, in essence protecting the patient from the study and research staff.

A caregiver may also lose interest in participation, especially if the patient experiences a favorable response to treatment and neither the patient nor the caregiver perceives a need to continue participating in the study. Not all cancer patients and their caregivers have an unfavorable response to the cancer disease and treatment. What is not yet known about these differences is whether they are due to psychological or physiological hardiness or an interaction between the two.

In order to enhance retention of patient–caregiver dyads in longitudinal studies, the rationale for repeated data collection should be explained at the time of recruitment. Helping cancer patients and their family caregivers to recognize that it is important for science to learn from those dyads who do *not* have difficulties, as well as from those who *do* have difficulties, is critical. This allows researchers the opportunity to further examine how these groups differ on specific outcomes measures or sociodemographic features.

Providing flexibility in conducting telephone interviews and intervention encounters is key to retaining busy caregivers. This research team has had instances in which study participants were only available after midnight, before 6:00 a.m., or on weekends for completing the telephone interviews. Study participants whose employment required a lot of travel posed a special challenge to adhering to the study protocols, as well as retention. Employing interviewers and intervention nurses who are willing to conduct study sessions beyond traditional business hours is imperative. This flexibility allows family caregivers who may have nontraditional work hours the opportunity to participate.

Educational levels of cancer patients and their family caregivers can be another factor in successful retention. Standardized instruments for data collection are not always developed for persons with lower literacy levels. Cancer patients and their family caregivers may become frustrated by the language/wording of questions if they do not understand the intent. Frustration can also result when questions are worded very similarly and have only very subtle differences.

Participants recruited from rural or community-based centers often travel great distances to receive treatment. Their lack of proximity to the treatment centers may impede their ability to participate in on-site behavioral interventions per protocols and may lead to their withdrawal from the study.

Given, Keilman, Collins, and Given (1990) designed a number of strategies to enhance subject retention in longitudinal studies that focused on specialized training for data collectors. Data collectors must be able to convey consideration and concern for the study participants while demonstrating enthusiasm for and commitment to the goals of the study. Interviewer consistency is one means of enhancing retention in longitudinal studies involving multiple data collection points. Cancer patients and their family caregivers are assigned to a particular interviewer for the duration of the project. This consistency allows rapport to be established between the interviewer and the study participant over time, fostering within the cancer patients and family caregivers the sense that they are more than merely study participants. In addition, continuous expressions of appreciation for the cancer patient and family caregiver's ongoing participation and contribution to science are essential to successful retention. It is imperative that telephone interviewers express appreciation at the beginning and the end of interviews. Over the years, this research team has utilized a number of strategies to enhance participant retention, including token gifts (e.g., a coffee mug with an imprint of the study name) and personalized thank-you letters at the completion of each data collection period, periodic newsletters, and annual study progress reports (Given et al., 1990).

SUMMARY

RCTs to test behavioral interventions for cancer patients and their family caregivers are often fraught with challenges due to accrual and retention issues. Some of these challenges can be overcome through the development of a research protocol that meets the needs of the patient–caregiver dyad, while affording investigators the capacity to answer the research questions and move the science forward. Protocol characteristics to facilitate success include:

1. Hiring racially and culturally diverse consultants to review all research instruments, consents, and intervention materials for cultural relevance
2. Utilizing multiple recruitment sites that provide access to a racially, culturally, and socioeconomically diverse sample
3. Hiring research personnel who are racially and culturally diverse
4. Assuring that all research personnel are culturally competent through training and inservice programs *prior* to implementing the study
5. Allowing for flexibility in the research protocol to prevent conflicts with cultural or religious practices

6. Hiring research personnel who are willing to conduct interviews or intervention sessions outside of normal business hours
7. Being sensitive to the many role obligations of family caregivers and appreciating that many are giving up leisure time in order to participate
8. Making every effort to ensure that data collectors remain consistent for participants over the course of their participation
9. Expressing gratitude to all participants after each data collection period

Other important points to consider when designing a RCT include tailoring explanations of the study to patients and family caregivers based upon cultural affiliation, race, emotional status, and/or existing role strains. Recruiters need to be sensitive to how these issues influence patients and caregivers in order to help potential dyads understand how they can participate and the potential benefits of their participation.

Research protocols may need to be adapted to fit the needs of patients and caregivers. How late can an interview or intervention session be conducted? Can an interview be conducted piecemeal, rather than all in one setting? Accommodation of patients' and caregivers' special needs is likely to result in appreciation, cooperation, and ongoing participation in the study. The extent to which a protocol can be altered must be determined by the research team in advance, with policies and procedures established to guide these adaptations.

REFERENCES

American Cancer Society. (2002). *Cancer facts and figures.* Atlanta, GA: Author.

Bakas, T., Lewis, R. R., & Parsons, J. E. (2001). Caregiving tasks among family caregivers of patients with lung cancer. *Oncology Nursing Forum, 28*(5), 847–854.

Brody, E. M. (1981). "Women in the middle" and family help to older people. *The Gerontologist, 21*(5), 471–480.

Emanuel, E. J., Fairclough, D. L., Slutsman, J., Alpert, H., Baldwin, D., & Emanuel, L. L. (1999). Assistance from family members, friends, paid care givers, and volunteers in the care of terminally ill patients. *The New England Journal of Medicine, 341*(13), 956–963.

Fogg, L., & Gross, D. (2000). Threats to validity in randomized clinical trials. *Research in Nursing & Health, 23,* 79–87.

Given, B. A., & Given, C. W. (1994a). Family home care for individuals with cancer. *Oncology, 8*(5), 77–83.

Given, B. A., & Given, C. W. (1994b). The home care of a patient with cancer: The mid-life crisis. In E. Kahana, D. E. Biegel, & M. Wykle (Eds.), *Family caregiver application series: Vol 4. Family caregiving across the lifespan* (pp. 240–261). Thousand Oaks, CA: Sage.

Given, B. A., & Given, C. W. (1998a). *Final report: Rural partnership linkage for cancer care* (Grant # R01CA56338), funded by the National Cancer Institute.

Given, B. A., & Given, C. W. (1998b). *Family home care for cancer—A community-based model* unpublished data (Grant #r01 NR 01915), funded by the National Institute for Nursing Research, Bethesda, MD.

Given, B. A., Given, C. W., Champion, V. L., Kozachik, S. L., Rawl, S. M., & White, N. (1999). *Final Report: Cancer care interventions to improve functioning and psychosocial outcomes in newly diagnosed cancer patients and their families.* Research conducted in collaboration with the Walther Cancer Institute, Indianapolis, IN.

Given, B. A., Given, C. W., Helms, E., Stommel, M., & De Voss, D. N. (1997). Determinants of family caregiver reaction: New and recurrent cancer. *Cancer Practice,* 5(1), 17–24.

Given, B. A., Keilman, L. J., Collins, C., & Given, C. W. (1990). Strategies to minimize attrition in longitudinal studies. *Nursing Research,* 39(3), 184–186.

Given, C. W., Given, B. A., Stommel, M., & Azzouz, F. (1999). The impact of new demands for assistance on caregiver depression: Tests using an inception cohort. *Gerontologist,* 39(1), 76–85.

Jansen, C., Halliburton, P., Dibble, S., & Dodd, M. J. (1993). Family problems during cancer chemotherapy. *Oncology Nursing Forum,* 20(4), 689–694.

Jemal, A., Thomas, A., Murray, T., & Thun, M. (2002). Cancer statistics. *CA: A Cancer Journal for Clinicians,* 52(1), 23–47.

Josipovic, P. (2000). Recommendations for culturally sensitive nursing care. *International Journal of Nursing Practice,* 6(3), 146–152.

Kart, C. S., Metress, E. K., & Metress, S. P. (1992). *Human aging and chronic disease.* Boston: Jones and Bartlett.

Kozachik, S. L., Given, B. A., & Given, C. W. (1999). Cancer patients at home: Activating nurses to assist patients and to involve families in care at home. *Oncology Nursing Updates,* 6(2), 1–11.

Kozachik, S. L., Given, C. W., Given, B. A., Pierce, S. J., Azzouz, F., Rawl, S. M., & Champion, V. L. (2001). Improving depressive symptoms among caregivers of patients with cancer: Results of a randomized clinical trial. *Oncology Nursing Forum,* 28(7), 1149–1157.

Krach, P., & Brooks, J. A. (1995, October). Identifying the responsibilities and needs of working adults who are primary caregivers. *Journal of Gerontological Nursing,* 21(10), 41–50.

McCorkle, R., & Pasacreta, J. (2001). Enhancing caregiver outcomes in palliative care. *Cancer Control,* 8(1), 36–45.

Mor, V., Masterson-Allen, S., Houts, P., & Siegel, K. (1992). The changing needs of patients with cancer at home. *Cancer,* 69(3), 829–838.

Motzer, S. A., Moseley, J. R., & Lewis, F. M. (1997). Recruitment and retention of families in clinical trials with longitudinal designs. *Western Journal of Nursing Research,* 19, 314–333.

Northouse, L. L. (1995). The impact of cancer in women on the family. *Cancer Practice,* 3(3), 134–142.

Oberst, M. T., Thomas, S. E., Gass, K. A., & Ward, S. E. (1989). Caregiving demands and appraisal of stress among family caregivers. *Cancer Nursing, 12*(4), 209–215.

Pasacreta, J., & McCorkle, R. (2000). Cancer care: Impact of interventions on caregiver outcomes. In J. Fitzpatrick & J. Goeppinger (Eds.), *Annual review of nursing research, 19* (pp. 127–148). New York: Springer.

Penning, M. J. (1998). In the middle: Parental caregiving in the context of other roles. *Journal of Gerontology, 53,* S188–S197.

Polit, D. F., & Hungler, B. P. (1999). *Nursing research: Principles and methods* (6th ed.). Philadelphia: Lippincott.

Robison, J., Moen, P., & Dempster-McClain, D. (1995). Women's caregiving: Changing profiles and pathways. *Journal of Gerontological Behavioral Psychological Science and Social Science, 50*(6), S362–S373.

Schumacher, K. L. (1996). Reconceptualizing family caregiving: Family-based illness care during chemotherapy. *Research in Nursing & Health, 19*(4), 261–271.

Schumacher, K. L., Dodd, M. J., & Paul, S. M. (1993). The stress process in family caregivers of persons receiving chemotherapy. *Research in Nursing & Health, 16*(6), 395–404.

Schumacher, K. L., Stewart, B. J., Archbold, P. G., Dodd, M. J., & Dibble, S. L. (2000). Family caregiving skill: Development of the concept. *Research in Nursing & Health, 23,* 191–203.

Siegel, K., Raveis, V. H., Mor, V., & Houts, P. (1991). The relationship of spousal caregiver burden to patient disease and treatment-related conditions. *Annals of Oncology, 2,* 511–516.

Stommel, M., Given, C. W., & Given, B. (1990). Depression as an overriding variable explaining caregiver burden. *Journal of Aging & Health, 2*(1), 81–102.

Stommel, M., Given, C. W., & Given, B. A. (1993). The cost of cancer home care to families. *Cancer, 71*(5), 1867–1874.

10

The Women's Health Initiative: Aspects of Management and Coordination

Barbara Cochrane, Bernedine Lund, Susan Anderson, and Ross Prentice

he Women's Health Initiative (WHI) is one of the largest and most complex clinical research undertakings ever carried out. From its initiation in 1992 through the present, this multisite, multicomponent, multiethnic, and multidisciplinary study has posed both management challenges and outstanding opportunities. Study management decisions, in response to ongoing experiences and new scientific findings, continue to require open discussion, careful consideration of scientific and budgetary implications, and appropriate systems for broad consensus gathering. Various WHI organizational entities, investigators, and staff share responsibilities for the management of the WHI. This chapter focuses primarily on WHI logistical and management activities at the Clinical Coordinating Center (CCC) at the Fred Hutchinson Cancer Research Center (FHCRC) in Seattle, Washington; other CCC activities and other aspects of the overall organization and management of the WHI have been described elsewhere (WHI Study Group, 1998).

OVERVIEW OF THE WOMEN'S HEALTH INITIATIVE

The overall objective of the WHI is lofty and comprehensive: to reduce the risk of major causes of morbidity and mortality in postmenopausal

Author Note: The research upon which this publication is based was performed pursuant to Contract N01-WH-2-2110 with the National Institutes of Health, Department of Health and Human Services.

women, including cardiovascular disease, cancer, and osteoporotic fractures. To achieve this objective, 40 Clinical Centers (CCs) across the United States are following a total of 161,809 postmenopausal women, ages 50 to 79 at baseline, for an average of eight years in one or more of three overlapping clinical trial (CT) components or an observational study (OS).

The WHI CT uses a partial factorial design to test three preventive interventions. *Hormone replacement therapy* (HRT component, including a trial of estrogen plus progestin and a trial of estrogen alone) was hypothesized to reduce the risk of coronary heart disease and, secondarily, other cardiovascular diseases and hip fractures, with an increase in breast cancer risk as a hypothesized adverse effect. Although the estrogen alone trial continues, the estrogen plus progestin trial was stopped early because overall health risks exceeded benefits (Writing Group for the Women's Health Initiative Investigators, 2002). *A low-fat eating pattern* (Dietary Modification or DM component) is hypothesized to reduce the risk of breast cancer and colorectal cancer, and, secondarily, coronary heart disease. *Calcium and vitamin D supplementation* (CaD component) is hypothesized to prevent hip fractures and, secondarily, other fractures and colorectal cancer. Eligible women were invited initially to join one or both of the HRT and DM components.

The rationale, eligibility criteria, and protocol requirements for each of the CT components are described elsewhere (WHI Study Group, 1998). Women who were ineligible for or not interested in the CT were invited to join the OS. These OS participants are being followed, without intervention, to determine risk estimates, find new risk markers, and examine the relationship between risk factor changes over time and disease risk.

Statistical projections for the CT and OS are described in the WHI protocol and the WHI design paper (WHI Study Group, 1998). Recruitment goals within the WHI were established to support specific subgroup analyses, including analyses within racial/ethnic minority groups and within specific age categories. The WHI aimed to recruit racial/ethnic minority women in proportion to their representation (about 17%) in the general population. Ten WHI CCs identified themselves as having access to large numbers of minority women and accepted specific minority recruitment goals. Age distribution goals for the CT were also established, and were 10% of participants in the age range 50 to 54 years, 20% in 55 to 59, 45% in 60 to 69, and 25% in the 70–79 range. Randomizations within age categories were closed as these goals were achieved. Age-eligible women were recruited using multiple strategies at each CC, with mass mailings the predominant method (Hays et al., in press) used to meet the daunting recruitment goals established for each CC.

Although there was some variability in how WHI screening visits were conducted locally, all potential participants had at least one screening visit during which CCs obtained an initial consent and the baseline and eligibility data for all study components (CT and OS). Women who remained eligible and willing for the CT proceeded through an additional two or three screening visits during which data were collected, further aspects of eligibility were assessed, and specific informed consent documents were presented for both the HRT and DM trial components. At each screening visit, women who were ineligible or unwilling for the CT were invited to join the OS. After one year from CT randomization, eligible women randomized in one or both of the HRT and DM CT components were invited to join the CaD component of the CT, which also had its own eligibility requirements.

The CT intervention activities, including DM intervention and maintenance sessions with participants, began soon after randomization and will continue up to study closeout. Follow-up of CT participants includes annual visits and semiannual contacts or visits. Observational Study participants have annual contacts and a clinic visit following three years of participation. Activities during these routine follow-up contacts include clinical outcomes (endpoints, events) data collection and, in the CT, safety monitoring, adherence assessment, and study pill dispensations (HRT and CaD). Additional follow-up activities vary by CC, but generally focus on strategies to promote CT intervention adherence and CT and OS participant retention.

BRIEF OVERVIEW OF THE WHI STUDY ORGANIZATION

The development of the WHI did not occur in isolation. Previous research in many relevant areas of inquiry informed the protocol and coordination of the WHI. Multiple women's health research agenda-setting conferences held at the National Institutes of Health (NIH) and elsewhere identified the most critical gaps in our scientific knowledge. The WHI, initially localized in the NIH Director's Office has, since 1997, been a program of the National Heart, Lung, and Blood Institute (NHLBI). The protocol, procedures, participant materials, and data and safety monitoring plans have been reviewed and commented upon by the Institutes of Medicine, the federal Office for the Protection of Research Risks and Office of Management and Budget, the CCC's Institutional Review Board (the *central* IRB), each CC's IRB, the WHI Data and Safety Monitoring Board (DSMB, an independent, multidisciplinary group of expert scientists), the independent Working Group of the National Heart, Lung, and Blood Advisory Council (made up of national organizational partners and women's health advocates), and a Consortium of NIH Directors. The DSMB, the Working Group, and the Consortium provide ongoing review and advice.

The study is overseen by the Program Office at the NHLBI, which reports to the NHLBI Director and participates in all studywide organizational entities (see Figure 10.1). The Steering Committee, composed of the 40 CC Principal Investigators (PIs), the WHI Clinical Coordinating Center (CCC) PI, two of the CCC Co-PIs, and one member from the NHLBI Program Office, provides overall scientific and operational direction to the WHI (see Appendix 1 for a listing of WHI PIs). The current Steering Committee configuration ensures that all CC PIs have input and a vote on studywide decisions. The committee selects the membership of and oversees an Executive Committee (which considers study issues, facilitates the final development of study proposals for Steering Committee vote, and monitors the completion of action items assigned to committees and other groups), nine Advisory Committees, and various ad hoc task forces and working groups. The WHI Advisory Committees (Behavioral, Calcium-Vitamin D, Design and Analysis, Diet Modification, Hormone Replacement Therapy, Morbidity and Mortality, Observational Study, Presentations and Publications, and Special Populations) review issues relevant to their specific areas of expertise and make recommendations and proposals to the Executive Committee and Steering Committee. In addition to these studywide committees, a Performance Monitoring Committee (consisting of CCC and Program Office investigators and two Clinical Center PI representatives) regularly reviews and facilitates performance enhancement activities at the 40 CCs.

The sheer number of CCs within the WHI poses a challenge to discussion and common understanding among staff and investigators. The Steering Committee, therefore, established a regional structure of communication for the consideration of issues, gathering of consensus, and mutual support. Clinical Centers are assigned to one of four regions: the Northeast, Southeast, Midwest, and West. Monthly or bimonthly PI and lead staff regional conference calls (which include CCC liaisons for each of the lead staff groups) facilitate communication among CCs in specific areas of responsibility. Regional chairs from each PI and lead staff group (Clinic Managers, Lead Clinic Practitioners, Lead Nutritionists, Data Coordinators, and Outcomes Coordinators) communicate issues to an Executive Committee point person, who then brings issues and proposals for consideration to the

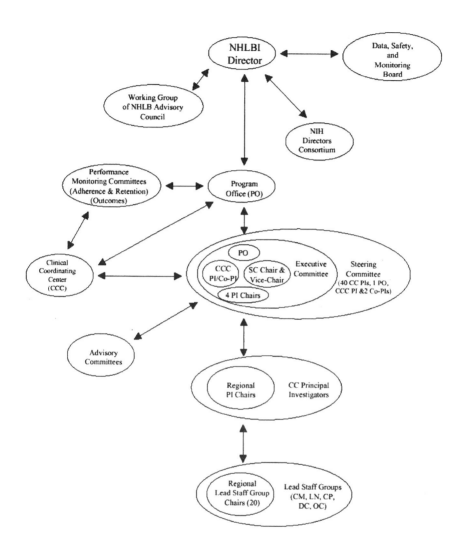

FIGURE 10.1 Organizational Structure of the Women's Health Initiative.

NHLBI: National Heart, Lung, and Blood Institute; NIH: National Institutes of Health; PI: Principal Investigator; SC: Steering Committee; CC: Clinical Center; CM: Clinic Manager; LN: Lead Nutritionist; CP: Clinic Practitioner; DC: Data Coordinator; OC: Outcomes Coordinator.

From Women's Health Initiative. (2000, December). *Study organization and management handbook* (Draft prepared by Marcia Stefanick). Retrieved May 31, 2002 from *http://www.whi.org*

Executive Committee. The lead staff regional representatives are also invited to semiannual Steering Committee meetings and are thereby able to report on meeting discussions to their lead staff constituencies.

CLINICAL COORDINATING CENTER MANAGEMENT RESPONSIBILITIES

The WHI CCC has contractual responsibilities for study coordination and focuses on the scientific and operational activities necessary to ensure the integrity of the study data, analyses, and progress. The planning and implementation of strategies to meet these responsibilities have involved consideration of previous experience in multicenter clinical trials (cf., Blumenstein, James, Lind, & Mitchell, 1995; Curb et al., 1983; Gassman, Owen, Kuntz, Martin, & Amoroso, 1995; Knatterud et al., 1998); appreciation of the sheer magnitude and complexity of the WHI as it exceeds previous experience; awareness of probable variations among CC resources, staffing, and experience; understanding of the budgetary and resource implications of changes, even modest changes in operational systems or in study protocol and procedures; and devotion of high priority to scientific rigor and the ability to achieve major study goals.

Over 60 staff and investigators work within the CCC at the Fred Hutchinson Cancer Research Center. Clinical Coordinating Center activities are led by the CCC PI, three Co-PIs, the Project Manager (with responsibilities for the coordination of budget, contracts, and other administrative activities), and the Technical Coordinator (with responsibilities for the coordination of day-to-day operational and quality assurance activities). Nine units within the CCC carry out its functional activities: Administration, Clinical and Follow-up, Data Operations, Data Management, Network Administration, Nutrition, Outcomes, Scientific Support, and Statistics. Additionally, other scientists at FHCRC provide expertise and consultation in areas relevant to CCC responsibilities and participate in WHI studywide organizational entities.

Aspects of our approach to fulfilling some of the CCC roles and responsibilities are described elsewhere, including data management (Anderson, Davis, & Koch, 2002), CC performance monitoring (Pottern et al., 2001), and statistical aspects of data and safety monitoring (Freedman et al., 1996; WHI Study Group, 1998). Here we focus on other responsibilities, namely, studywide materials and communications, logistical support, subcontractor coordination, quality assurance activities, outcomes ascertainment coordination, and data analysis and reporting. Finally, Section 10 describes how CCC management activities have varied as the clinical trial and observational study have progressed through various phases.

STUDYWIDE MATERIALS AND COMMUNICATIONS

A study as large, complex, and long as WHI generates a large number of records. Any documents used studywide are duplicated at least 50 times so that all CCs, satellite CCs (there are eight CCs with remote sites that function fairly independently), and appropriate central institutions have copies. Study forms and participant materials typically apply to tens of thousands of women, and some of these documents (e.g., data collection forms) are used on a semiannual basis.

Although the CCC coordinates the development and distribution of most studywide materials, many individuals and groups within the program review these materials more broadly before they are finalized and distributed. All participant materials are reviewed meticulously for appropriate content, accuracy, readability (goal of a sixth grade reading level), and formatting. In addition, all participant materials (including audiovisual and other materials, such as the name of the study on pill organizers) are translated into *broadcast* Spanish, a neutral type of Spanish that is understood by most Spanish speakers regardless of their country of origin or ethnic background. Correcting participant misunderstandings or compensating for errors of communication is problematic for any study, but when tens of thousands of copies of a document are printed before it is used, the consequences of an error or even a regional colloquialism can be extraordinarily burdensome. Revisions to study forms and materials, while sometimes necessary and appropriate, are also expensive and are therefore evaluated carefully before implementation. Such revisions require version tracking, not only to ensure that CCs have a mechanism for checking that they are using the correct version of a form or document, but also for historical and analytic purposes.

The WHI has some 50 forms for collecting data on WHI participants; over 20 of these forms collect self-report data by self-administration or interview. Some WHI forms are component-specific (for HRT, DM, CaD, or OS specifically) or a combination of components (e.g., clinical trial participants only). For example, *Form 10—HRT Safety Interview* is used only with HRT participants. *Form 62—Four-Day Food Record* is administered only to DM participants. All forms that collect self-report data have also been translated into broadcast Spanish for Spanish-speaking WHI participants. Appendix 2, from the WHI protocol, lists data collection forms and provides some detail on their content and collection schedule.

Each WHI form is numbered and associated with a current version number. The form number and version number support tracking of when each version of a specific form was implemented, facilitates database management, and helps the CCs track the current version of the form in use. Most data are collected on scannable forms that are scanned at the CCs for inclusion in the local CC database.

A protocol and procedures manual (sometimes called a *manual of operations*) is standard in most multisite research studies. There are eight such manuals in the WHI: Protocol and Policies, Procedures, Forms, Diet Modification (Nutritionist and Participant manuals), Data System, DXA Bone Density Quality Assurance, Quality Assurance, and Outcomes.

As much as possible, the WHI manuals include all policies, procedures, guidelines, templates, resources, participant materials, data collection forms, data systems capabilities, studywide expectations (e.g., performance goals, priorities), and supplemental reference guides (e.g., a table that includes a time line of tasks to be performed for each study component). The CCC releases WHI Manual *Bulletins* on a regular basis to communicate updates to procedures, forms, and other materials. Accompanying these *Bulletins* are reference tables that inform CC staff when new or revised procedures are to be implemented, exactly where the updates are to be inserted, and what to do with previous materials. The CCC also maintains a list of all current versions of forms and manual pages as a reference for CCs to check that their materials are current.

Other studywide materials include required and optional materials for participants (HRT handbook, welcome to WHI handouts, WHI membership cards, model letters), for health care providers (WHI chart labels for patient charts, model letters), and for staff and investigators (questions and answers on relevant topics, orientation memos to new staff, CCC contact lists, WHI Directory, and a Consulting Gynecologist Handbook). The CCC also routinely develops and finalizes three CT participant *WHI Matters* newsletters annually (one of which also goes to OS participants), and a quarterly *WHIse Choices* newsletter for DM intervention participants. A *WHI Times* newsletter for staff and investigators is distributed biweekly, and includes procedural reminders and clarifications, tips, relevant information from the Project Office, a listing of materials recently distributed studywide, and upcoming conference calls and meetings.

Communications and distribution of study information occur via computer network systems, mailings, conference calls, and meetings. A standardized computer configuration was established for the CCs, including application software, peripheral hardware, and planned upgrades during the course of the study. Such standardization was critical to ensuring that centralized support of the network and database met study requirements in a cost effective manner. A Wide Area Network (WAN) connects the Program Office, CCC, CCs, and selected CCC subcontractors. The WAN, in conjunction with CCC-configured Local Area Networks (LANs) at the CCs, facilitates electronic communications among WHI staff and investigators. The LANs also support CC management of their local data. The WAN allows centralized electronic consolidation and backup of all WHI data collected in the WHILMA database. The WHI e-mail system is accessible to WHI staff and investigators on their local CC computer network systems and a website on the World Wide Web.

The CCC established several routine systems for the distribution of study materials, including electronic mailings to WHI group lists (staff inquiries with CCC responses, *WHI Times* newsletters, conference call information), weekly mailings to CCs (hard copies of monthly reports, forms, and supply order forms), publication in the e-mail system Public Folders (e.g., archived *WHI Times*, Executive and Steering Committee minutes, studywide performance monitoring reports, resource documents), and monthly Steering Committee packets to principal investigators.

The CCC also distributes some study materials directly to participants, including the *WHI Matters* newsletters for all participants and annual mailings of data collection forms for OS participants (except during year 3 when all OS participants have a CC visit). Thousands of questionnaire packets, with appropriate participant labels and CC-addressed return mail envelopes, are sent out monthly, based on an OS participant's annual target date. The CCC also sends out follow-up mailings to OS participants who do not respond to the initial questionnaire packet.

LOGISTICAL SUPPORT

CCC administrative and scientific support staff coordinate many of the logistic arrangements for studywide conference calls, meetings, and workshops. Monthly conference calls of 10 to 15 investigators are the forum within which many discussions related to studywide issues occur. The CCC coordinates studywide committee calls (including calls for the Executive committee and selected Advisory Committees, ad hoc task forces, and working groups). For these calls, scientific support staff provide a government-contracted phone service with the call schedule and list of participants, assure timely notification of conference call participants (including the call focus, the schedule for three to five time zones, and instructions for handling last-minute phone number changes), solicit for agenda items and materials to distribute before the call, and mail out materials to call participants. On some conference calls (e.g., Executive Committee, Morbidity and Mortality Advisory Committee), CCC staff also take and distribute minutes of the call.

The CCC provides logistical support for regular meetings of WHI investigators and workshops for lead staff groups. A full Steering Committee meeting occurs each spring and fall; the fall meeting usually includes additional coinvestigators, CC staff from at least one of the lead staff groups, and scientific session presenters. The Executive Committee also meets face-to-face four times a year (twice in conjunction with Steering Committee meetings). Staff workshops are conducted as the need arises for training and discussion about specific topics or new initiatives (e.g., adherence and retention of special populations, motivational enhancement training for DM interventionists, HRT and CaD updates, aging). These workshops have occurred at least annually and usually involve one or two representatives (e.g., nutritionists, clinic managers, adherence and retention staff) from each CC, depending on the focus of the workshop. Most of these meetings involve 50 or more participants and necessitate logistic arrangements that begin months in advance and are similar to those needed for a medium-sized national conference. A training and meeting coordinator at the CCC, along with program assistants, works with the meeting or workshop planning committee to plan and carry out communications, travel considerations, hotel arrangements, meeting room set-up, banquet planning, and materials preparation.

MAINTENANCE OF CCC SUBCONTRACTOR ACTIVITY

The CCC uses the specialized services and expertise from several other organizations to help fulfill its responsibilities. These specialized services include study drug distribution and storage of blood and urine specimens, specialized labs for specimen analyses and DNA extractions, Nutrient Data Systems analysis, ECG analysis and quality control, bone density analysis and quality control, cardiovascular disease expertise, and performance monitoring. Each of these organizations is funded through a subcontract with the CCC, and CCC staff coordinate the activities and budget separately with each subcontractor.

One CCC staff person is designated as the primary contact person for each subcontract. Three of the subcontractors also have routine direct contact with the CCs, both through the WHI e-mail system and through transfer of materials and data. For example, the drug distribution and specimen repository communicates directly with the CCs to supply study drugs, blood draw, and storage supplies, and to receive frozen blood and urine specimens.

The CCC prepares CC-specific reports concerning the data and specimens that CCs routinely send to subcontractors. These reports include data on ECG data sent to the ECG subcontractor, frozen blood and urine specimens sent to the central repository, and bone densitometry results sent to the Bone Density Center. The CCC, CCs, and subcontractors use these reports to monitor and track the collection and submission of data and specimens, such as data that are not matched with a participant. The ECG and Bone Density Center are responsible for reviewing the reports in their respective areas and recommending or implementing corrective action as needed. Problems identified by these two centers are communicated to the CCs and CCC directly for correction. CCs use the reports to identify mismatches and investigate the reasons for mismatched data.

QUALITY ASSURANCE ACTIVITIES

The WHI quality assurance (QA) priorities were developed to focus activities on aspects critical to the main components of WHI. The highest priority (Priority 1) was given to fundamental elements of the CT, including informed consent, randomization, participant safety, interventions, adherence and retention, and primary outcomes. These areas receive rigorous routine review and monitoring, both at the CCs and the CCC. Second priority (Priority 2) was given to elements of the CT that are important for interpretive analyses and to key elements of the OS, including blinding to the CT interventions, CT eligibility and follow-up predictive data, CT and OS baseline predictive and biological data, and OS outcomes. These areas receive review at a reduced level, often with only CC monitoring and with CCC review limited to data monitoring. Lower priority (Priority 3) was given to other elements, such as CT and OS secondary outcomes, which are addressed on a time-available basis.

Implementation of the QA program includes activities performed at the CC as well as those initiated and coordinated by the CCC. Standardized methods WHI uses to assure data quality include documentation, training and certification, direct observation, meaningful standards and goal setting, monitoring, and feedback. Each aspect of WHI can be evaluated using one or more of these methods.

The primary resource documents are the WHI Manuals, which contain the protocol, forms, and required and recommended procedures. Routine manual updates and a written system for providing responses to procedural inquiries not included in the WHI Manual help keep the WHI Manual current over the course of the study.

Training all WHI staff is the responsibility of both the CCC and CCs. The purpose of training within WHI is to teach staff the WHI protocol and procedures for implementation at the CCs. To facilitate training, CC staff duties and responsibilities were divided into the following six areas of responsibilities, also called lead staff areas: clinic management, recruitment, clinic practitioner, nutrition, data management, and outcomes management. The CCC conducts training sessions for all lead staff positions; replacement lead staff trainings are held every 6 to 12 months, as needed. The content and materials covered in replacement sessions are similar to those from the initial training sessions, addressing all activities that fall within the lead staff group's area of responsibilities. Supplemental training sessions may be offered on routine lead staff conference calls or on separate conference calls as needed. After the training session for some lead staff groups, additional training activities take place at the CC. CC lead staff are, in turn, responsible for training CC non-lead staff. The CCC developed training/QA Checklists that contain step-by-step procedures for performing specific tasks. These Checklists are completed by an observer while a staff person performs the specific task. The Training/QA Checklists are used during training, certification, recertification, peer observations for routine monitoring, and CCC QA visits. Specific tasks also have materials such as videos and training modules for use at the CCs.

Lead staff and all other CC staff responsible for data collection or performing specific WHI procedures must be initially certified and annually recertified for the specific tasks they perform in order to ensure that they have received adequate training, can perform a task consistent with studywide criteria, and have maintained their skills. In general, the certification process asks that staff members read relevant WHI documents and show they can perform the specific tasks according to predefined guidelines. The CCC developed Certification Forms that list required and/or recommended steps in the training process for each specific task. CC staff are required to read the listed manual sections for initial certification, to review the same section as a reminder of the current procedures, and to note any changes for annual recertification. CCs are responsible for ensuring all CC staff are appropriately certified and recertified for the WHI tasks they perform. The CCC is responsible for reviewing the certification documentation at routine QA visits.

Observation of CC performance occurs at routine QA visits at CCs every one to three years. These visits usually are conducted by both a clinical and nutrition CCC QA field representative. Occasionally, additional CCC liaison staff participate in the QA visit to train staff or to provide specific support in their specialized area of responsibility. The visits usually last two to three days and involve observations and discussions focusing on the QA Priority areas. A preliminary debrief is conducted with CC staff and investigators at the end of the visit. A formal report with required and recommended action items is sent to the CC after the visit. This report and the CC's formal response to the action items are also provided to the Project Office.

Performance goals set for many WHI tasks are based on criteria appropriate to assure the scientific integrity of the data, previously published standards of quality and safety, or ranges of performance. Goals are quantified as Meets/Exceeds Goal and Borderline for each of the QA Priority 1 and 2 activities, wherever possible. In most cases, the Meets/Exceeds Goal levels are greater than the protocol-defined goals to maintain high standards of performance. Borderline levels will not meet the protocol-defined goals and require prompt action. CCs with good performance are encouraged to share their strategies with other CCs on their routine staff group conference calls. CCs performing below performance goals are encouraged to discuss strategies for improving their performance with other CCs and with CCC staff liaisons.

Both the CCs and the CCC monitor CC performance relative to established goals on a wide variety of activities from meeting goals in recruitment and adherence to appraising the quality of data collected. The primary method used to monitor the CCs is the production and review of general and specific reports. The type, frequency, and detail of these monitoring reports are largely dictated by the QA priorities. Examples of reports include those that show CC progress in recruitment, adherence, retention, completeness of WHI specified tasks and associated data collection, maintenance of participant safety, validity and accuracy of the data collected, and timeliness and reliability of data collection. In addition, the CCC performs an audit of selected participant files to evaluate the quality of CC data collection and documentation with every QA visit. Additional file audits may also be conducted at other times locally or by the CCC. In general, files are selected at random, although they may also be selected based on particular problem areas.

CCs have the ability to produce many specific monitoring reports from their own database. Using these CC-produced reports, CCs can evaluate many aspects of their operations, compare their performance to studywide goals, identify issues and procedures that need review, and monitor individual staff performance. The reports also allow the CCs to take corrective action early, before performance issues have a major effect on other areas of study operations and before they appear on centrally produced monitoring reports.

The CCC also prepares a set of quarterly reports showing data for activities such as follow-up, adherence and retention, and outcomes. The reports are prepared from the quarterly consolidated database and show quarterly and cumulative data by CC, allowing comparisons between CCs. Examples of distributed quarterly reports include DM performance, HRT and CaD pill collection and adherence, retention or follow-up of all participants, and specific monitoring of safety events requiring discontinuation of HRT or CaD study pills. New reports are added as new stages in the study occur, and other reports are dropped as activities stop (e.g., recruitment). Footnotes on each table indicate the routine reports CCs can use to monitor their own performance.

Providing feedback in a timely and useful way is important for maintaining and improving performance at all levels. The means of providing such feedback include manual updates, training and recertification, CC observations, and QA visits. Taking into account each CC's circumstances and depending on the source of performance information (e.g., questions from the CC, database reports, QA visits), the appropriate CCC action may include encouraging the CC to maintain its performance level, discussions to help identify problems and investigate ways to improve performance, recommendations to perform additional observations, requests to retrain and recertify staff, or requests to plan and document strategies for addressing performance issues.

The performance of all CCs is reviewed and feedback offered on a regular basis following a four-step Performance Monitoring Plan. CCC QA staff and lead staff liaisons routinely contact the lead staff from each clinic to review database reports and discuss CC activities. Liaison staff also monitor clinic-specific performance in key areas to provide timely and routine feedback and assistance regarding performance concerns to clinics where appropriate. This Performance Monitoring Plan also integrates regular Performance Monitoring Committee (PMC) review of CCs, followed by general feedback or more targeted performance enhancement efforts (e.g., conference calls, visits) (Pottern et al., 2001).

OUTCOMES ASCERTAINMENT COORDINATION

The CCC has established systems for supporting CC outcomes or events ascertainment (data collection of participant-reported health events), investigation (requesting and assembling relevant medical records), and local and central adjudication (physician determination of an outcome event based on study-established criteria). The CCC has developed an outcomes database subsystem that supports analysis of medical history update forms, identifies WHI outcomes, generates medical records requests, assembles appropriate documents into case adjudication packets, and monitors each step of outcomes processing. Documentation for outcomes also includes the outcomes procedures manual, data collection forms specific for outcomes adjudication, and central training of CC Outcomes Coordinators.

To determine the primary outcome diagnosis, adjudication of WHI outcomes is carried out by local CC physicians trained in WHI adjudication protocols, who complete the outcomes forms that are entered in the local CC database, thus providing data on events and endpoints in the WHI. For quality assurance purposes and under the oversight of the Morbidity and Mortality Advisory Committee, the CCC coordinates central adjudication of the primary outcomes for the WHI Clinical Trial. These primary outcomes include deaths and cardiovascular events (by a central committee of physician adjudicators); breast, colorectal, ovarian, and endometrium cancer outcomes (by trained tumor coders at the CCC); and hip fractures (by the bone density quality control subcontractor). These central adjudication activities necessitate creation and maintenance of a central adjudication database subsystem, CCC archive of copied CC case adjudication packets, assignment of central adjudicators to specific cases, coordination of mailings to adjudicators, receipt of adjudicator decisions, and annual meetings of adjudicators to reach final agreement in selected cases.

ANALYSIS AND REPORTING OF DATA

Many of the routine reports on recruitment (completed in 1998, except for the CaD component of the CT), for quality assurance, for performance monitoring, and selected other purposes in WHI have already been described. Beyond these reports there are two main categories of data analyses. Biannually the CCC prepares both a semiannual progress report and a report for the external Data and Safety Monitoring Board. On an ongoing basis CCC staff interrogate the WHI database toward the production of scientific papers. In addition, specialized data analyses may be conducted to address scientific or operational issues arising in the study, often in conjunction with one or more of the advisory committees previously mentioned. Specialized analyses may also be carried out to facilitate the planning or conduct of ancillary studies that build on the WHI infrastructure using external funding.

The biannual progress reports serve primarily to update study investigators and the sponsoring institute on key aspects of both the CT and OS. Initially, there was major focus on recruitment rates in relation to corresponding expectations. Then the emphasis moved to retention and to intervention adherence in the CT. Other elements of these reports include the numbers of adjudicated disease events and deaths for a broad range of disease categories, along with routine analyte results (blood lipids, antioxidants, and clotting factors) and bone density results. These outcome and intermediate outcome numbers and distributions are shown only in the aggregate across the intervention groups in each CT component (i.e., unblinded data with randomization group assignment are not included). In addition, updates are presented on performance monitoring activities, on the timeliness of outcome adjudication and other program activities, and on the status of WHI publications and ancillary studies.

The biannual DSMB report covers much of this same territory for the CT, but its emphasis is on the presentation and updating of data on participant safety and on participant clinical outcomes by randomization group. Formal statistical comparisons are presented to compare randomized groups with respect to primary and secondary clinical outcomes for each CT component and for a designated global outcome that is intended to provide an informative assessment of overall health benefits versus risks. Graphs of test statistics across time for primary and for global outcomes are presented in conjunction with predetermined boundaries that may trigger DSMB discussion of early stoppage of a CT component, based on evidence of efficacy or harm. Displays by intervention arm are also given for a broad range of other diseases and symptoms, which contribute to the Board's overall evaluation of the usefulness of, and role for, the interventions under test.

CCC Statistical Unit staff devote much of their time to supporting the development of scientific papers, aside from the times of the year when

DSMB and progress reports are under development. With an Observational Study of nearly 94,000 postmenopausal women having an average follow-up (in early 2002) of nearly five years, substantial data on personal characteristics and exposures, and a substantial system for clinical outcome ascertainment, there are many opportunities for association studies. In fact, about 100 papers are currently underway or recently completed using this resource. The CT data also contribute to some of these papers, but, of course, the key papers must await the termination of a CT component and unblinding of the data. There are also close to 100 ancillary studies underway or in the planning stages. These studies typically require some merging of data collected under the ancillary study with data from the central WHI database and may require data management, and statistical and scientific support from the CCC. In fact, providing the personnel and resources needed to facilitate the planning and funding of ancillary studies is one of the more difficult management challenges for the CCC.

CCC MANAGEMENT ACTIVITIES IN RELATION TO STUDY PHASE

Some of these roles and responsibilities have changed qualitatively as the study has moved from one phase to the next, based on evolving data or issues within the study and in response to scientific findings or other events external to the WHI. This section highlights some of the changes in CCC management activities over the time period 1992 to 2002. Activity at the CCC began in October 1992, before the first 16 vanguard CCs were named in 1993 (the final set of 24 CCs were named in 1994, after developing and testing the protocol and procedures for a year). In collaboration with the Program Office and scientific experts across the United States, the CCC developed the protocol, data collection forms, study manuals, and intervention materials. All of the CCC functional units were involved in developing study procedures and drafting the WHI manuals. Operational systems were established for communications, documentation, distribution of study pills, collection and storage of biological specimens, and data collection and computer data entry.

After the 16 vanguard CCs were named, CCC activities expanded to include the implementation of materials and operational systems based on study phase and priorities, sequenced communications to facilitate CC start-up, coordination of an investigator meeting, and central training of lead staff. Recruitment Coordinators from the 16 CCs also met centrally to share expertise, plan strategies, and develop a studywide recruitment brochure. The CCC coordinated and led monthly conference calls with each of the lead staff groups to facilitate start-up and respond to questions. CCC QA staff (one clinical liaison and one nutrition liaison) conducted initial QA visits within the first year of CC start-up.

The implemented protocol, procedures, and operational systems were carefully scrutinized by all WHI entities during the first year of vanguard CC activity. The CCC participated in a streamlining task force of study investigators and staff to refine the protocol and activities before the final 24 CCs were named. CCC activities to facilitate start-up of the 24 new CCs then followed a model similar to that used with the vanguard CCs: a sequenced set of communications, distribution of study materials, installation of the WAN/LAN, coordination of an investigator meeting, central training of lead staff, monthly conference calls with each of the lead staff groups, and initial QA visits. The monthly conference calls continued with the vanguard CC lead staff groups, but were held separately from these other CC calls because of different needs related to their phase of activity.

CCC responsibilities during the recruitment phase initially included monthly reporting of screening activities, CT randomizations, and OS enrollments at each CC and studywide. Based on these data, CCs could calculate yields at each step of the recruitment and screening process and plan catch-up activities as needed (Hays et al., in press). When an identifiable study logo was chosen, the CCC ensured that the logo, stylized "Women's Health Initiative," recruitment message ("Be part of the answer"), and/or logo colors were included as much as possible in studywide materials. The CCC incorporated recruitment materials (e.g., brochures, magnets, buttons, and stickers) in its system for regular CC ordering of studywide supplies.

A National Recruitment and Public Awareness Campaign, which was spearheaded by a public affairs firm (Porter-Novelli) was also initially under CCC auspices to facilitate recruitment efforts. The CCC coordinated the activities of an advisory group of selected WHI investigators and Recruitment Coordinators that reviewed and advised on the planning, implementation, and evaluation of campaign activities. The first year of the national campaign coincided with a meeting of all 40 CC Recruitment Coordinators to plan and share recruitment strategies. Print, audio, and video materials for national release were also prepared and used by CCs (Hays et al., in press). A 1-800 recruitment line was established to support the national campaign. Potential participants could call this number and, based on their area code and prefix, be automatically routed to a recruitment line at the clinical center in their area or to a message line that was administered by the CCC.

Follow-up is the longest phase of WHI activities and continues through 2005. CCC management responsibilities during the follow-up phase include replacement lead staff training (every 6 to 12 months, as needed) and updating or maintaining communications, study documents and participant material distribution systems, computer and network systems, database systems, and quality assurance monitoring that support ongoing activities at the CCs. Outcomes ascertainment is an area of activity that has increased dramatically and has become progressively more complex during the follow-up phase. The CCC has responsibilities for monitoring and supporting CC efforts to promote participant adherence and retention, another major focus of the follow-up phase. Activities include the ongoing development and revision (based on review by WHI organizational entities) of quarterly DM maintenance sessions for DM intervention participants, and participant newsletters. Additionally, the CCC coordinates the development and implementation of new strategies to address adherence and retention challenges, including a series of specialized maintenance activities for DM intervention participants and study updates and handouts for all CT participants. The CCC provides logistical and some program coordination support for one adherence and retention training workshop each year, the focus of which is defined by high-priority study challenges faced during that year. Workshops have focused on issues related to special populations, motivational enhancement skills for Group Nutritionists, the HRT and CaD components, and aging.

Some preliminary strategies for study closeout (in 2004 and 2005) were defined in the original study protocol. The WHI investigator community began more intensive planning for closeout activities in 2001 (three to four years before participants would actually attend their last WHI clinic visit). That planning is still ongoing in 2003. CCC responsibilities related to study closeout are consistent with activities at other phases of the study: documentation and distribution of procedures, finalizing participant materials, developing appropriate database support, and monitoring and reporting on study activities.

CCC activities continue for two years beyond CC closeout. Activities during that time will be finalizing outcomes adjudication, data management and clean-up, data analyses, and final reporting of study results.

SUMMARY

The WHI, with a multifaceted, randomized, controlled clinical trial that includes 68,133 postmenopausal women, and a cohort study that enrolled over 93,676 postmenopausal women, extends over a 15-year period. Two of the CT components involve significant challenges: the HRT components in view of the need for careful safety monitoring, and the DM component because of the need to effect and maintain a substantial behavioral change over a lengthy time period. Furthermore, the size and scope of the WHI imply organization and management issues that far exceed those for previous studies. Clinical Center investigators and staff, the NHLBI Program Office, and the CCC have endeavored to develop an organization and a set of procedures that can meet these challenges. This has required various adjustments and adaptations over the past ten years. In fact, it took some period of time for investigators and staff, who mostly had not worked together previously, to learn how to effectively contribute to the achievement of study goals. This chapter summarizes some of the activities of the WHI Clinical Coordinating Center in these evolutions, and in the management of this exciting women's health research program.

REFERENCES

Anderson, G. A., Davis, S., & Koch, F. (2002). *A comprehensive data management system for multicenter studies.* Manuscript submitted for publication.

Blumenstein, B. A., James, K. E., Lind, B. K., & Mitchell, H. E. (1995). Functions and organization of coordinating centers for multicenter studies. *Controlled Clinical Trials, 16,* 4S–29S.

Curb, J. D., Ford, C., Hawkins, C. M., Smith, E. O., Zimbaldi, N., Carter, B., & Cooper, C. (1983). A coordinating center in a clinical trial: The Hypertension Detection and Followup Program. *Controlled Clinical Trials, 4,* 171–186.

Freedman, L., Anderson, G., Kipnis, V., Prentice, R., Wang, C. Y., Rossouw, J., Wittes, J., & DeMets, D. (1996). Approaches to monitoring the results of long-term disease prevention trials: Examples from the Women's Health Initiative. *Controlled Clinical Trials, 17,* 509–525.

Gassman, J. J., Owen, W. W., Kuntz, T. E., Martin, J. P., & Amoroso, W. P. (1995). Data quality assurance, monitoring, and reporting. *Controlled Clinical Trials, 16,* 104S–136S.

Hays, J., Hunt, J. R., Hubbell, A., Anderson, G., Limacher, M., Allen, C., & Rossouw, J. (in press.) Recruitment of postmenopausal women in the Women's Health Initiative. *Annals of Epidemiology.*

Knatterud, G. L., Rockhold, F. W., George, S. L., Barton, F. B., Davis, C. E., Fairweather, W. R., Honohan, T., Mowery, R., & O'Neill, R. (1998). Guidelines for quality assurance in multicenter trials: A position paper. *Controlled Clinical Trials, 19,* 477–493.

Pottern, L., Naughton, M., Lund, B., Cochrane, B., Brinson, Y., Kotchen, J., McTiernan, A., & Shumaker, S. (2001). *Innovative strategies for monitoring and enhancing clinic performance in the WHI Clinical Trial: The creation of the Performance Monitoring Committee.* Manuscript in preparation.

Women's Health Initiative Study Group. (1998). Design of the Women's Health Initiative clinical trial and observational study. *Controlled Clinical Trials, 19,* 61–109.

Writing Group for the Women's Health Initiative Investigators. (2002). Risks and benefits of estrogen plus progestin in healthy postmenopausal women: Principal results from the Women's Health Initiative randomized clinical trial. *Journal of the American Medical Association, 288,* 321–333.

APPENDIX 1.   WHI INVESTIGATORS

We wish to acknowledge all WHI Centers and their Principal Investigators for their participation in this research. A list of key personnel involved with this research follows.

Program Office: (National Heart, Lung, and Blood Institute, Bethesda, MD) Jacques E. Rossouw, Linda Pottern, Shari Ludlam, Joan McGowan, Nancy Morris

Clinical Coordinating Center: (Fred Hutchinson Cancer Research Center, Seattle, WA) Ross Prentice, Garnet Anderson, Andrea LaCroix, Ruth Patterson, Anne McTiernan, Barbara Cochrane, Julie Hunt, Lesley Tinker, Charles Kooperberg, Martin McIntosh, C. Y. Wang, Chu Chen, Deborah Bowen, Alan Kristal, Janet Stanford, Nicole Urban, Noel Weiss, Emily White; (Bowman Gray School of Medicine, Winston-Salem, NC) Sally Shumaker, Pentti Rautaharju, Ronald Prineas, Michelle Naughton; (Medical Research Labs, Highland Heights, KY) Evan Stein, Peter Laskarzewski; (University of California at San Francisco, San Francisco, CA) Steven Cummings, Michael Nevitt, Maurice Dockrell; (University of Minnesota, Minneapolis, MN) Lisa Harnack; (McKesson Bioservices, Rockville, MD) Frank Cammarata, Steve Lindenfelser; (University of Washington, Seattle, WA) Susan Heckbert, Bruce Psaty.

Clinical Centers: (Albert Einstein College of Medicine, Bronx, NY) Sylvia Wassertheil-Smoller; (Baylor College of Medicine, Houston, TX) Jennifer Hays; (Brigham and Women's Hospital, Harvard Medical School, Boston, MA) JoAnn Manson; (Brown University, Providence, RI) Annlouise R. Assaf; (Emory University, Atlanta, GA) Lawrence Phillips; (Fred Hutchinson Cancer Research Center, Seattle, WA) Shirley Beresford; (George Washington University Medical Center, Washington, DC) Judith Hsia; (Harbor-UCLA Research and Education Institute, Torrance, CA) Rowan

Chlebowski; (Kaiser Permanente Center for Health Research, Portland, OR) Cheryl Ritenbaugh; (Kaiser Permanente Division of Research, Oakland, CA) Bette Caan; (Medical College of Wisconsin, Milwaukee, WI) Jane Morley Kotchen; (Medstar Research Institute, Washington, DC) Barbara V. Howard; (Northwestern University, Chicago/Evanston, IL) Linda Van Horn; (Rush-Presbyterian St. Luke's Medical Center, Chicago, IL) Henry Black; (Stanford Center for Research in Disease Prevention, Stanford University, Stanford, CA) Marcia L. Stefanick; (State University of New York at Stony Brook, Stony Brook, NY) Dorothy Lane; (The Ohio State University, Columbus, OH) Rebecca Jackson; (University of Alabama at Birmingham, Birmingham, AL) Cora Beth Lewis; (University of Arizona, Tucson/Phoenix, AZ) Tamsen Bassford; (University at Buffalo, Buffalo, NY) Maurizio Trevisan; (University of California at Davis, Sacramento, CA) John Robbins; (University of California at Irvine, Orange, CA) Allan Hubbell; (University of California at Los Angeles, Los Angeles, CA) Howard Judd; (University of California at San Diego, LaJolla/Chula Vista, CA) Robert D. Langer; (University of Cincinnati, Cincinnati, OH) Margery Gass; (University of Florida, Gainesville/Jacksonville, FL) Marian Limacher; (University of Hawaii, Honolulu, HI) David Curb; (University of Iowa, Iowa City/Davenport, IA) Robert Wallace; (University of Massachusetts, Worcester, MA) Judith Ockene; (University of Medicine and Dentistry of New Jersey, Newark, NJ) Norman Lasser; (University of Miami, Miami, FL) Mary Jo O'Sullivan; (University of Minnesota, Minneapolis, MN) Karen Margolis; (University of Nevada, Reno, NV) Robert Brunner; (University of North Carolina, Chapel Hill, NC) Gerardo Heiss; (University of Pittsburgh, Pittsburgh, PA) Lewis Kuller; (University of Tennessee, Memphis, TN) Karen C. Johnson; (University of Texas Health Science Center, San Antonio, TX) Robert Schenken; (University of Wisconsin, Madison, WI) Catherine Allen; (Wake Forest University School of Medicine, Winston-Salem, NC) Gregory Burke; (Wayne State University School of Medicine/Hutzel Hospital, Detroit, MI) Susan Hendrix.

APPENDIX 2.   WHI DATA COLLECTION
FORMS (AND TIMING)

Eligibility Screen (Form 2 or 3, All WHI participants during screening)—name; mailing address; telephone numbers and best times to call; date of birth; residing in area for next three years; current involvement in other research studies; history of cancer (site, diagnosis in past 10 years); ethnicity; recruitment source; hormone use (present, in last three months); osteoporosis-related fracture and hormone use as treatment; hysterectomy history; last menstrual bleeding; number of meals prepared away from home; special diets (type); history of diabetes, deep vein thrombosis, pulmonary embolus, stroke, transient ischemic attack, myocardial infarction; history of sickle cell anemia, heart failure, liver disease, bleeding problem; loss of 15 pounds in last six months; renal failure requiring hemodialysis; other chronic illness; emotional or mental problems; ability to get to clinical center; interest in DM; interest in HRT (willingness to stop current hormone medications).

HRT Washout (Form 4, HRT participants taking HRT during screening)—date stopped hormones; assessment of symptoms after stopping (HRT for those on hormones at Initial Contact).

Final Eligibility Assessment (Form 6, All WHI participants during screening)—confirmation of eligibility due to medical conditions, depression, substance abuse, staff assessment.

CaD Eligibility Review (Form 16, All CaD participants for screening)—confirmation of eligibility due to medical conditions, personal supplement, and staff assessment.

Initial, HRT, DM, CaD, OS Consents (Form 11–Consent Status, All WHI participants during screening)—date signed or refused; reasons refused; genetic studies consented or refused.

Participation Status (Form 7, All WHI participants as needed to change intervention or follow-up status)—date of change, type of change, and reason for change.

Personal Information (Form 20, All WHI participants during screening)—name, address, address and telephone number of contacts not living with participant, social security number, education, employment status, occupation, marital status, partner's name, social security number, education, employment status, occupation; total family income; primary health care provider's name, address, phone number; recent history of mammogram, pelvic exam, endometrial aspiration; insurance coverage.

Personal Information Update (Form 21, CT participants semi-annually, OS participants at Annual Visit (AV) 3)—name, address, and phone numbers, best time to call; names, addresses, and phone numbers of contacts not living with participant; primary health care provider's name and address.

Medical History (Form 30, All WHI participants during screening)—hospitalization history; history of medical conditions; history of heart, circulatory, or coagulation problems; history of arthritis, gallbladder disease, thyroid disease, hypertension, angina, peripheral arterial disease and related procedures, colonoscopy or sigmoidoscopy, stool guaiac; history of cancers (site, age at diagnosis); recent history of falls or syncopal episodes; history of fractures (site, age, number).

Medical History Update (Form 33 and Form 33Detail as needed, CT participants semi-annually, OS participants annually)—hospitalization since last contact; hospitalization for heart, circulatory, or coagulation problems; stroke or transient ischemic attack, number of falls or syncopal episodes, fractures update; cancer (type, where diagnosed, hospitalization); mammogram; breast biopsy, needle aspiration, or lumpectomy; tests and procedures; electrocardiogram; diagnosis of new conditions; hip or other joint replacement.

Addendum to Medical History Update (Form 40 all WHI participants, one time only)—family history of deep vein thrombosis and pulmonary embolus; expanded ethnicity

Reproductive History (Form 31, All WHI participants during screening)—age at menarche; history of menstrual irregularity and amenorrhea; history of menopausal symptoms; history of pregnancy, pregnancy outcomes, infertility; history of breast feeding; history of gynecologic and breast surgeries.

Family History (Form 32, All WHI participants during screening)—number of full-blooded sisters and brothers, daughters, and sons; parental age or date of death; relatives' history of diabetes, myocardial infarction, stroke, cancers; fractures in parents (site, age).

Personal Habits (Form 34, All WHI participants during screening)—coffee consumption; smoking history; alcohol history; weight change; special diets; history of physical activity and exercise (frequency, duration).

Personal Habits Update (Form 35, CT participants at AV1, 3, 6, and 9)—physical activity and exercise, alcohol consumption, current cigarette smoking.

Thoughts and Feelings/Daily Life (Form 37, All WHI participants during screening)—social support; social integration; caregiving; social strain; optimism; negative emotional expressiveness; hostility; quality of life; symptoms; life events; depression; sleep disturbance; urinary incontinence; sexual functioning.

Daily Life (Form 38, CT participants at AV1, CT subsample at AV3, 6, and 9; OS at AV3)—quality of life; symptoms; life events; depression; sleep disturbance; urinary incontinence; sexual functioning.

Cognitive Status (Form 39, HRT participants 65 years or older at AV1, 3, 6, and 9)—expanded minimental status examination (MMSE).

Hormone Use (Form 43, All WHI participants during screening)—current and past hormone replacement; history of oral contraceptive, diethylstilbestrol, depo-provera use.

Current Medications (Form 44, All WHI participants during screening, CT participants at AV1, 3, 6, and 9, OS participants at AV3)—current medication inventory.

Current Supplements (Form 45, All WHI participants during screening, CT participants at AV1, 3, 6, and 9, OS participants at AV3)—current dietary supplements inventory.

Change of Medications (Form 54, All HRT and CaD participants as needed to change study pill regimen)—date of change, new regimen, duration of change, reason for change.

Food Frequency Questionnaire (Form 60, All WHI participants during screening, CT participants at AV1, DM subsample at AV2 through 9; OS participants at AV3)—food frequency questionnaire.

Four-Day Food Record (Form 62, all DM participants during screening and DM subsample at AV1).

24-hour Dietary Recall (DM subsample during screening and at AV1 through 9).

Physical Measurements (Form 80, All WHI participants during screening, CT participants annually, OS participants at AV3)—blood pressure; resting pulse; height, weight, waist and hip circumference.

Functional status (Form 90, CT subsample of participants age 65 and older at baseline and AV1, 3, 6, and 9)—grip strength; chair stand; time to walk 18 feet.

Pelvic Exam (Form 81, HRT participants at screening, HRT participants with a uterus annually).

Pap Smear (Form 92, HRT participants at screening, HRT participants with a cervix at AV3, 6, and 9).

Endometrial Aspiration (Form 82, HRT participants with a uterus during screening, HRT subsample at AV3, 6, and 9).

Clinical Breast Exam (Form 84, CT participants at screening, HRT participants annually).

Mammogram (Form 85, CT participants at screening, HRT participants annually, DM participants biannually).

ECG (Form 86, CT participants at screening and AV3, 6, and 9)—Resting 12-lead electrocardiogram.

Blood Collection (Form 100, CT participants at screening and AV1, CT subsample at AV3, 6, and 9, OS participants at screening and AV3)—Hematocrit, white blood cell count, platelet count, fasting triglycerides (as needed for HRT eligibility at baseline); fasting serum, plasma (citrate and EDTA), buffy coat, RBCs for storage.

Medication Dispensation (HRT participants during screening, HRT and CaD participants at randomization and semiannually or annually thereafter).

Medication Adherence (HRT participants during screening, HRT and CaD participants at randomization and semiannually or annually thereafter).

HRT Safety Interview (Form 10, HRT participants during screening, 6 weeks after randomization, and semiannually while on intervention)—presence and amount of vaginal bleeding; changes in breasts; presence of other symptoms or worries, health changes that might require stopping study pills, pill-taking behaviors.

CaD Safety Interview (Form 17, CaD participants at 4 weeks after randomization and semiannually)—presence of gastrointestinal symptoms or other symptoms or concerns, health changes that might require stopping study pills, pill-taking behaviors.

HRT Calendar (Form 53, given to HRT participants at Baseline and Semi-Annual Visit 1, to turn in at SAV1 and AV1)—days and amount of vaginal bleeding (HRT women with uterus).

Observational Study Questionnaire (Form 42, OS participants during screening)—birth weight, birth status, breast feeding at birth; coffee/tea consumption; alcohol history; smoking history; history of breast examination, history of benign breast disease, recent history of mammogram; history of the use of powders in genital area or on sanitary napkins; history of diaphragm; history of electric blanket use; religious affiliation; recent history of physical activity and exercise (frequency, duration); occupational history; height and weight history, weight change; state of residence history.

Observational Study Exposure Update Questionnaires (e.g., Form 48 at AV1, Form 143 at AV3, Form 144 at AV4, Form 145 at AV5, Form 146 at AV6, OS participants, Form 147 at AV7, Form 148 at AV8)—annual updates of key exposure information and assessment of selected new exposures.

Bone Density Scan (Form 87, Three bone density sites only—All WHI participants at screening, CT participants at AV1, 3, 6, and 9; OS participants at AV3, 6, and 9)—Bone densitometry scan.

Urine collection (Form 101, Three bone density sites only—All WHI participants at screening, CT participants at AV1, 3, 6, and 9, OS participants at AV3 and 9)—Urine for storage.

11

The Early Head Start Research and Evaluation Consortium: Collaborations and Partnerships

Rachel F. Schiffman

BACKGROUND

Early Head Start is a child development program consisting of comprehensive, two-generation services to enhance child development and support families. In addition to the child development and family domains, Early Head Start programs provide staff development for professional growth and community development, particularly in the areas of child care and services for children and families (Early Head Start, n.d.; Paulsell et al., 2000).

In 1995, the first wave of Early Head Start programs was funded by the Administration on Children, Youth and Families (ACYF) of the Department of Health and Human Services (DHHS) to serve low-income pregnant women and families with infants and toddlers. The stimuli for this new Head Start initiative came from multiple sources including (1) a Carnegie Corporation report, *Starting Points*, which identified a "quiet crisis" facing families with very young children (Carnegie Task Force, 1994), (2) recommendations from the DHHS Advisory Committee on Services for Families with Infants and Toddlers (Early Head Start, n.d.; Paulsell, Kisker, Love, & Raikes, 2000), (3) a growing need for services for infants and toddlers in communities (Early Head Start; Paulsell et al.), and (4) the Head Start Act Amendments of 1994, which established a special initiative with progressively increasing percents of Head Start funding directed to Early Head Start. The Coats Human Services Reauthorization Act of 1998 continued and increased the set aside for funding Early Head Start. Funding for Early Head Start went from 3% of Head Start funding in 1995 to 10% set aside in 2002 and the number of programs grew from 68 to 664 in the same period.

My association with the Community Action Agency (CAA) in Jackson, Michigan, began in the early 1990s when my colleague from the College of Nursing, Dr. Mildred Omar, and I conducted an evaluation of the agency's Center for Healthy Beginnings, a primary care center for women. In 1995, following the successful completion of this evaluation, I was asked to write the evaluation/continuous quality improvement plan for the Early Head Start program proposal being submitted to DHHS by the CAA. The CAA was successful and was funded as one of the first wave of 68 Early Head Start programs. In this chapter I discuss this multisite research from my experiences as the principal investigator (PI) of one of the evaluation sites and as a member of the Consortium formed to coordinate the national evaluation of the Early Head Start program.

With the notification of funding came an announcement indicating that each newly funded site was eligible to participate in the national evaluation of the Early Head Start program by establishing a community–university partnership and proposing site-specific research. The university partner was expected to submit a competitive proposal to ACYF that addressed research questions relevant to the community partner's program and that would enhance, enrich, or expand the national evaluation and provide rich background that might explain outcomes. The community partner was expected to participate in a clinical trial and enroll a sufficient number of families to meet the research design requirements. How many researchers are fortunate enough to be *asked* by a community agency to participate in a randomized trial? The agency was willing to withstand the community pressures of participating in an experimental design and the university was committed to assist me in putting together a multidisciplinary team to meet the requirements of the RFA. The community–university partnership between Michigan State University and the Community Action Agency has been described elsewhere (Schiffman, Fitzgerald, & DeLuca, 2002).

The Early Head Start Research and Evaluation Project was a high-stakes, policy-relevant research endeavor mandated by the public laws that funded the Early Head Start programs. Although the content of the evaluation was not legislated, the timing was. The results of the impact study were due to the relevant Congressional committees by June 1, 2002 (Coats Human Services Reauthorization Act of 1998; Head Start Act Amendments of 1994).

Mathematica Policy Research, Inc., a private policy research organization, and the Center for Children and Families at Teachers College, Columbia University, conducted the Early Head Start Research and Evaluation Project in collaboration with ACYF, 15 universities, and 17 Early Head Start programs.

The project had multiple components, including an impact study, an implementation study, local (site-specific) research studies, policy studies on emergent issues, and continuous quality improvement (Paulsell et al., 2000). All programs were heavily involved in the national implementation study and in continuous quality improvement for their programs. Smaller groups within the consortium were formed to address policy issues, notably welfare reform. The local research teams represented partnerships between university-based researchers and representatives from Early Head Start programs (one university was partnered with two programs and one program did not have a local research partner; one of the sites was from the second wave of program funding). The local researchers were selected through a competitive application process. Local research teams were most involved with the impact study and their own site-specific research.

As part of the application submitted in response to the RFA, we had not only to describe our site-specific research but we had to agree to be a site for the national evaluation and to participate in the Consortium. Our program partners had to agree to participate in the experimental design and recruit a sufficient number of qualified families for random assignment to the two arms of the study. In addition to the scientific merit of the local research proposal, criteria for selecting community/university partnerships to participate in the research were aimed at constituting a balanced group across many domains such as type of program, geographic area, and accessible population (Early Head Start, n.d.; Paulsell et al., 2000). The proposal submitted to ACYF by the Michigan State University (MSU) team was focused on family health and was developed with our program partners to capture the central components of their model of care delivery, their close relationship with the community's primary care center, and the strengths of the multidisciplinary MSU team in nursing, developmental and community psychology, family and child ecology, and nutrition.

The funding mechanism for this study at the site level was multifaceted. Funding for the local research was from ACYF in the form of a cooperative agreement. A cooperative agreement implies that the grantor is more involved with the conduct of the research than in a traditional grant and sets boundary conditions for both the grantor and the grantee. Funding for the national data collection component was through a contract between the university and Mathematica Policy Research, Inc. (MPR). The initial contract required 10 supplements as adjustments were made in cost estimates and new work was added, notably spinoff research on the role of fathers in the lives of these very young children. In addition, the MSU team has had contracts with the Community Action Agency for supplemental studies on fathers, welfare reform, and continuous quality improvement.

The formal working of the Consortium began with the advent of funding and the first meeting of the Consortium in early May of 1996. The Consortium met a total of 13 times with the last formal meeting in November 2001. There were two separate local researcher meetings and three Head Start Research Conferences, which we were required to attend. In addition, Consortium members and workgroups took advantage of professional meetings, such as the Society for Research in Child Development's biennial meeting, to get together. Being a member of the Consortium has been a wonderful experience. I worked closely with my funding agency through my project officer; with other members of ACYF who were responsible for the national research project and the Early Head Start programs; with researchers from the prime contractor MPR; with Columbia University researchers; with 30 to 40 other university researchers from a wide variety of worldviews including nursing, early childhood education, developmental psychology, child psychiatry, pediatrics, language and linguistics, among others; and with Early Head Start program directors from across the country. From the very first meeting we formed a bond that has lasted through the six years of the project and that continues, albeit in a reformulated Consortium moving beyond the initial funding and into the next phase with a pre-Kindergarten follow-up study. We are united in our mantra to "keep our eye on the prize," the prize being the children in our study and in the many Early Head Start programs across the country.

Participation in this project had many aspects that were similar to other multisite studies (Hogg, 1991; Powell, Lloyd, & Olajide, 1999; Smith, Salyer, Geddes, & Mark, 1998) such as core measures collected in a standardized fashion and regular meetings. Yet there were differences, particularly in the locus of decision making and in the relationship between the research sites and the funding agencies. The multiple levels of collaboration and partnership needed to make this project succeed are described from my perspective at the level of my individual site and at the level of my participation in the Consortium.

DEVELOPING RELATIONSHIPS—THE LOCAL PERSPECTIVE

Although this was a positive experience, that is not to say that there were no bumps in the road either at the local site level or at the Consortium level. At the site level, I had to develop relationships with two masters. One was my federal project officer at ACYF, who oversaw the local research component; the other was MPR, including the project director, principal investigator, and relevant staff, who oversaw the national evaluation component. For the most part, the local research cooperative agreement was very much like a grant. I was responsible for the science and the budget. For the science, there was determination of the instruments and measures to be used and the day-to-day management of the data collection, data entry, and data analysis relevant to the local research. Quarterly progress reports, that were later changed to semiannual reports, were expected, as was a final report. The budget was relatively standard; however, there was a yearly maximum of $150,000, inclusive of indirect costs and out-of-state travel that could include trips to attend the Consortium meetings, local researcher meetings, and the biennial Head Start Research Conference. These meetings were a condition of the cooperative agreement.

In addition, unlike most grants, the funding was approved on a yearly basis and each year was treated as new funding. The requirements for the noncompeting continuation application were streamlined to include only major changes from the original proposal and the budget for that year. This meant that each grant year received a different account number at the university and each required a six-month financial statement and a final statement. I had to request any funds not used in the preceding grant year to be carried over into the next grant year through an amended application and award process. Because of the cooperative agreement and consortial arrangement I had multiple and frequent interactions with my ACYF project officer on line, on the telephone, and in person, over six years. As a result, we developed a professional and personal relationship that may be different than other researchers have in a more traditional multisite funding arrangement. We were collaborators in the scientific component of the national evaluation. We discussed and debated the merits of measures, procedures, analytic strategies, and interpretation of findings within the context of the Consortium.

Also at the site level, a contract had to be negotiated with MPR, the prime contractor for the evaluation. Negotiations for the final contract took some time; however, during the contract development, MPR offered a letter of intent to the university with start-up funds since subject enrollment, data collector training, and data collection would begin within a very short time. MPR has a long history of conducting research in the field. The new wrinkle in this project for MPR was the injection of a middleman, the local researcher. The purpose of the contract with MPR was solely to collect the data for the national evaluation. MPR's practice was to work with a local site coordinator who oversaw all aspects of data collection, including return of the data to MPR. However, in most sites, including MSU, that site coordinator was not the faculty local researcher but rather the project manager for the local research.

Developing a relationship with MPR for this research at the site level required MPR to make adjustments in their usual mode—working with the PI as part of the local site team was the primary one. Local researchers had to make adjustments in their usual autonomy and control over the data collection situation in order to have consistency across sites. Although consistency of data collection is critical to any multisite study (Hoggs, 1991; Smith et al., 1998) in this case the protocols and data management were conducted through a primary contractor. MPR had a standard method for calculating cost per case that was different from what I was used to and from how I had budgeted for the companion local research component. In addition, it was difficult to determine adequate time allocation for the site coordinator and faculty local researcher and then to fit it into the MPR budget template. In our case, there was a co-PI to consider as well (after a few years, the MSU situation changed and there was only the PI to consider). These issues were resolved through negotiation, and adjustments were made over time as necessary.

Many aspects of the project, such as instrument preparation and respondent incentives for the national evaluation component, were managed centrally by MPR. It was difficult to determine how much administrative time was needed locally for these activities. For example, respondent incentives were not included in the site budgets from MPR. Normally, the university has a system by which the PI can access monies allocated in grants for respondent incentives and for accounting for the distribution. Some of the MPR incentives were in the form of checks made out to respondents and were sent with contact materials when a case window opened. In order to develop and maintain our relationships with the participants, we had to devise a system locally to allow for those participants who did not have access to free or reasonable check-cashing services. Data collectors asked participants if they would be able to cash the check easily. If the participant indicated that it would be a hardship, the data collector gave the participant the amount of the check in cash borrowed from the cash on hand for other incentives and had the participant sign the check. Data collectors returned the signed checks to the research office where they were deposited in the cash incentive account. Other problems with checks included stale checks that occurred when we had difficulty finding or scheduling visits with families, and unused checks for respondents whom we could not contact to schedule a visit.

Another incentive was in the form of a gift, in this case a gift certificate. MPR was able to negotiate with national chains such as Kmart and Wal-Mart for gift certificates that would then be sent to the sites. However, our community program partners recommended that gift certificates from a regional chain would be more appealing and convenient for our participants. MPR was willing to accommodate our site's preferences. This required the site coordinator to negotiate with the regional chain to accept MPR's check. She then had to request the check from MPR, wait for it to arrive, and then travel to a particular store branch to obtain the gift certificates. Eventually, MPR provided the PI with a check for incentives for a predetermined number of data collections. This made the process of obtaining incentives much easier and allowed us more choice in the type of incentive to give respondents.

We kept track of the money in a manner similar to that used with the University for funds that are accessed through grants and gave a careful accounting to MPR. However, initially determining how much of the site coordinator's time to allocate for such tasks was difficult and I seriously underestimated it. Fortunately, I was able to make adjustments through supplements to the contract.

I had to work with multiple levels of staff at MPR. Various staff were negotiating and managing the budget; others had responsibility for data collector training and for data collection, and these individuals changed over time. At first MPR was working through the site coordinator only—I had to be sure that I was copied on e-mails and included in the weekly telephone call to review progress of data collection. Eventually it became customary for the PI to be included in all interactions. As data collection was drawing to a close, the frequency of the calls decreased.

The national or cross-site data collection was guided very much as described by Smith and colleagues (1999); however, the problem they identify of attrition of site coordinators was attenuated in the Early Head Start study by having the PI (or coinvestigator) remain a constant. The MSU site has been very fortunate to have had only three site coordinators in six years, the most recent one for the last four years. This provided considerable stability despite high attrition among our data collectors.

Several performance reviews were held over the course of the contract. During these telephone conferences, MPR staff would review with the co-PI, the site coordinator, and me, the MSU site's completion rate for each of the data collection points and the completeness, quality, and timeliness of the data returned to MPR. The benchmarks utilized were the predetermined minimum acceptable completion rate of 80% for each data collection point and our site's position relative to the national average. We were also given the opportunity to comment on MPR's performance with respect to timeliness of receipt of materials and appropriateness and promptness of responses to our concerns and queries. The MSU site submitted high quality data and had completion rates consistently higher than the benchmarks and the national average for all data points. Having a site coordinator who was a consistent day-to-day manager for the MSU site was one of the major reasons for the success of this project.

BLENDING LOCAL AND NATIONAL RESEARCH

Data for the national evaluation were collected from multiple sources—parent reports, direct assessments of children, observations by trained observers, and videotaping and coding of parent–child interactions in problem solving and free-play situations—and at varied times—when the child was 14, 24, and 36 months of age and after the family had been enrolled in the research for 6, 15, and 26 months, and at the time of exit. In addition, if the children were involved in out-of-home care that met the established criteria at the 14, 24, and 36 month of age visits, we sought permission to visit the child care provider. If the child care provider agreed, child care data collection visits were made when the child was present at the day care home or center. All research sites were contracted to collect these data at these times.

Based on their local research, some sites collected additional data at the same time as one or more of the data points or at times other than those identified for the national evaluation. The MSU site used both of these approaches by adding a data collection point at or near the time of enrollment, adding medical and program records reviews, and supplementing the national measures at each data point with parent, child, or family measures; parent–child observations; or structured qualitative questions consistent with our local research focus on family health. Other sites focused their local research on a subsample from their site with intensive qualitative studies of a few families, while still others were focused only on the intervention children and families in their site with intensive studies of program participation.

Although the responsibility for collecting the core data for the national impact study for each site rested with the PI in that site, training was centralized and standardized by MPR. I hired the data collectors and was responsible for the training related to the site-specific measures and methods, but the data collectors and the project manager, who was considered the site coordinator, were trained by MPR, initially in a week-long training session in Princeton, New Jersey, where MPR is located, and subsequently in a shorter training session held in Kansas City, Missouri; final training took place locally with the site coordinator as the trainer. After training, data collectors had to be certified by MPR by way of video and audio taping of the national data collection protocols with non-research families. Quality control protocols were also implemented with periodic audio or video taping of the data collection visit to assess fidelity to the protocols.

As the prime contractor, MPR controlled the random assignment; the notification of the opening and closing of data collection windows; the production of the questionnaires and other data collection instruments for the national evaluation; the necessary equipment, including video cameras, videocassettes, laptop computers, booster chairs, toys, and the materials for mailing the data to MPR when collected. I was responsible for the equipment, for locating subjects, for collecting the data within the time windows, for checking the completeness of the data, and for sending the completed data to MPR. In return, our site received its site-specific data collected as part of the national evaluation and we were free to use some or all of the data to answer questions of local interest. We planned to use selected measures to answer our local research questions.

One of the drawbacks of this approach was that the national data were returned according to a set schedule after MPR had entered and cleaned the particular data set. Once we received the data, it took some time to make the MPR data set compatible with our local data set. At times we were held back in our local analyses because we did not have the national data for that time point.

One benefit of this approach was that we had access to measures collected for the national evaluation that we initially had not considered using. Another unexpected benefit was the return to us of a copy of the videotape of the child at play and the parent–child interactions. We had been searching for an appropriate gift to send participants between our waves of data collection as one strategy to minimize attrition (Given, Keilman, Collins, & Given, 1990) and the videotapes were a wonderful solution. Parents were quite pleased to receive copies of these videotapes and looked forward to the next wave of data collection, frequently asking when they could expect the videotape.

Managing the multiple budgets was also a challenge. Doing the payroll each week was an adventure. The cost for most data collection points was split between two accounts, one for the national data and one for the local data. Data collectors might do visits for local data collection that were charged to a separate account or for the supplementary fathers' study, a subaccount of the national data with a local component as well. Travel related to the data collection or other project business was likewise distributed among accounts. It was conceivable that one data collector's pay and reimbursement for expenses would be divided among four or five different accounts. This was also true for the office staff, primarily students, who had to carefully log their work with the accurate amount of time so that the appropriate accounts could be charged. The allocation of supplies and expenses had to be distributed appropriately across accounts as well. This included printer paper, phone bills, copying costs, and other miscellaneous expenses. All of these demanded careful attention on the part of the staff. As PI, I had to review and approve many of the requisitions or purchase orders to ensure that the charges would appear on the correct accounts; this would not have been usual or necessary with a simpler budget structure. The task also demanded careful scrutiny of each account's monthly ledger.

A final aspect of the blending of local and national perspectives was the preparation and maintenance of protocols for the protection of human subjects in research. Although this project was funded through multiple sources, the chair of the institutional review board (IRB) at MSU (University Committee on Research Involving Human Subjects—UCRIHS) advised me to prepare one application for review primarily because the common denominator across all of the components was the child. The initial application was a challenge to compile. The components had to be described in a meaningful way to distinguish between local and national components, measures, and instruments, many of which were in draft stages. Multiple consent forms were developed either by MPR, by the co-PI and me or by a combination of the two. For a period of time in the middle years of the project, the study of fathers in Early Head Start had a separate human subjects review, but the fathers study component was rolled back into the primary study protocol. The most difficult to develop was the main consent form. It had to cover random assignment, all the various levels of national and local data collection, and access to medical records for the child and the mother. In addition, the main consent form had to be acceptable to MPR as well as to UCRIHS. MPR provided a template and I was able to modify it to meet all the requirements. Other forms included special consents for videotaping the child, for use of the videotape for training and education, for permission to contact the child care provider and the child's father or father figure, as well as consents for the director of the child care center, for the direct provider of child care, and for the various combinations of resident, nonresident, biological and nonbiological fathers among others. At the time of the last data collection for the Early Head Start impact study, we added consent to contact in the future and consent to access preschool, day care, and school records as we anticipated doing a follow-up study. Very few of the participants refused to be contacted in the future.

DEVELOPING RELATIONSHIPS— THE CONSORTIUM PERSPECTIVE

The Early Head Start Research Consortium was a large, multilayered entity that functioned relatively well during the project, considering its size. The format of other multisite research may differ, but the importance of good communication with periodic face-to-face meetings is stressed not only for its professional and scientific value but also for its social value in building relationships (Hogg, 1991; Powell et al., 1999). The work of the Consortium exemplified one model of how multisite research can be done. Consortium meetings were held on average twice a year. During the meetings, the group as a whole conducted business such as issues of policy and procedure, while topical workgroups provided for more in-depth discussions that were later brought before the entire group. The workgroups ranged in scope from interest in concepts such as parent–child relationships and welfare reform to methodological areas such as data analytic strategies. Groups were often scheduled to meet during the formal meeting times but there were also breakfast, lunch, dinner, and evening meetings arranged ad hoc during the meeting days.

Some social activities were planned, such as a welcoming reception on the evening before the meeting began. Other activities evolved spontaneously as clusters of members gathered for dinner or to take advantage of the arts and entertainment available in the Washington, DC area where meetings of the Consortium were held.

The focus of the Consortium meetings changed from a concern about subject enrollment and data collection measures and methods in the early meetings to data analysis and inclusion of local research findings in the national reports in the later meetings. Attendees also changed over time. Researchers and the Technical Work Group were the primary participants at the early meetings. The MSU research team was represented by at least two members at each Consortium meeting. In the true spirit of partnership, program directors became integral members of the Consortium with the seventh meeting in May of 1998. What a great way to model research/ practice partnerships!

The CAA was a strong proponent of the integration of program directors. The program directors were able to set their own agenda for a portion of the meeting that was not combined with the researchers. This gave them an opportunity to share with each other and support each other in their unique positions as Early Head Start research programs. It also provided them with opportunities to dialogue with their federal program funders at Head Start and ACYF, an opportunity not afforded many Head Start/Early Head Start program directors as programs are generally supervised at the regional level.

The MSU team and research and program partners found the time together at the Consortium meetings to be extremely valuable. We were able to focus and discuss the implications of issues presented to the Consortium for our site. We also began a tradition of going out to dinner together on one night. These were the times when we got to know each other better and cemented our working relationships in walks along the Potomac in Alexandria, Virginia, where the Consortium frequently met.

MODES OF COMMUNICATION

A Steering Committee was established, composed of representatives from MPR and Columbia University, the ACYF project officer for the local research, the ACYF liaison/project officer for the national evaluation, and three representatives from the local researchers. A representative of the program directors was added when program directors were integrated into the Consortium. Each research site was expected to serve for one year on the Steering Committee. Some sites with multiple researchers involved were able to serve more often. The Steering Committee met monthly between Consortium meetings. It addressed problems that arose between meetings and planned the next Consortium meeting. Minutes were sent to all members of the Consortium. I served on the Steering Committee, as did two other members of the MSU team. A listserv was established early in the Consortium and was a useful communication tool. Conference calls were also utilized in a number of ways.

Although measures for the first round of data collection were predetermined, local researchers, through a series of conference calls, provided input and guidance for subsequent rounds. We appreciated the opportunity to make our case for retaining measures that were of particular interest to our site. This also provided local researchers with some lead time to add a measure to their local research that was being dropped or altered from the national battery. Later in the project a similar mechanism of conference calls was used to present results of the psychometric testing of the measures and again to seek input from the local researchers about analytic strategies. Many of the work groups also used the conference call mechanism to continue momentum gained at the Consortium meetings.

WORKGROUPS

The workgroups functioned in multiple ways and at different levels and provided synergy across the Consortium. A few of them are described to illustrate how this mechanism was utilized to advance and expand the work of the Consortium. From the first meeting, it was apparent that most of the parent report data for the national evaluation would be collected from mothers. A number of sites, including our site with its family focus, had identified fathers as a special supplementary research focus. There was sufficient interest in pursuing avenues, particularly funding mechanisms, to include fathers into the Early Head Start project that a workgroup was formed. The timing for this endeavor was ideal to tap into the Clinton Administration's Fatherhood Initiative (National Fatherhood Initiative, n.d.).

Through the concerted efforts of ACYF, MPR, and others across governmental agencies such as the National Institute for Child Health and Human Development and the Office of the Assistant Secretary for Planning and Evaluation of DHHS (ASPE) working with the Ford Foundation, funds were secured to support two waves of data collection from fathers, one when the child was 24 months old and another at 36 months. In addition, two other smaller, separate studies about fathers and father involvement in programs were funded (Fatherhood Research in the Early Head Start Research and Evaluation Project, n.d.). Twelve of the 17 sites participated in the 24- and 36-month father study, including ours. The funding was administered through MPR and was rolled into the existing contract. In addition, we had funding from CAA to supplement the national effort on fathers with local measures. The workgroup was very involved in developing the measures and procedures to be used for the study of fathers in Early Head Start. We had to deal with issues of how much of the father data should parallel the mother data and how much should be unique.

Because there was minimal research done with low-income fathers, the literature did not provide much guidance. A thin layer of open-ended qualitative questions was included to allow the fathers to talk about their experience of fathering and of being fathered. Three of the MSU team, including me, were active participants in this workgroup. One other member and I continue as active members in the follow-up study. The Fathers Workgroup has disseminated descriptive findings from the first round of data at national and international meetings.

Another workgroup, focused on the impact of welfare reform, was able to secure outside funding to support additional conference calls, meetings, and a separate study. Seven of the 17 sites participated in this spin-off, including the MSU site. Michigan was among the first states to implement changes in the welfare system. These changes were perceived to have an impact on the CAA's clients, particularly in Early Head Start, so this study was of special interest to our program partners. One of our team members was very active in this workgroup and led the MSU team that conducted this separately funded study. The workgroup developed a protocol that involved interviews from the top levels of state government through the local administration of the welfare programs to participants and former welfare participants from our sample. A number of white papers have been disseminated to policy makers as well as other presentations of the findings at national and international meetings.

A third workgroup focused on children with disabilities, functioning solely within the Consortium and doing their work at Consortium meetings and by e-mail and telephone conferences. This workgroup was interested in the enrollment and identification of children with disabilities and in the application of the measures and protocols to these children. The workgroup made recommendations to the Consortium for procedures to deal with children whose scores on cognitive and other measures were in the range indicating a need for referral. The workgroup was also involved in analysis of data for the subgroup of children in the study identified with disabilities.

POLICIES AND PROCEDURES

The smooth running of the Consortium required procedures and policies that were understood and agreed upon by the members. It was important to know under what circumstances the local researchers gave advice to the chair of the Consortium, who was the project director for the national evaluation, and when they had decision-making authority. Another interesting twist had to do with voting. There were issues where the sense of the whole was important regardless of site affiliation, while other issues were handled with one vote per site. These distinctions applied whether the Consortium was meeting in person or whether the issue was raised on the listserv. The Consortium was an example of blending and compromise. There were several nationally and internationally known and respected researchers as members of the Consortium. The measures and methods for the national evaluation may not have been what they would have selected if they were doing a project; nonetheless, they were members of collaborative teams in their sites and were committed to making the project work. Likewise, MPR and ACYF had to make adjustments and incorporate suggestions from the researchers and programs when these made sense. *All* of us were interested in maintaining the integrity of the research and obtaining the best data possible.

One of the major policies that had to be formulated dealt with publications and other dissemination of findings and data sharing. Issues of data ownership and authorship are essential for multisite research (Hogg, 1991; Powell et al., 1999) and, in this case, one of the conditions of the cooperative agreement dealt with abiding by the publications guidelines developed by the Consortium. Because of the policy-sensitive nature of the project, great care was taken to ensure that the findings of the national impact study, in the form of the preliminary and final reports, were completed and delivered to Congress as required prior to the release of any other evaluative information whether written or oral, local or national. In the same vein, all members of the Consortium, of local research teams including all project staff, and of program staff had to sign confidentiality agreements not to divulge or discuss findings until the reports were released. A committee was formed to develop the policy and to establish implementation procedures.

The policy included the definition of "evaluative," the multiple modes of dissemination (e.g., reports, manuscripts, papers, and posters), and a procedure for review of materials if there was a question as to whether evaluative findings were included. The policy also included guidelines for authorship (e.g., when the Consortium would be considered as author, how to recognize the Consortium members, and boilerplate for appropriate acknowledgments for the national evaluation team and for other local researchers).

Another aspect of this policy focused on data sharing across sites. This exemplified the sensitivity of the Consortium leaders and members to site-specific data. A process was established by which individuals or workgroups that wished to access data collected for the national evaluation from more than one site posted the request on the listserv with research questions, identified variables, and rationale. Principal investigators had to approve the use of their site-specific data before MPR would release the data. Although data from this project will become a public use data set, MPR did not have the budget or the resources to prepare multiple interim data sets without identifiers.

ADVANTAGES AND CHALLENGES

There were a number of advantages as well as some challenges to participation in this type of multisite research arrangement. I have framed the advantages as opportunities afforded by the Consortium:

- The opportunity to develop relationships and work with a multidisciplinary and diverse group of professionals, many of whom were recognized experts in their fields: This not only enriched the research project as a whole but also enhanced my own professional development. It was through the interactions I had in the Consortium that I was guided to seek a policy fellowship through the Society for Research in Child Development. As a result I spent a year in Washington, DC, as a policy fellow at the National Institute on Drug Abuse at the National Institutes of Health.
- The opportunity to model collaborative partnerships across multiple borders including research, practice, government, and funding: The concern that efficacious models of intervention in biobehavioral research are not implemented in the field speaks to the need to include the program or practice side in the research. Programs become invested in the research as a vehicle to improve practice and to make contributions to the field. That is not to say that all individual university-program partnerships were successful, but most were. It is also not to say that all activities, methods, and products of the Consortium were met with unanimous, enthusiastic approval, but most were. Individuals were generally able to leave their egos at the door and work together toward a common goal.
- The opportunity to have access to a large, national data set prior to its public use release: Local researchers benefited from procedures that were put in place to provide early access to this data set. This process was well thought out from access to data files through acknowledgments, and authorship for publications. Many questions

of interest at the local level can only be adequately addressed with the power inherent in large samples. The Early Head Start data set with about 3000 low-income families collected in the context of an experimental design is a gold mine to a researcher.

- The opportunity to see the interface of science, policy, and politics firsthand: Early Head Start and the Early Head Start Research and Evaluation Project were born through policy. The first wave of Early Head Start children has entered school. The future of funding for Early Head Start programs depends, in part, on the findings from the research project. As researchers we want to have the data "speak for themselves" and provide clear directions for policy. This is not always the case; science may or may not shape policy.

The challenges, from my perspective, are few. They should, however, be considered when one is making a decision about whether to participate in multisite studies, especially consortium arrangements.

- The lag time in the receipt of site-specific data collected as part of the cross-site data: This was important to the MSU research site because we planned on using many of the measures in our site-specific data. We could not complete the analyses to our research questions within the time frame we had allotted. If I were going to proceed in this way in the future, I would be better prepared to plan for data analyses.
- The added time required of the investigator to take part in the activities of the consortium: Certainly part of this was my naïveté in the initial planning. Without a good barometer, I planned as one would for the management of a single-site study. By the time I had a realistic picture of the time I needed for this project, I was not able to make all the adjustments necessary in the budget to adequately provide for it. There were two related constraining factors. One was the funding limit for each site. The other was the commitment made to the coinvestigators who wanted to be part of this project. As a result we were all contributing more time than was allocated for each of us in the budget. It was also difficult to convince departmental administration to match at least some of the time allocation as most were operating from the perspective of an individual grant rather than from a multisite study.
- To maintain the involvement and investment of team members in the national evaluation when many could not attend the Consortium meetings: I originally thought that team members would be able to

take turns in attending the Consortium meetings. However, I soon realized that as the team members who attended the first Consortium meetings became involved in workgroups and other activities of the Consortium the rotation would not be a feasible option. One of the members was able to fund his attendance at some of the Consortium meetings through other sources, freeing up resources for others. Every attempt was made to bring the national perspective to the local level by reporting on the national data collection, preparing summaries of the Consortium meetings, and discussing important topics at monthly team meetings.

• The mechanism of this project's inception and the tight time line made input into the initial decisions for design and measures impossible. However, some adjustments in measures were made in subsequent rounds of data collection. In addition, some programs were not fully implemented when the evaluation began. This latter challenge provided an opportunity to study the process of program implementation and its influence on expected outcomes. These challenges may, in some ways, be unique to this particular project and projects like it in which certain aspects are legislated, but they may also apply to other multisite studies.

SUMMARY

There are great benefits to consortium arrangements, particularly when the partners are willing to engage in true collaboration. The Early Head Start Research Consortium was akin to a family; we worked, laughed, and played together. We experienced births among our members, the death of one of our members, illnesses, and divorces, as well as welcoming new members into our midst. We were inspired by the chair of the Consortium with the music played to start meetings and call us to order after breaks, with representations of art that illustrated our commitment to children, with poetry that reflected our mission, and with meaningful quotes from literature at the end of e-mail messages. We were committed to the thought that "we" is better than "I" and that together we could and did accomplish a considerable feat.

ACKNOWLEDGMENTS

The Early Head Start Research and Evaluation Project was funded by the Administration on Children, Youth, and Families (ACYF), U.S. Department of Health and Human Services under contract 105-95-1936 to Mathematica Policy Research, Princeton, NJ, and Columbia University's Center for Children and Families, Teachers College, in conjunction with the Early Head Start Research Consortium. The independent research conducted by Michigan State University with the Community Action Agency in Jackson, Michigan, was funded by the Head Start Bureau at ACYF through grant #90YF0010, *Pathways Project: Research into Directions for Family Health and Service Use*, to Michigan State University, Rachel F. Schiffman, PhD, RN, Principal Investigator.

In the spirit of true partnership I would like to extend my appreciation to the present and past members of the Michigan State University/Community Action Agency Early Head Start Research Team for their participation and support: Holly Brophy-Herb, PhD, Mary Cunningham-DeLuca, BA, Hiram E. Fitzgerald, PhD, Cynthia L. Gibbons, RN, PhD, Marshelle Hawver, MSW, Sharon Hoerr, RD, PhD, Dennis R. Keefe, PhD, Marsha Kreucher, MA, Lorraine M. McKelvey, MA, Seung-yeon Lee, MA, Mildred A. Omar, RNC, PhD, Angela Smith, BA, Thomas M. Reischl, PhD, Martha York, MSW, the many data collectors and students, and the staff of the Early Head Start program.

For the national evaluation and the Consortium, I also extend my thanks to: ACYF (Rachel Chazan Cohen, Judith Jerald, Esther Kresh, Helen Raikes, and Louisa Tarullo); Columbia University (Lisa Berlin, Jeanne Brooks-Gunn, and Alison Fuligni); Mathematica Policy Research (Kimberly Boller, Ellen Eliason Kisker, John M. Love, Diane Paulsell, Christine Ross, Peter Schochet, and Welmoet van Kammen); and to the local researchers and program directors from the other 14 universities and 16 sites.

REFERENCES

Carnegie Task Force on Meeting the Needs of Young Children. (1994). *Starting points: Meeting the needs of our youngest children*. New York: Carnegie Corporation. Retrieved February 1, 2002 from *http://www.carnegie.org/starting_points/index/html*

Coats Human Services Reauthorization Act of 1998, 42 U.S.C. § 9831 et seq. Retrieved February 8, 2002 from *http://law2.house.gov/uscode-cgi/fastweb.exe?getdoc+usc view+t41t42+6168+0++%28Head%20Start*

Early Head Start. (n.d.). Retrieved January 30, 2002, from the ACYF Commissioner's Office of Research and Evaluation Web site: *http://www.acf.dhhs.gov/programs/core/ongoing_research/ehs/ehs_intro.html*

Fatherhood Research in the Early Head Start Research and Evaluation Project. (n.d.). Retrieved January 30, 2002, from the ACYF Commissioner's Office of Research and Evaluation Web site: *http://www.acf.dhhs.gov/programs/core/ongoing_research/father/father_intro.html*

Given, B. A., Keilman, L. J., Collins, C., & Given, C. W. (1990). Strategies to minimize attrition in longitudinal studies. *Nursing Research, 39,* 184–186.

Head Start Act Amendments of 1994, 42 U.S.C. § 9831 et seq. Retrieved February 8, 2002 from *http://law2.house.gov/uscode-cgi/fastweb.exe?getdoc+uscview+t41t42 +6168 +0++%28Head%20Start*

Hogg, R. J. (1991). Trials and tribulations of multicenter studies. *Pediatric Nephrology, 5,* 348–351.

National Fatherhood Initiative. (n.d.). Retrieved February 8, 2002, from *http://www.fatherhood.org/*

Paulsell, D., Kisker, E. E., Love, J. M., & Raikes, H. (with Boller, K., Rosenberg, L., Coolahan, K., & Berlin, L. J.). (2000). *Leading the way: Characteristics and early experiences of selected Early Head Start programs. Executive summary, volumes I, II, and III.* Retrieved January 25, 2002 from *http://www.acf.dhhs.gov/programs/core/ongoing_research/ehs/leading_summary/lead_sum_title.html*

Powell, R. A., Lloyd, K. R., & Olajide, D. (1999). Negotiating the minefield: Multisite collaborative psychiatric research. *Journal of Mental Health, 4,* 321–324.

Schiffman, R. F., Fitzgerald, H. E., & DeLuca, M. C. (2002). Community–university partnerships: The best vintage. *NHSA Dialog, 5,* 325–339.

Smith, C. S., Salyer, J., Geddes, N., & Mark, B. A. (1998). Strategies to enhance internal validity in multi-center longitudinal research. *Outcomes Management for Nursing Practice, 2,* 174–179.

Epilogue:
Final Words, Many Voices

Joellen W. Hawkins and Lois A. Haggerty

T he mural our contributing authors have painted is the first of many and is as multifaceted as their projects. Each of the studies these authors have described will continue to generate new work and, in that process, create new panels for the mural. As researchers, we will continue to learn to work together as members of diverse disciplines, inculcate more complete understanding of the perspectives our colleagues and research participants bring to projects, and find more effective and productive ways to manage multiple research sites. With what we have learned through conducting investigations, we hope to mentor researchers for the next decades. They, in turn, will create studies even more important and complex to answer the questions that inform practice, guide the preparation of new generations of health and human services professionals, and lay the path for the next investigations.

We hope the lessons we have learned will enrich the investigations of our readers. We don't believe we have found the one and only true way to conduct multisite research with a multidisciplinary team and multicultural samples. What we have created are diverse paths to the same goal: the best possible research design to answer the questions of interest, and the means to select the most representative sample of subjects or respondents who can inform us about their experiences, physical parameters, behaviors, and other relevant variables.

Relationships underlie each and every project but are far more complex with multisite, multidisciplinary, and/or multicultural studies. These relationships evolve and change much as natural light is ever-changing, while funding, creating a research team, planning project management strategies, integrating students and research assistants into the project, planning and implementing the study protocols, and achieving IRB approval are the paint and brushes. Then it is time to get down to the work of painting the mural—collecting and analyzing the data and disseminating the findings.

What we have tried to create for our readers is a multidimensional mural of multidisciplinary, multicultural, and multisite research. The many artists who contributed chapters have truly done that.

Index

MIXEG/MIXOR, in international multisite studies, 131
Monitoring of research assistants, 64–65
Morale, in multisite team management, 93
Motivation
  of patient, to partake in research, 60
  in research project management, 16
Multicenter research. *See* Multisite research
Multidisciplinary research
  collaborative research model, complications, 4–5
  communication, 6–7
  interorganizational planning, 4–9
  management, 3–19
  methodology, 9–14
    data analysis, 12–13
    data collection, 12
    ethical issues, 13–14
    measurement issues, 12
    project design, 9–11
    report writing, 12–13
    sampling, 11
  planning, 6–9
  political considerations, 17
  political issues, 14–15
  protocols, 6–7
  report writing, 12–13
  research team
    collaboration, 8–9
    tasks, 7–9
Multiethnic research, 145–159
  collaborative research model, complications, 4–5
  communication, 6–7
  cultural competence, 146–152
  data analysis, 12–13
  data collection
    fidelity, 156
    site preparation, 154–155
  domestic violence organizations, working with, 157
  Hispanic Journal of Behavioral Sciences, 149
  hospitals, working with, 153

interorganizational planning, 4–9
Journal of National Medical Association, 149
Journal of Poor and Undeserved, 149
Koop, C. Everett, 145
management, 3–19
Nursing Network on Violence Against Women International, 145, 158
Nursing Research Consortium Against Violence and Abuse, 145, 158
planning, 6–9
political considerations, 17
political issues, 14–15
protocols, 6–7
report writing, 12–13
research assistants, training as data collectors, 155–156
research team
  collaboration, 8–9
  tasks, 7–9
subject location, 156–157
trainers, training of, 154
Multisite research, 71–80
  Belmont Report, 76
  collaborative research model, complications, 4–5
  communication, 6–7
  consent forms, 76
  cultural competence, 146–152
  data collection fidelity, 156
  data collection site preparation, 154–155
  design, 153–154
  domestic violence organizations, working with, 157
  feasibility, 72
  guidelines, 73–74
  Hispanic Journal of Behavioral Sciences, 149
  hospitals, working with, 153
  institutional review board
    resubmissions to, 76–77
    submission, 75–77
    submission of proposals to, 73
  internal principal investigators, 74

Time lines, 17, 96, 123
Timing, in multicenter research, 74–75
Trainers, training of, 154
Training
  of data collectors, 94
  in Women's Health Initiative, 192
TRAM: Research Funding Opportunities
    and Administration, 45
Turnover, of staff, 94
Tuskegee Syphilis Study, 117, 119

Uganda, 120
  placebo controlled trials in, 117
Universal Declaration of Human Rights,
    international multisite studies
    and, 119
Urine Collection Form, 207
U.S. Department of Justice, 45
U.S. management team, international
    sites, communication between,
    123

Varmus, Harold, 118
Violence, against partner, prevalence of,
    47–59
Vitamin D supplementation, 181–207
Vitamin D Supplementation Eligibility
    Review Form, 203
Vitamin D Supplementation Safety Inter-
    view Form, 206

Women's Health Initiative, 181–207
  Addendum to Medical History Update
    Form, 204
  analysis of data, 195–197
  Blood Collection Form, 206
  Bone Density Scan Form, 207
  calcium supplementation, 181–207
  Calcium Supplementation Eligibility
    Review Form, 203
  Calcium Supplementation Safety Inter-
    view Form, 206
  Change of Medications Form, 205
  Clinical Breast Exam Form, 206
  clinical coordinating center, 181
  Cognitive Status Form, 205

communication, 187–189
Consents Form, 203
Current Medications Form, 205
Current Supplements Form, 205
Daily Life Form, 205
data collection forms, 202–207
Dietary Recall Form, 205
Electrocardiogram Form, 206
Eligibility Screen Form, 202
Endometrial Aspiration Form, 206
Final Eligibility Assessment Form,
    203
Food Frequency Questionnaire Form,
    205
Four-Day Food Record Form, 187,
    205
Fred Hutchinson Cancer Research
    Center, 181
Functional Status Form, 206
hormone replacement therapy,
    181–207
Hormone Replacement Therapy Calen-
    dar Form, 207
Hormone Replacement Therapy Safety
    Interview Form, 187, 206
Hormone Replacement Therapy Wash-
    out Form, 203
Hormone Use Form, 205
logistical support, 189–190
low-fat eating pattern, 181–207
Mammogram Form, 206
materials, 187–189
Medical History Form, 204
Medical History Update Form, 204
Medication Adherence Form, 206
Medication Dispensation Form, 206
Observational Study Exposure Update
    Questionnaires, 207
Observational Study Questionnaire
    Form, 207
organizational structure, 185
outcomes ascertainment, coordination
    of, 195
Pap Smear Form, 206
Participation Status Form, 203
Pelvic Exam Form, 206

Springer Publishing Company

Spirituality In Nursing
From Traditional to New Age
2nd Edition

Barbara Stevens Barnum, RN, PhD, FAAN

Praise for first edition:

"A fascinating look at spirituality's growing role in nursing...from the early days of the profession through today." —**Nurse's Book Society**

"Powerful...this book is a pocket guide for visiting a wonderful and rich place, written by someone who knows its value well."

—**Journal of Nursing Staff Development**

Thoroughly updated, the new edition of this award-winning book looks at spirituality and nursing from many perspectives: theoretical, historical, religious, psychological, and physiological.

2003 216pp 0-8261-9181-9 hard

536 Broadway, NY, NY 10012
Order on-line: www.springerpub.com • Order Toll-Free: 877-687-7476

Springer Publishing Company

Religious Organizations in Community Services

A Social Work Perspective

Terry Tirrito, PhD and Toni Cascio, PhD, Editors

"This book comprehensively addresses the role that religious organizations could play in providing services to those in need. It represents a wake-up call for faith communities, many who may have lost their vision and purpose in today's secular society."
  --**Harold G. Koenig**, MD, Director, Center
    for the Study of Religion/Spirituality and
    Health, Duke University Medical Center

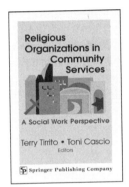

Beginning with the origins of social work, back to the earliest civilizations and religious traditions, the editors establish precedent for a fruitful commingling of religion and social welfare. The contributors propose that faith organizations can assume responsibilities for social welfare, using the Korean Church as one example of an effective provider of social services.

Partial Contents:
Part I: The Historical Role of Faith Organizations and Religion
• Religious Foundations of Charity, *T. Cascio*

Part II: The Contemporary Role of Religious Organizations
• American Congregations and their Social Programs, *T. Wolfer and M. Sherr*
• Spirituality and the Life Cycle, *I. Nathanson*
• Health, Spirituality, and Healing, *C. Corely*
Part III: New Models for the 21st Century
• The Role of the Korean Church as a Social Service Provider, *G. Choi*

2003   216pp   0-8261-1548-9   hard

536 Broadway, NY, NY 10012
Order on-line: www.springerpub.com Order Toll-Free: 877-687-7476